Historical Dictionaries of Intelligence and Counterintelligence
Jon Woronoff, Series Editor

Historical Dictionary of Air Intelligence

Glenmore S. Trenear-Harvey

Historical Dictionaries of Intelligence and Counterintelligence, No. 9

The Scarecrow Press, Inc.
Lanham, Maryland • Toronto • Plymouth, UK
2009

SCARECROW PRESS, INC.

Published in the United States of America
by Scarecrow Press, Inc.
A wholly owned subsidiary of
The Rowman & Littlefield Publishing Group, Inc.
4501 Forbes Boulevard, Suite 200, Lanham, Maryland 20706
www.scarecrowpress.com

Estover Road
Plymouth PL6 7PY
United Kingdom

British Library Cataloguing in Publication Information Available

Library of Congress Cataloging-in-Publication Data
Trenear-Harvey, Glenmore S., 1940–
  Historical dictionary of air intelligence / Glenmore S. Trenear-Harvey.
    p. cm. — (Historical dictionaries of intelligence and counterintelligence ; no. 9)
  Includes bibliographical references.
  ISBN-13: 978-0-8108-5982-1 (cloth : alk. paper)
  ISBN-10: 0-8108-5982-3 (cloth : alk. paper)
  ISBN-13: 978-0-8108-6294-4 (eBook)
  ISBN-10: 0-8108-6294-8 (eBook)
  1. Aerial reconnaissance–History–Dictionaries. 2. Military intelligence–
History–Dictionaries. I. Title.
  UG760.T74 2009
  358.4'1343203–dc22   2008043110

♾™ The paper used in this publication meets the minimum requirements of
American National Standard for Information Sciences—Permanence of Paper
for Printed Library Materials, ANSI/NISO Z39.48-1992.
Manufactured in the United States of America.

Contents

Editor's Foreword

Ever since airplanes, or indeed hot air balloons, appeared air intelligence has been one of the most productive sources of information on enemies or potential enemies. It has stood the test of time, developing successive and greatly improved generations of planes and photographic equipment specially designed for the task. Among the best known, but hardly the only one, was the U-2. This form then took a huge leap forward during the space age, with the utilization of satellites for reconnaissance purposes, then returning to earth with the use of smaller and simpler drones, whose main advantage was getting closer to the terrain but without endangering a pilot or crew. Indeed, it looked as if nothing could surpass air intelligence over the long decades from World War I and World War II, through the Cold War and assorted hot wars in Korea, Vietnam, Afghanistan, and Iraq—that is, until 11 September 2001, and the increasing use of suicide bombers reminded us that there are still some things human operatives can do better. Still, when it comes to war, and for other purposes as well, nothing has and nothing is likely to surpass air intelligence.

That explains the need for a special volume in this growing series of *Historical Dictionaries of Intelligence and Counterintelligence*. Like others in the series, it starts off with a list of acronyms, indispensable merely to read the literature. It is followed by a chronology that traces the rapid evolution over a relatively short period of time for air intelligence. The introduction then inserts it in the broader context, showing which methods and equipment were used in which periods and during which wars, and even helping us peep into the future somewhat. The bulk of the information, however, is provided in several hundred dictionary entries on the more significant persons, places, and equipment, the various operations and other events, the more notable successes, and some deplorable failures. Although the literature on air intelligence is not that large—only enhancing the value of this volume—it is there to be learned from and the bibliography offers access to it.

This *Historical Dictionary of Air Intelligence* was written by someone coming directly from the field, Glenmore Trenear-Harvey. After serving in the Royal Air Force as a jet fighter pilot, an intelligence officer, and on the staff of the Signals Command Headquarters, he did a stint supervising work on confidential ciphers. Since then he has become a specialist on air intelligence, lecturing on the topic to the general public and more select audiences at the British Defence Intelligence and Security Centre. A member of the main bodies dealing with defense and intelligence studies, he is also associate editor of a specialized magazine, *Eye Spy*, and editor of *IntelDigest* as well as heading a consultancy, IntelResearch. With more than four decades of experience under his belt, it was indeed fortunate to have him as the author of this handy and informative guide to a field all intelligence professionals and buffs regard as particularly vital.

Jon Woronoff
Series Editor

Acronyms and Abbreviations

AFESC	Air Force Electronic Security Command
AFOSI	Air Force Office of Special Investigations
AFSA	Armed Forces Security Agency
AFSS	Air Force Security Service
AIA	Air Intelligence Agency
ARIES	Airborne Reconnaissance Integrated Electronic System
ASA	Army Security Agency
ASW	Anti-Submarine Warfare
AVMF	Aviatsiya Voenno Morskova Flota (Soviet Naval Air Service)
BND	Bundesnachrichtendienst (Federal German Intelligence Service)
BTTR	Brothers to the Rescue
C	Chief of the Secret Intelligence Service
CAZAB	Canadian, American, New Zealand, Australian, and British counterintelligence liaison
CIA	Central Intelligence Agency (United States)
CIAA	Coordinator of Inter-American Affairs
CIC	Counter-Intelligence Corps
CIO	Central Imagery Office
CSDIC	Combined Services Detailed Interrogation Centre
CSE	Communications Security Establishment (Canada)
CSIS	Canadian Security Intelligence Service
CSO	Composite Signals Organization
DARO	Defense Airborne Reconnaissance Office
DGSE	Direction Générale de Securité Extérieure (French intelligence service)
DIA	Defense Intelligence Agency

DIAS	Defence Intelligence Analysis Staff
DIS	Defence Intelligence Staff
DMI	Director of Military Intelligence
DNI	Director of Naval Intelligence
DO	Directorate of Operations
ECM	Electronic Counter-Measures
ELINT	Electronic Intelligence
FARC	Armed Front of the Republic of Colombia
FBI	Federal Bureau of Investigation (United States)
FRA	Forsvarets Radioanstalt (Swedish Signals Intelligence Agency)
FRG	Federal Republic of Germany
GC&CS	Government Code and Cypher School
GCHQ	Government Communications Headquarters
GDR	German Democratic Republic
GRU	Glavnoe Razvedyvatel'noe Upravlenie (Soviet Military Intelligence Service)
HARM	High-speed Anti-Radiation Missile
ICBM	Inter-Continental Ballistic Missile
IDF	Israeli Defense Force
INS	Immigration and Naturalization Service
IRBM	Intermediate Range Ballistic Missile
JIC	Joint Intelligence Committee
KGB	Komitei Gosudarstevnnoi Bezopasnosti (Soviet Intelligence Service)
LAKAM	Israeli Bureau of Scientific Liaison
MAV	micro air vehicles
MI5	British Security Service
MI6	British Secret Intelligence Service
MRBM	Medium Range Ballistic Missile
MSIC	Missile and Space Intelligence Center
NATO	North Atlantic Treaty Organization
NIE	National Intelligence Estimate
NIMA	National Imagery and Mapping Agency
NIO	National Intelligence Officer
NISC	Naval Intelligence Support Center
NPIC	National Photographic Intelligence Center
NRO	National Reconnaissance Office

NSA	National Security Agency
OSS	Office of Strategic Services
PR	Photographic Reconnaissance
PRC	People's Republic of China
PRU	Photographic Reconnaissance Unit
RAF	Royal Air Force
RSM	Radio Squadron Mobile
SAM	Surface-to-Air Missile
SDECE	Service de Documentation Extérieure et de Contre-Espionage (French Intelligence Service)
SHAPE	Supreme Headquarters Allied Powers Europe
SIGINT	Signals Intelligence
SIS	Secret Intelligence Service (Great Britain)
SRBM	Short-Range Ballistic Missile
TACAN	Tactical Air Navigation
UNMOVIC	United Nations Verification and Inspection Commission
UNSCOM	United Nations Special Commission
VPVO	Voiska Protivovozdushnoi Oborony (Soviet Air Defense Force)

The nation with the best photographic intelligence will win the next war.

General Werner von Frisch
Commander in Chief of the Wehrmacht, 1935–1938

For all the billions of dollars spent on satellite and other overhead surveillance, on electronic eavesdropping, on export controls, on the debriefing of defectors and on human espionage, I have to conclude that the failure in the case of Iraq was monumental.

Hans Blix
Chairman, UNMOVIC, 2000–2003

Chronology

1783   Montgolfier brothers fly in a balloon.

1793   A balloon corps formed in France.

1794   Captain J. M. J. Coutelle is the first soldier in the air under fire at the Battle of Fleurus.

1797   A Companie d'Aérostiers deployed during the siege of Mantua.

1798   Companie d'Aérostiers sent to Egypt by Napoleon.

1856   French experiments in aerial photography end in failure.

1858   Felix Tourachon carried a darkroom into the air on a balloon to process images on glass plates.

1860   Aerial photographs taken of Boston, Massachusetts, from 1,200 feet.

1861   Meteorologist Thaddeus Lowe arrested as a Union spy when he lands accidentally in South Carolina in the *Eagle*.

1862   Confederates employ Professor Lowe's balloon, the *Intrepid*, during the Battle of Fair Oaks in the American Civil War.

1863   The Royal Society attempts to photograph the tops of clouds.

1870   Balloons used during the Franco-Prussian War to fly agents and documents out of besieged Paris.

1879   Triboulet photographs Paris from a balloon.

1883   Shadbolt and Dale take aerial photographs of England.

1884   British Army in Bechuanaland equipped with balloons.

1885 Sudan Expedition uses observation balloons.

1886 Kronstadt photographed from a balloon.

1890 Royal Engineers introduce a Balloon Section. U.S. 9th Infantry Regiment experiments with kites and cameras.

1897 Drachen kite balloons developed by von Parseval and von Sigsfeld.

1900 Royal Engineers Balloon Section deployed in Natal during the Boer War.

1903 A pigeon camera patented by Dr. Julius Neubonner in Germany. The Wright brothers achieve first powered flight at Kitty Hawk.

1907 Washington, D.C., photographed from a high-altitude balloon.

1908 U.S. Army establishes balloon unit at Fort Myer, Virginia.

1909 The holder of a private pilot's license, Mansfield Smith-Cumming, appointed chief of the new British Secret Service Bureau.

1910 His Majesty's airship *Beta* enters service with the British Army.

1911 Italian aircraft used to spot Turkish troops in Libya.

1912 Commodore Sulsi takes ciné-film from the airship P.3. Royal Flying Corps formed. Italians pick up agents behind enemy lines during war with Turkey.

1913 American reconnaissance aircraft deployed in the Philippines.

1914 The Royal Flying Corps sends four squadrons to France. Captain Joubert flies first British reconnaissance over enemy territory. A French pilot lands a scout behind the German lines and collects him.

1915 German Fokker fighters decimate RFC BE-2c reconnaissance planes. An Italian pilot lands an observation officer behind enemy lines and then collects him.

1916 Lieutenants Falk and Schultheiss bomb Cairo railway station and photograph the pyramids.

1917 School of Military Aeronautics opened at Cornell University.

1918 Fighter ace Frank Luke Jr. shoots down eight enemy balloons in five days. Bill Barker parachutes an agent behind Austrian lines.

1919 The Ordnance Survey publishes a photo-map of Salisbury.

1920 RAF Duxford commences mapping project using aerial photography.

1921 The supposedly impregnable *Ostfriesland* sunk with a single 2,000-pound bomb dropped by the U.S. Army Air Corps.

1922 Carl Norden invents his bombsight.

1923 First nonstop flight across the United States. Air-refueling allows Lieutenant Lowell Smith to remain aloft for a record 36 hours.

1924 The first stereo survey of Hong Kong completed.

1927 Captain Malcolm Christie appointed air attaché at the British embassy in Berlin.

1928 Captain St. Clair Streett reaches a record 37,854 feet in a two-seater plane.

1929 Captain A. W. Stevens photographs Mount Rainier from 227 miles.

1930 Fred Winterbotham appointed head of the Secret Intelligence Service's air section. Hansa Luftbild GmbH starts to map Germany.

1932 Aeroflot established in Moscow as a civil airline.

1934 George Goddard maps 20,000 square miles of Alaska in three days.

1935 Cabinet enquiry into Luftwaffe bomber strength. Arrest of Herman Goertz in Broadstairs.

1936 Air Section established at Bletchley Park.

1937 Roy Fedden visits the Messerschmitt aircraft factories in Germany.

1938 Fred Winterbotham hires pilots Sidney Cotton and Bob Niven.

1939 Aerial photography flights flown over Germany by SIS. The *Graf Zeppelin* tests radar sites along the east coast of England.

1940 The Royal Air Force introduces a Photographic Reconnaissance Unit.

1941 Photographic Reconnaissance Unit equipped with Spitfires and Mosquitoes at Benson. German paratroops capture Crete.

1942 1474 Flight inaugurated by the Royal Air Force. Northwest African Photographic Reconnaissance Wing established. 5 PRU formed at Dum Dum.

1943 V-2 missiles spotted at Peenemünde.

1944 First operational sortie by a Mosquito PR 34 of 344 Squadron. One hundred and sixteen photo missions flown on D-Day. *Tirpitz* sunk.

1945 Army Security Agency created from Army Signals Security Agency. After the PRF disbanded, 347 (PR) Wing established.

1946 BIG SAFARI operations initiated. Deportation of German missile scientists to the Soviet Union begins. Two C-47 transports lost over Yugoslavia.

1947 Tu-4 *Bull* bombers seen at Tushino air display.

1948 LEOPARD oblique photography of Chukotsky Peninsula begins. Defection of Grigori Tokaev. Air Force Security Service created. Royal Air Force Mosquito shot down by an Israeli Mustang.

1949 The first Soviet atomic test detected by a WB-29 from Alaska. Four Royal Air Force PR Spitfires shot down by Israeli fighters.

1950 U.S. Navy PB4Y2 Privateer shot down over the Baltic off Latvia with loss of all 10 crew.

1951 U.S. Navy P2V Neptune shot down near Vladivostock with loss of all 10 crew. A U.S. Air Force C-47 lost over Hungary.

1952 U.S. Air Force RB-29A shot down in Sea of Japan by MiG-15s. Swedish DC-3 and Catalina shot down over the Baltic. Royal Air Force fly RC-45C missions from Sculthorpe. A U.S. Air Force B-29 lost while dropping leaflets in Manchuria, and a CIA C-47 forced to land in China.

1953 U.S. Air Force RB-50 shot down near Vladivostock by a MiG-15. British RB-45s radar map Soviet targets. Polish MiG-15 *Fagot* defects to Bornholm. P2V-5 Neptune shot down over Swatow. Royal Air Force Lincoln shot down by MiG in East Germany with loss of six aircrew. B-29 shot down over Liaoning province and crew of 11 captured.

1954 Loss of a U.S. Air Force P2V-5 Neptune and a RB-29, both in the Sea of Japan. MOBY DICK balloons launched from Scotland. An RB-47 attacked by MiG-17s over the Kola Peninsula. Syrian airliner hijacked to free Israeli commandos.

1955 President Dwight D. Eisenhower proposes an Open Spies policy. U.S. Air Force RB-47 shot down over Kamchatka. A U.S. Navy P2V shot down in the Bering Straits, seven of the crew injured.

1956 First U-2 overflight of the Soviet Union. U.S. Navy P4M-IQ Mercator shot down over the Chengszu Islands with the loss of 16 crew. A U.S. RB-50 lost over the Sea of Japan.

1957 U-2 photographs Kapustin Yar. First successful Soviet Inter-Continental Ballistic Missile (ICBM) test at Tyuratam to the Pacific. *Sputnik 1* placed into orbit by an SS-6.

1958 AQUATONE overflights begin and Tyuratam discovered. A CIA C-118 courier flight shot down over Yerevan, Armenia. An EC-130 shot down over Armenia with loss of 17 crew.

1959 First Corona satellite launched in orbit. P4M-IQ Mercator attacked off Wonsan. Israeli Super-Mystere fails to intercept a U-2. Soviet Luna I and Luna II spacecraft reach the moon on SS-6 rockets.

1960 Francis Gary Powers shot down over Sverdlovsk. Three-month blackout of surveillance over the Soviet Union until August. A National Intelligence estimate calculates Soviet bomber strength at 120–185. U.S. Air Force RB-47H shot down over the Barents Sea. *Sputnik 5* takes an animal into space.

1961 Tu-16 Badgers deployed over the Atlantic and Pacific. Bay of Pigs invasion of Cuba.

1962 Rudolph Abel swapped for Gary Powers. Rudolf Anderson's U-2 shot down over Cuba. Taiwanese U-2 shot down over the People's

Republic of China. An RB-47 crashes on takeoff in Bermuda, killing all four crew.

1963 Loss of Taiwanese U-2 over China. Israeli Mirages force an RB-57A to land at Lod.

1964 Loss of a T-39 and an RB-66 over East Germany. Mahmoud Himli defects to Israel in an Egyptian Yak. Taiwanese U-2 shot down over China.

1965 Loss of U.S. Air Force RB-57F with two crew over the Black Sea. Taiwanese U-2 shot down over China.

1966 Defection of Munir Redfa with a MiG-21. Australia signs agreement for American satellite ground station at Pine Gap. A Soviet Yak-28 crashes into the Havelsee in Berlin.

1967 Loss of Taiwanese U-2 over China. Six Syrian MiGs shot down in dogfight with Israeli jets over Damascus.

1968 Tu-16 Badger-F crashes near USS *Essex*. Loss of a U.S. Air Force DC-8 near the Kurile Islands.

1969 Loss of Taiwanese U-2 over China. Israelis dismantle Egyptian radar station at Ras-al-Ghaleb. EC-121M shot down by two North Korean MiG-21s with loss of all 31 crew.

1970 Loss of U-8 over Armenia. Nurrungar satellite ground station opened in Australia. A nuclear-armed B-52 crashes into the Mediterranean off Palomares. Phantoms strike Egyptian SA-2 sites.

1971 KH-9 Big Bird satellite launched and remains in orbit for 54 days. Defense Mapping Agency established.

1972 Incidents at Sea Pact agreed by Soviet and U.S. navies.

1973 RC-130 from Hellinikon attacked by Libyan Mirage fighters. An EC-47Q Skytrain shot down over Laos with loss of all four crew.

1974 MiG-25R Foxbat overflies Tel Aviv from Cairo-West. India tests an atomic weapon.

1975 Cypriot police accidentally arrest American U-2 pilots near Akrotiri. U-2 photos of Berbera released.

1976 Defection of Viktor Belenko with MiG-25 Foxbat. Christopher Boyce sells details of the RHYEOLITE and ARGOS satellites to the KGB. A Japanese P-2V Neptune is fired on by a Soviet Su-15.

1977 Adolf Tolkachev compromises Phaestron avionics. Five Foxbat-Bs deployed to Okra Ben Nafi in Libya. Loss of a CH-47 over North Korea.

1978 HAVE BLUE stealth aircraft tested at Area 51. Orion P-3 rescued in the Pacific by a Soviet trawler. William Kampiles imprisoned for selling a KH-11 handbook to the KGB. Cosmos 954 crashes in Canada. KAL 902 shot down by a Su-15 in the Barents Sea.

1979 NSA intercept sites at Kabkan, Meshed, and Behshahr in Iran closed. F-15 Eagles shoot down five MiG-25s over the Lebanon.

1980 Tu-16 Badger crashes into the Sea of Japan. OFEQ-1 launched by the Israelis. An RC-135 from Hellenikon attacked by two Libyan MiG-23s over the Mediterranean.

1981 COBRA BALL RC-135 crashes on Shemya Island. Syrian MiG-23 Flogger-E shot down by an Israeli F-15 Eagle. The Osiraq research reactor destroyed by Israeli jets. Ana Montes joins the Defense Intelligence Agency.

1982 Argentine invasion of the Falkland Islands. A Syrian MiG-25R Foxbat shot down over Beirut by a Hawk missile.

1983 KAL 007 shot down over the Pacific.

1984 Samuel Morison imprisoned for disclosing KH-11 imagery. The National Reconnaissance Office launches a VORTEX satellite. Cosmos 1603 launched.

1985 A Titan-IIID rocket carrying a KH-11 satellite is destroyed when it malfunctions. Cosmos 1625 breaks up over Romania. Air India flight 182 sabotaged. Three Americans murdered aboard a hijacked Jordanian airliner by Fawaz Yunis.

1986 A Titan-III rocket carrying a KH-9 satellite explodes shortly after takeoff. European SPOT 1 satellite launched from Kourou, French Guiana, on an Arianne rocket. Loss of the *Challenger* space shuttle.

1987   A KH-11 satellite detects deployment of Soviet SS-24 Sickle rail mobile missiles, and SS-25 Scalpel 10-warhead ICBMs. The last KH-11 is launched.

1988   Australia signs 10-year agreement for Pine Gap and Nurrungar. China sells three DFA-3 ballistic missiles to Saudi Arabia.

1989   Israelis launch a Jericho-II missile from Palmikhim. South Africans launch a SRBM from the Arniston test site. India tests MRBM at Balasore.

1990   Iraq test fires three Scud-B missiles.

1991   Iraq fires 88 Scud-B missiles at Saudi Arabia, Bahrain, and Israel. A Scud kills 28 Americans at Dhahran.

1992   The U.S. Central Imagery Office established. The National Reconnaissance Office is officially acknowledged.

1993   North Korea tests the Nodong-1. A Black Hawk helicopter shot down in Mogadishu.

1994   French launch the HÉLIOS satellite. Nuclear weapons production is detected at Yongbyon in North Korea.

1995   OFEQ-3 launched successfully by the Israelis.

1996   The United States agrees to share ballistic missile defense technology with Israel.

1997   The third generation LACROSSE radar imaging satellite launched.

1998   India completes a successful nuclear test on the Pokharan range in Rajastan. Chemical factory in Khartoum bombed.

1999   An F-117A Nighthawk stealth fighter shot down by a SA-3 Goa missile in Yugoslavia. Chinese embassy in Belgrade bombed.

2000   The Israelis launch the Eros A-1 photo-reconnaissance satellite. An Orion P3V makes an emergency landing on Hainan Island. Brian Regan arrested at Dulles Airport.

2001   President Jiang Zemin's Boeing 767-300ER found to contain listening devices installed before delivery. Arrest of Ian Parr.

2003   National Imagery and Mapping Agency (NIMA) established. An RC-135S aircraft intercepted by four North Korean MiGs.

2004   Launch of the Israeli OFEQ-5 fails. Bunker-busting bombs purchased by the Israeli Air Force. China puts Nanosatellite-1 into orbit.

2005   RAF C-130 Hercules shot down in Iraq by al-Qaida. U-2 pilot killed at Al Dafra airbase. Predators kill al-Qaeda terrorists in Pakistan. Iran launches Sinah-1 surveillance satellite.

2006   Chinese KJ-2000 crashes in Guangde. North Korea tests a nuclear weapon.

2007   The Air Force Intelligence, Reconnaissance and Surveillance Agency created.

Introduction

From the moment man learned how to ascend from the ground, the strategic significance of air intelligence became apparent. It was, classically, the Duke of Wellington's desire "to see over the other side of the hill" and thereby instantly obtain an advantage over an adversary massing for a surprise attack. But what makes the discipline of air intelligence unique are its relative newness and the astonishing speed with which it has developed. Naval intelligence is as old as the first warships that put to sea, and military intelligence might be said to date back to biblical times, when we read in the Old Testament that Joshua sent men to "spy out the land of Canaan." However, the earliest air intelligence missions are much easier to document, for they can be said to have commenced with the very first hot-air balloons. Probably the first dedicated air reconnaissance missions were undertaken in 1870 during the siege of Paris, when tethered French balloons were employed to spot enemy positions and direct artillery fire onto them.

In the century since the Franco-German War, air intelligence developed to include satellites placed in geostationary orbit, high-flying U-2 and SR-71 reconnaissance aircraft, unmanned drones, and numerous other sophisticated solutions to the challenges of the modern era. Curiously, air intelligence has received scant attention from historians, in part because during the Cold War, this particular component of the intelligence jigsaw puzzle largely had to remain top secret. Often, the countermeasures for an ingenious innovation can be relatively simple, as Francis Gary Powers discovered when, on 1 May 1960, his Central Intelligence Agency aircraft was shot down over Sverdlovsk by a Soviet SA-2 surface-to-air missile that detonated close enough to destabilize his fragile U-2. On that occasion, the exposure of what had intended to be a clandestine mission would have worldwide political implications, with Nikita Khruchchev canceling a scheduled summit meeting with

President Dwight Eisenhower, when the latter had been entrapped into a very public lie to maintain the CIA's flimsy cover of a harmless weather flight.

The pressure to produce accurate air intelligence has always been critical and politically charged. In 1936, Prime Minister Stanley Baldwin was forced to return to the House of Commons to correct a gross underestimate of German fighter and bomber strengths submitted days earlier. The crisis had arisen after the government's official figures had been challenged by intelligence professionals and a Cabinet subcommittee had been impaneled under the chairmanship of Sir Philip Cunliffe-Lister, the former air minister, to investigate the conflicting assessments. Seventy years later, policy makers would be equally wracked by controversy over the existence of weapons of mass destruction in Iraq. In the intervening period, air intelligence had made a powerful impact on history.

Air intelligence, conducted by so many nations before World War II, enabled the Nazis to accurately locate Royal Air Force airfields in England and the British to monitor the covert expansion of the Kriegsmarine. During the war itself, air intelligence fulfilled a vital role, collecting information about technical breakthroughs that allowed an adversary some distinct advantage in the field of night navigation, radar, secret weapons, proximity fuses, parachute tactics, glider-borne troops, and a hundred other innovations that altered the way warfare was conducted. Electronic countermeasures were introduced to redress the balance, and ingenious projects were pursued to deceive the enemy. Because of the urgency of war, some extraordinary inventions were introduced, and some equally ingenious countermeasures were developed in a remarkably short, concentrated period of intense scientific activity that ushered in the operational use of radar, navigation beams, jet engines, atomic weapons, and ballistic missiles.

With the stakes so high and the risks well understood by politicians on both sides, resources that might have been applied over decades in peacetime to particular scientific projects were made available almost instantly. The result was an era of unprecedented innovation in which some unusual and eccentric characters, who might not have been allowed to thrive in other conditions, were empowered to achieve some astonishing technical breakthroughs, including the development of guided missiles, jet fighters, and the uranium and plutonium bombs.

With research into these projects cloaked in secrecy, air intelligence agencies on all sides adopted great ingenuity in their efforts to penetrate the closely guarded facilities where the classified work was being conducted. Thus air intelligence came to rely not just on the collection and interpretation of photoreconnaissance imagery, but also encompassed prisoner of war interrogations, the recruitment of sources inside the target establishments, cryptography, diplomatic reporting, the study of captured documents, postal censorship, and even the scrutiny of submissions to the Patent Office. This synthesis, sometimes referred to as the mosaic effect, drew on many different intelligence disciplines to complete a comprehensive picture of the target issue. Whereas air intelligence had played a relatively minor role in previous conflicts, in World War II it proved decisive in every field and theater.

Unlike previous conflicts, World War II (1939–1945) was fought very largely in the air. Innovative tactics introduced by the Luftwaffe during the Spanish Civil War had brought the terror of air raids to the civilian populations of Madrid and Barcelona. Close coordination between fast-moving armored forces, supported by ground-attack aircraft, established *blitzkrieg* as a new and highly effective strategy that left concentrated pockets of defenders in Poland, France, Belgium, and Holland isolated, their roads clogged with terrified refugees harassed by Stuka dive-bombers. Winston Churchill termed Hermann Göring's assault on southern England during the late summer of 1940 as the Battle of Britain, and intelligence played a significant role in vectoring "the few" to the enemy bombers, thereby enabling the country to at least survive the onslaught. Thereafter, scarce resources were channeled into the areas that offered an advantage over a vastly superior adversary. Radar transformed air combat in much the same way that the development of sonar altered the balance underwater against the U-boat wolf packs. Projects that in peacetime might have taken years to nurture—such as the introduction of antiaircraft shells that could emit radio waves to detect a target and detonate nearby, instead of exploding at a preset altitude or upon impact—were treated as priorities and rushed into production. The British talent for improvisation led the avionics specialists to exploit the enemy's navigation beams and literally bend them so the Luftwaffe's deadly cargos were delivered harmlessly into empty fields instead of over vital population centers and military targets.

Undeterred by such setbacks, Nazi industry responded with a bewildering array of aerial devices that Adolf Hitler believed, even as late as October 1944, would win him the war. As well as the V-1 Doodlebug cruise missile, the V-2 ballistic missile, a variety of jet fighters, and two very sophisticated air-launched guided weapons, he had confidence in radar-controlled flak, radar-guided nightfighters, and an atomic warhead, even if he suspended research on the latter project in favor of the rockets he believed would bring more immediate results. Indeed, German industrial output reached its zenith in late 1944, gaining far greater statistics than anything achieved earlier in the war. If it had not been for the crucial contribution made by Allied air intelligence, these innovations might well have altered the outcome, or at least delayed events to enable the Reich to acquire a viable nuclear device. Hitler's last offensive, in the Ardennes in December 1944, exploited a lack of Allied air intelligence in the region, and almost succeeded in reversing the tide of war, but as the weather cleared, Allied air supremacy was quickly reasserted, with disastrous consequences for the Reich.

Nor was air intelligence decisive only in the European theater. Airborne deception schemes were perpetrated in southeast Asia, and the events at Hiroshima and Nagasaki might be described as the culmination of one of the greatest air intelligence operations ever contemplated by mankind. Indeed, much of the island-hopping strategy adopted across the Pacific was intended to secure airstrips for the forward deployment of fighters to provide air cover for the fleet and for land operations. Without the acquisition of these landing fields, built with unprecedented efficiency by U.S. Marine Corps "Seabee" engineers while often under fire, Allied operations would have been wholly dependent on carrier-borne aircraft, limited in range and vulnerable to the enemy's kamikaze tactics.

In the immediate postwar period, when the only members of the nuclear club were the United States and Great Britain, the major intelligence preoccupation was to determine when the Kremlin would develop a viable nuclear warhead. In the absence of any other means of gathering the necessary data, this top-priority information could only be ascertained from air intelligence. Considerable effort was devoted to experimenting with various techniques until high-altitude air-sampling was perfected to the point that the secret test in August 1949—conducted thousands of miles inside the Soviet Union in a well-guarded, remote desert location, far from the nearest seismograph—was detected within hours and confirmed within days by analysts examining filters containing bomb debris caught in mid-air over the northern Pacific. Thus, the news that the Soviets had perfected plutonium implosion was known in Washington, D.C., and London, and was announced to the world by President Harry Truman, even before Joseph Stalin had been given enough time to consider what public position his regime should take on the breakthrough.

For a decade after the end of World War II, the issue of Soviet strengths and intentions had been the top item on every Western political agenda, but the available information came almost exclusively from a combination of refugee interviews and oblique photography taken by aircraft flying along the Soviet periphery. While these flights eventually demonstrated that there had not been any threatening buildup of airstrips in locations that would bring the United States within range of a surprise first strike, there remained a significant problem that could only be overcome by flying directly over potential targets deep inside the Soviet Union. At the time, the nuclear deterrent consisted of free-fall atomic weapons that were to be dropped by U.S. Strategic Air Command and British Bomber Command aircraft. However, the effectiveness of the deterrent was entirely dependent on the weapons being delivered to their targets accurately, and the bombardiers' aiming systems required radar ground-mapping of every site. This procedure demanded advance reconnaissance of each target, which in turn necessitated a vertical radar survey that could only be undertaken by long incursions into hostile air space. Thus, during the Cold War there were a variety of reasons for the many reconnaissance flights flown into Eastern Bloc airspace. There was the need to locate Warsaw Pact radar stations and air defense systems, then a requirement to map the Soviet Union and survey potential targets, and finally the long-term commitment to monitoring hostile communications channels as an early-warning precaution against a surprise first strike.

During the uneasy postwar period, American and British aircraft routinely penetrated the Soviet Bloc, and Red Air Force Tupolev-95 Bears constantly tested the North Atlantic Treaty Organization's air defenses. These risky provocations continued throughout the Cold War and between 1950 and 1970, 252 American aircrew were shot down by Soviet fighters. But as reliance on technical intelligence sources grew, and on signals in particular, the use of airborne platforms to intercept telemetry and other communications increased, especially in those parts of the world where safe land sites were unavailable. Although the National Security Agency established eavesdropping facilities in friendly countries such as Turkey, Japan, and Germany and developed relationships with the British and Norwegians, the U.S. Air Force was often required to fill the gaps when, for instance, the sites at Kagnew, Eritrea, and the three in Iran had to be evacuated because of changes in the local regime. In the absence of convenient ground sites in strategic locations, aircraft were deployed to intercept the target traffic.

The issue of Soviet strategic bombers and missiles was equally crucial, and until the U-2 began regular overflights of Red Air Force bases, the science of judging the Kremlin's military capability became almost as arcane as the art of predicting the Politburo's decisions. Soviet secrecy and the repressive nature of the regime effectively prevented use of the "Mark I Eyeball" to study production figures, accumulate published statistics, monitor factory output, watch airbases, or photograph naval installations. Indeed, in the absence of even Soviet roadmaps, the postwar intelligence analysts were obliged to rely on ancient prerevolutionary maps of Russia and aerial photographs taken by the Luftwaffe. Yet the need to find the submarines, aircraft, nuclear facilities, railway lines, test sites and training areas became increasingly important, and it was not until the U-2 imagery became available that analysts could grasp the scale of Nikita Khrushchev's breathtakingly ambitious bluff, which culminated in the Cuban missile crisis. In November 1959, he had boasted that a single factory had produced 250 hydrogen warheads over the previous 12 months. It had seemed incredible that any responsible leader would blatantly lie about such an important issue yet the frequent claim that a "missile gap" had left the United States vulnerable to a more powerful potential enemy had a significant influence on American domestic politics, especially during the presidential campaign won by John F. Kennedy.

The mystery of the Kremlin's true strength would eventually be solved by the U-2 and then by the deployment of satellites, but Khrushchev's ingenious remedy to the relative weakness of his atomic arsenal was simply to move his short-range weapons closer to their target, and the result was the Cuban missile crisis, the catalyst for which was the discovery by U.S. air intelligence of his scheme. Although the resulting naval blockade of Cuba was enforced by warships, the whole confrontation was essentially about aircraft, with Soviet missiles detected by American aircraft. Indeed, the only fatality of the entire incident was a U.S. Air Force pilot, Major Rudolph Anderson, whose U-2 spy plane was shot down by a Soviet SA-2.

Many of the other conflicts fought during the Cold War, often proxy battles in which the adversaries were equipped by the superpowers, served to update intelligence analysts on the relative potency of air power. Following the invasion of South Korea, Soviet aircraft and pilots skillfully outmaneuvered and outgunned their U.S. counterparts until new equipment and tactics could be deployed in the skies over the peninsula. Initially, the MiG-15, powered with a reverse-engineered Rolls-Royce jet engine, proved invincible, at least until the F-86 Sabre evened the balance. This was to be the last time American fighter jocks would ever engage the Soviets in sustained aerial dogfights, leaving future confrontations to surrogates, apart from some suspected incidents over North Vietnam. In that war, overwhelming and permanent air superiority proved no substitute for political support at home and Vietnamese tactics in an environment that favored the insurgents and limited the effectiveness of comprehensive air cover.

Most future tests of relative equipment, personnel, and avionics would occur in simulated environments over secret airbases in the western United States or in real conditions, with Israelis pitted against Syrian, Egyptian, Jordanian, and Iraqi aircrews. For decades, the Middle East provided a highly realistic scenario for American manufacturers to bench test new jets and electronic countermeasures against Eastern Bloc interceptors and ground defenses. Captured Warsaw Pact military equipment, ranging from an entire Egyptian radar station to a defecting Iraqi MiG Fishbed, ended up in American laboratories, so all their most secret components could be examined and the appropriate countermeasures devised. While politicians picked over the consequences of 1967's Six Day War and the participants on both sides reexamined the strategic lessons, the air intelligence analysts were assessing the strengths and weaknesses of the opposing forces, confident that the outcome of the next clash again would be decided in the air.

As well as providing aircraft to undertake the many air intelligence roles, the discipline also encompasses fulfillment of the requirement to collect data on an adversary's order-of-battle and equipment. During the

Cold War, air intelligence represented good value for money. Weapon systems often took years to develop before they entered service, and would remain in use for years, sometimes decades. In those circumstances, early discovery of technical data could have a lasting impact. The opportunity to learn the secrets of a MiG-21 or to recruit an avionics engineer with access to technical manuals can pay long-term dividends. To examine a captured missile or electronic jammer offers the chance to develop the apparatus that can neutralize an investment worth millions. Conflict in the Middle East also provided opportunities for the Cold War protagonists to pit Western innovation, such as the Phantom F-4, against the SA-2 Guideline missile, which would be principal air defense system deployed in Vietnam.

American U-2 overflights had been conducted with minimal interference from Soviet air defenses, but once the KGB had learned of the astonishing plane's operating altitudes, elaborate arrangements were made to bring one down. Similarly, when the Central Intelligence Agency traitor William Kampiles sold the KH-11 handbook to his Soviet contacts in 1978, he compromised an entire satellite surveillance system that cost millions of dollars and thereby enabled the most sensitive sites in Russia to be concealed during daylight hours.

During the 40 years of superpower confrontation that followed the first Soviet nuclear test, air intelligence was in the forefront of the constant search conducted by the protagonists for information about each other's strategic capabilities that might offer an advantage. The North Atlantic Treaty Organization concentrated on collecting evidence of Warsaw Pact strengths while the Soviets took elaborate measures to prevent effective intelligence collection within its territory, to the point of shooting down more than two dozen intruders into its airspace. With the advent of powerful antiaircraft missiles and supersonic interceptors, both sides came to rely on satellites to provide overhead imagery, and when the era of arms control, nonproliferation, and weapons reduction dawned, this same technology supplied the means to verify compliance with treaty obligations.

The final proxy war between the superpowers, which would bring the Soviet Union to its knees, also proved to be a conflict very dependent on air technology. With the Red Army able only to exercise its authority across Afghanistan after the invasion of December 1979, with the lethal gunships that cowed the local populations and kept the Mujahideen isolated in mountain hideouts, the introduction of shoulder-held heat-seeking missiles called Stingers eliminated the threat from the ubiquitous Hind helicopters. The first deliveries of this remarkable weapon, which previously had never been fired in combat, brought instant results, with Soviet aircrews limiting their operations to altitudes above 10,000 feet, a height that rendered them harmless to the guerrillas far below. Within weeks of the first casualties inflicted by the Stinger missile, the entire course of the war had changed and ultimately the Cold War was doomed. Once the last Soviet soldiers had been withdrawn from Afghanistan, the myth of Soviet military strength had been exposed, and the totalitarian states in Eastern Europe, bolstered only by the Brezhnev doctrine of repression, quickly opted for democracy and freedom.

The collapse of the Soviet Bloc proved to be another significant milestone in the development of air intelligence, although the heavy reliance built up over so long on technical sources made the West vulnerable to the new adversary, the suicide bomber who was not easily deterred from committing atrocities and was not dependent on the sponsorship of any state. Indeed, the first major American overseas military commitment, following the conventional deployment after DESERT STORM, was in 1993 in Mogadishu, where the world's most sophisticated hardware was defeated by ill-disciplined ragtag tribesmen led by a Somali warlord. This was a turning point, even if a subsequent brief NATO commitment in the former Yugoslavia in 1998 served to accentuate the impressive superiority of Western technology. In Kosovo, virtually every Serbian armored vehicle was to be swiftly eliminated during nighttime air raids conducted by American stealth ground-attack aircraft exploiting the infrared profiles of Warsaw Pact tanks, which though skillfully camouflaged required their engines to be turned over daily, thereby making them visible to airborne sensors and the heat-seeking missiles that they heralded.

Even so, since the conclusion of the Cold War, air intelligence remains dominant and effective, even if aerial photography cannot predict the intention of a dictator to invade his neighbor, nor any satellite cover every potential hotspot on the globe, nor any airborne intercept platform prevent a terrorist incident. Nevertheless, modern air intelligence technology does allow a pilotless Predator to monitor the activities of a terrorist and provide a platform for the Hellfire missile that, remotely controlled from an operations room hundreds of miles away, destroys a particular vehicle in a convoy traveling across a Yemeni desert, as happened in November 2002. Unmanned drones can take the battlefield risks in situations where commanders are reluctant to jeopardize their troops and can snoop on suspect North Korean and Iranian nuclear facilities, while satellites can scoop up the cell phone conversations and e-mail messages of high-value insurgents. Nor is such sophisticated technology available only to the superpowers, and as the lead time for the general introduction of military applications shortens, the knowledge required to develop such weapons spreads. Thus, in August 2006, an Israeli gunboat on patrol off the Lebanese coast sustained a direct hit from an Iranian-supplied drone packed with explosives and guided to its target by Hezbollah gunmen based in southern Beirut.

Today, arguably more than ever, the world of air intelligence is as relevant to the survival of states as much as it was when Adolf Hitler planned his vengeance weapons. Pilotless aircraft have the ability to penetrate deep into hostile territory undetected, collect valuable imagery, and empower a tactician thousands of miles away to unleash highly sophisticated weapons and destroy targets with breathtaking accuracy. Of course, overreliance on imagery or signal intercepts can result in poor intelligence and ultimately lead to an attack on a building occupied by a Chinese diplomatic mission in Belgrade or on a factory making harmless baby food in Khartoum—such accidents can have lasting political consequences. Old-fashioned deception techniques duped British photo interpreters during the Falklands conflict, and the simple expedient of burying fighters in the sand saved some of the Iraqi Air Force from total annihilation in 2003. However, for all the sophistication boasted by the cutting-edge systems deployed and refined in the skies over Kandahar and Baghdad, mastery of the air and gadgetry will have only a limited utility against an insurgency that is next to impossible to define against a largely civilian backdrop. Just as air superiority in Vietnam could not distinguish a Vietcong guerrilla from an innocent rice grower or spot North Vietnamese regulars sheltering under the jungle canopy, so a Sunni suicide bomber looks much the same as everyone else in the bazaar, especially from an altitude of several thousand feet.

Over the past century, air intelligence has moved from hazardous observation balloons to the microcircuitry that can send pictures from a video camera mounted on a remote-controlled vehicle the size of a hummingbird. The discipline is essentially technology-led, and therefore the need to record its progress is as essential as it is fascinating.

The Dictionary

– A –

A-4. The designation for the Aggregat-4, a German-designed and German-constructed liquid-fueled ballistic missile weighing 12 tons capable of carrying a one-ton warhead at 4,000 miles per hour to a target 150 miles away. The first two A-4 rockets had been successfully test-fired at Borkum in December 1934. Development continued, sponsored by the Wehrmacht, at **Peenemünde**, on the Baltic island of Usedom, until a launch of the military variant in June 1942. Following a demonstration for Hermann Göring in October 1942, the project gained the approval of Adolf Hitler, who in July 1943 ordered the A-4 into production, to be manufactured at Peenemünde, Friedrichshafen, Ahrweiler, and Wiener-Neustadt at a rate of 900 a month. The plan called for 3,080 missiles to be ready by December 1944, when the production rate would rise to 930 a month.

The A-4 was intended to be deployed in northern France for launches against London, controlled from a major underground bunker at Watten, with 43 other smaller sites preprepared in the region to handle the missiles, fuel, and associated equipment. The plan was significantly disrupted by air intelligence operations conducted by the British from December 1942, which culminated in a massive raid on Peenemünde in August 1943. This was followed by a **U.S.** Army Air Force attack on Watten and another on 7 September that totally destroyed the site.

The raids, which delayed production for no more than two months, forced the Germans to transfer rocket development work to a cavern at Traunsee, near Salzburg, and the main missile assembly plant to an underground Volkswagen factory at Nordhausen in the Harz mountains. Watten was abandoned in favor of another bunker complex at

Wizernes. The test range was switched, out of the Allies' reach, to Blizna, near Dubica in Poland. Codenamed HEIDELAGER, the site's operations were monitored by the interception of the Schultes-faffel's Enigma channel between Peenemünde and Blizna, codenamed CORNCRAKE, and by the local resistance organization, which was in wireless contact with London. After Blizna was overrun by the Red Army, British scientists sought Soviet permission to visit the site, which was granted in September 1944.

After the war, captured German scientists were employed at the White Sands Proving Ground in New Mexico to improve the V-2's design, and between April 1946 and June 1951, a total of 67 A-4s were test launched. The result was a further program, conducted at the Redstone Arsenal at Huntsville, Alabama, on a derivative with a range of 200 miles, which was tested in 1953 as the Redstone missile. *See also* BODYLINE; CROSSBOW; V-WEAPONS.

AARHUS RAID. In the middle of October 1944, the Danish resistance signaled London for a low-level attack on the Nazi headquarters in Aarhus, following the successful raid on Amiens prison, Operation **JERICHO**, in February and another similar raid on 11 April 1944 in The Hague, where six Mosquito FB-VIs of 613 Squadron had bombed the local Gestapo headquarters, destroying its entire archive.

On 31 October, Mosquitoes from 140 Wing attacked two buildings in Aarhus University occupied by the Gestapo (headed by Eugen Schwitzgebel), the Sicherheitsdienst (led by Obersturmbannführer Lonechun), and the **Abwehr** (commanded by Oberstleutnant Lutze). Conveniently, the location had been photographed only days earlier by 544 Squadron on a routine reconnaissance mission. The need for the raid was considered urgent as the local resistance organization had been betrayed and feared widespread arrests were imminent.

The raiders took off from Thorney Island, refueled at Swanton Morley for the 1,200-mile flight, and reached the target just as a conference of senior German intelligence officers was being convened. Between 150 and 160 Germans were killed, including Schwitzgebel and Lonechun, and most of the records in their protected archive were destroyed. Also, several prisoners under interrogation were able to make their escape. Of the 30 Danes believed to have been killed in the raid, most were informers employed by the Nazis. Only one aircraft, piloted by Wing Commander W. W. L. Thomas of 487 Royal

New Zealand Air Force, failed to return to base safely. It landed in Sweden, having been damaged by a bomb blast.

ABWEHR. In 1933, in defiance of the terms of the Versailles Treaty, the new Nazi government in Germany created a foreign intelligence agency, the Abwehr, headed by Captain Conrad Patzig. He was replaced in January 1935 by Admiral Wilhelm Canaris, who developed an organization split into three *Abteilung* devoted to secret intelligence, sabotage, and security. Each of the three sections included air branches, designated as I Luft, II Luft, and III Luft respectively. Although run from headquarters in Berlin, Abwehr operations were dispersed to *Abwehrstellen*, regional centers corresponding to the German military districts, and to *Kriegsorganisationen* established in neutral and occupied territories, with internal structures mirroring the head office at 72 Tirpitzufer.

Abteilung I Luft was responsible for preparing a prewar survey of airfields in England, and in 1935 dispatched a lawyer, Dr. **Herman Goertz**, to tour the country accompanied by a girl he claimed as his niece, but his indiscretion led to his arrest and imprisonment. As a result of this episode, the Abwehr was banned from conducting further similar operations and was obliged to rely on photographs taken from aircraft flown by **Theodor Rowehl**. *See also* LUFTWAFFE.

ACE. The codename assigned a Soviet spy, an aeronautical engineer working in England in 1967, for the KGB's Line X. Identified in 1992 by a defector, Vasili Mitrokhin, ACE had died some years earlier, but according to notes he had made while serving as one of the KGB's archivists, he had been of exceptional value and had supplied documents filling 500 volumes, each containing 300 pages, related to aircraft and their power plants. The material covered Concorde and the Super VC-10, and the aero engines included the controversial RB-211, the SNEY-505 and the Rolls-Royce Olympus-593. ACE also sold the KGB details of the flight simulators for the Lockheed L1011 and the Boeing 747, and apparently recruited another source from a rival company, codenamed SWEDE.

AEROFLOT. Founded in 1932, Aeroflot was the world's largest airline, and during the Cold War provided cover for clandestine reconnaissance missions, as Tupolev-104 airliners frequently strayed from their flight plans to overfly military installations. Several military transports, including the Antonov AN-12 Cub, the Tu-134, Tu-154, and the Ilyushin Il-67 often flew in Aeroflot livery. In 1968, Aeroflot initiated a direct, twice-weekly Tu-144 Cleat flight to New York from Moscow, but the route was canceled as a sanction following the imposition of martial law in Poland in December 1981. The Moscow to Washington, D.C., route had been suspended for a week the previous month when two Aeroflot flights on 8 November had deviated from their flight plans and overflown the Trident submarine base at New London, Connecticut, and the Pease Strategic Air Command base in New Hampshire.

During the Vietnam War Aeroflot flew Il-76 Candid, An-22 Cock, and An-12 Cub transports of the Voeynmo Transportnaya Aviatsyva (VTA) to supply weapons to Hanoi. In February 1979, there were six An-22 flights a day to Vietnam, routed through either Bombay or Calcutta, and regularly overflying military bases in Thailand and Laos.

At the height of the Cold War, Aeroflot flew 7,000 planes and helicopters and controlled 3,600 Soviet airfields. The main international airliner, the Tu-104, which opened the Moscow to Amsterdam route in 1958, was a civilian version of the Tu-16 Badger bomber. *See also* SOVIET UNION.

AFGHAN WARS. During the latter part of the guerrilla war conducted in Afghanistan, following the Soviet invasion of December 1979, more than 1,000 Scud IRBMs were fired against the Mujahideen resistance, and during the siege of Jalalabad in 1989 more than 400 missiles were launched, all of which were monitored by American satellites.

Satellite imagery played an important role in the conflict, and provided the **Central Intelligence Agency**'s (CIA) Afghan Task Force with a means of verifying claims of aircraft successes claimed by Mujahideen groups equipped with **Stinger** missiles. When the Stinger was first deployed, against a flight of Soviet Hind helicopters coming in to land at Jalalabad airport on 25 September 1986, confirmation that four of the gunships had been shot down was quickly available to the Task Force commander in Islamabad.

The invasion of Afghanistan in October 2001 to remove the Taliban, Operation ENDURING FREEDOM, proved more reliant on paramilitaries infiltrated into the country and the deployment of Special Forces rather than sophisticated technology, as demonstrated by the use of horses by CIA Special Operations personnel in preference to their specially adapted all-terrain vehicles. While imagery played a role in assisting the troops on the ground, overhead reconnaissance was exploited to provide features for maps rather than pinpoint enemy concentrations, a significant departure from Cold War military doctrine.

While the coalition forces exercised total air superiority over Afghanistan throughout all the phases of ENDURING FREEDOM, air intelligence made only a limited contribution to the guerrilla conflict that followed when the al-Qaeda leadership retreated into deep caves dug into the Tora Bora mountains and the Taliban regrouped in the rural areas of Waziristan. The introduction of **unmanned aerial vehicles** improved the quality of tactical aerial reconnaissance during ANACONDA and the bombing of Tora Bora. On the very first deployment of a **Predator**, it captured images of a tall figure dressed in white, identified as Osama bin Laden, in a compound near Khost. Since then air intelligence has provided high-quality imagery to support ground operations, but it is recognized that the contribution of the coverage in a guerrilla environment is bound to be limited.

AGNI. The Hindu word for "fire." The 14-ton, two-stage Agni missile, with an estimated range of 1,000 to 1,500 miles, was test-fired over the Bay of Bengal from a launch site 750 miles southeast of Delhi in May 1989. A second generation, designated as the Agni-Plus and Agni-B MRBM, went into development in December 1996, together with a submarine-launched variant, the Sagarika.

AI-2. Air Ministry intelligence branch designation during **World War II** of the section responsible for the analysis of enemy aircraft production.

AI-2(g). In 1942, the Air Ministry introduced a research unit, designated as AI-2(g), to undertake research into new enemy aircraft to anticipate the introduction of new equipment. At the time, the **Luftwaffe** was known to have more than 40 different models under development, including jet fighters and rockets. AI-2(g) deployed inspection teams to all theaters to examine downed planes and established an operations center in the Air Ministry to coordinate new information from all sources. *See also* PRISONERS OF WAR.

AI-3. The Air Ministry intelligence branch designation during **World War II** of the section responsible for assessing Axis air power. The AI-3(b) prepared estimates of the enemy's order-of-battle and was heavily reliant on intercepted **Luftwaffe** communications enciphered on the Enigma machine. Various keys, like RED, were broken early in the war and continued to be read continuously and contemporaneously, giving the Allied analysts a tremendous advantage and impressive accuracy. Other methods of monitoring Nazi aircraft production proved less efficient, such as the airframe sequential numbering system, which was altered by the Germans in the spring of 1943 when they introduced random gaps in the numbers.

The subsection AI-3(c), based at Hughenden Manor, near High Wycombe, produced operational target intelligence for Bomber Command. By the end of the war, AI-3(c) employed a staff of 370 personnel and sifted through information from the Central Interpretation Unit, **prisoners of war**, refugees, academic societies, insurance companies, and professional associations. AI-3 (e) was created in August 1941 to coordinate information about the Luftwaffe derived from Enigma.

AI-4. The Air Ministry intelligence branch designation during **World War II** of the section supervising the **Royal Air Force** Y Service, which managed the intercept sites that monitored enemy signals traffic. In Great Britain, the Y Service stations were located at Montrose in Scotland, Cheadle in Staffordshire, Chicksands Priory in Bedfordshire, West Kingsdown in Kent, and **Waddington** in Lincolnshire.

AI-K. Air Ministry intelligence branch designation during **World War II** of the section supervising the interrogation of captured enemy aircrew at Wilton Park, Latimer, and Trent Park, Cockfosters.

AIR AMERICA. A **Central Intelligence Agency** (CIA) proprietary company, owned by the Delaware-registered Pacific Corporation, Air America operated scheduled and charter flights, as well as undertaking clandestine missions across southeast Asia for the CIA. Created in 1959 as an offshoot of Civil Air Transport, Air America contracted for U.S. government business across the region and established separate, dedicated air terminals in South Vietnam, Laos, and Thailand. Air America's largest base, inside the **U.S.** Air Force airfield at Adorn in Thailand, became the hub for operations into Laos and Cambodia. Air America employed 5,000 staff and nearly 500 pilots, and operated 125 aircraft that not only flew scheduled services, but also dropped rice to Moe tribesmen, parachuted CIA paramilitaries and mercenaries on secret missions, trained pilots for the Thai National Police, and even bombed North Vietnam. Before Air America was dissolved, it was ranked the second largest airline in the United States. Some 85 Air America aircrew were killed in action in Vietnam.

AIR ASIA. In 1950, following the breakup of Civil Air Transport, Air Asia was formed as a **Central Intelligence Agency** (CIA) proprietary, as a subsidiary of the Pacific Corporation, to manage the huge aircraft maintenance facilities at Taipei. By 1955, Air Asia was the largest civilian aircraft service organization in the entire Pacific, employing 8,000 staff. *See also* VIETNAM WAR.

AIRBRIDGE DENIAL PROGRAM. The **Central Intelligence Agency** (CIA) operation introduced to deter cargo flights of cocaine from Peru to Colombia during the 1990s. It provided the local administrations with the technical means of finding and identifying the aircraft operating near the Brazilian border that were responsible for importing an estimated 310 tons of coca paste for refinement before being smuggled elsewhere, mainly to lucrative markets in the **United States** and Europe. The project became public after some 38 planes had been detected and destroyed, when in April 2001 an amphibious aircraft was shot down by Peruvian fighters over the Amazon. The plane had been spotted by a CIA surveillance aircraft, crewed by contractors, and Peruvian fighters had been vectored to intercept it. However, due to language difficulties, the pilot, Kevin Donaldson, was unable to identify himself as a member of an evangelical Baptist missionary group flying from Islandia, and his passengers, James and Veronica Bowers and their adopted baby daughter, were killed.

AIR FORCE ELECTRONIC SECURITY COMMAND (AFESC).
The U.S. Air Force principal cryptographic organization, AFESC collected signals intelligence for the National Security Agency. Created in 1947 and based at San Antonio, Texas, AFESC employs 10,000 military personnel and 877 civilians. During the Cold War, it operated from numerous ground sites across the globe. In the Pacific area, the AFESC is based at Hickam Air Force Base in Hawaii, with ground sites at Osan in Korea, Misawa and Kadena in Japan, Clark Air Base in the Philippines, and Wheeler Air Force Base in Hawaii. In Alaska, the AFESC is represented at Elmendorf and Eielsen Air Force Bases. In Europe the facilities are at Lindsey Air Base, Hahn, Tempelhof, Sembach, Bad Aibling, and Augsburg in Germany; Hellenikon in Greece; San Vito in Italy; Heraklion in Crete; and Alconbury, Mildenhall, and Chicksands in England. In the United States, the tactical headquarters of AFESC's electronic security is at Langley Air Force Base in Virginia, with subordinate detachments at Hurlburt Field in Florida, Bergstrom Air Force Base in Texas, Nellis Air Force Base in Nevada, Shaw Air Force Base in South Carolina, Homestead Air Force Base in Florida, and Tinker Air Force Base in Oklahoma. *See also* FORT GEORGE G. MEADE.

AIR FORCE INTELLIGENCE SERVICE (AFIS). The principal intelligence branch of the U.S. Air Force, AFIS consists of nine directorates, covering escape and evasion, data management, targets, attachés, operational intelligence, personnel, Soviet affairs, and security.

AIR FORCE OFFICE OF SPECIAL INVESTIGATIONS (AFOSI). The principal U.S. Air Force counterintelligence organization, based in Boulder, Colorado, AFOSI collects information about hostile intelligence agencies, runs penetration operations, and investigates breaches of security.

AIR FORCE SECURITY SERVICE (AFSS). Created in October 1948 as the U.S. Air Force's cryptographic organization, also responsible for airborne interception operations, the AFSS initially consisted of the 8th Radio Squadron Mobile (RSM), which moved from its headquarters at Vint Hill Farms in Virginia to Brooks Air

Force Base, Texas. Soon afterward it absorbed the 1st RSM, based at Johnson Air Force Base near Tokyo, and the 136th Communications Security detachment at Fort Slocum, New York. The new AFSS deployed the 2nd RSM to Darmstadt in Germany, to cover Soviet Morse and voice traffic west of the Urals, with the 1st RSM in Japan collecting traffic in the Far East. A 3rd RSM in Alaska was formed to cover the Arctic. The AFSS's name was later changed to the Electronic Security Command. *See also* BLUE SKY.

AIR FORCE SPECIAL ACTIVITIES CENTER (AFSAC). Previously the 1127th Field Activities Group and then the 7612th Air Intelligence Group, AFSAC is headquartered at Fort Belvoir, Virginia, with a detachment at Wright Patterson Air Force Base in Ohio, and collects intelligence from human sources through the interrogation of prisoners, the debriefing of defectors, and other clandestine means. In 1981, the declared establishment was 447 military personnel and 144 civilians. Overseas, AFSAC is represented in Hawaii at Hickam Air Force Base, with detachments at Yokota, Japan, and Yongsan, Korea, and in Germany at Lindsey Air Force Base with detachments at Munich, Nierrod, and Bitburg.

AIR FORCE SPECIAL PROJECTS OFFICE (AFSPO). Located at the Air Force's Space Division in El Segundo, California, the AFSPO collects strategic satellite intelligence for distribution to other intelligence agencies, and was subordinate to the **National Reconnaissance Office**.

AIR FORCE SPECIAL PLANS OFFICE (AFSPO). Created in 1982 as part of a U.S. Department of Defense expansion into strategic deception, the AFSPO undertakes classified deception operations.

AIR FORCE SPECIAL SECURITY OFFICE (AFSSO). A component of the **U.S. Air Force Intelligence Service**'s Directorate of Security and Communications Management, AFSSO is responsible for the security and handling of signals intelligence within the Air Force.

AIR FORCE TECHNICAL APPLICATION CENTER (AFTAC). Headquartered with a staff of 1,400 at Patrick Air Force Base in

Florida, AFTAC monitors nuclear proliferation through squadrons deployed to Wheeler Air Force Base in Hawaii, McClennan Air Force Base in California, and Lindsey Air Force Base in Germany. AFTAC manages the Atomic Energy Detection System and verifies treaty compliance in 30 foreign countries from overt and covert ground sites.

AIR FRANCE. Following permission granted to make scheduled flights to Moscow in 1959, the state-run Air France was persuaded by the **Central Intelligence Agency** to equip some Sud-Aviation Caravelles with covert photoreconnaissance equipment. Only selected flight-deck crew, who were Air Force reservists, knew about the equipment, which was activated over Moscow's air defenses, and during the course of 100 flights some five previously unidentified missile sites were photographed. In 1981, Air France's chairman, Pierre Marion, was appointed chief of his country's principal intelligence agency, the Direction-Générale de Sécurité Extérieure (DGSE).

AIR INDIA. On 23 June 1985, Air India's Flight 182 to New Delhi via Montreal and London was destroyed in midair over the Atlantic, 90 miles off Cork, by a bomb planted on the Boeing 747 jet in Toronto, killing all 329 crew and passengers aboard. Almost simultaneously, a bomb detonated at Narita Airport, Tokyo, killing two baggage handlers, as they unloaded it from a Canadian Pacific plane from Vancouver, destined for another Air India flight.

The sabotage, perpetrated by Sikh separatists, prompted the largest and longest investigation conducted by the Canadian Security Intelligence Service (CSIS), then headed by director general Ted Finn. Since its creation in July 1984, CSIS and its predecessor, the Royal Canadian Mounted Police Security Service, had been aware of the existence of a Sikh terrorist organization, the Dashmesh Regiment, dedicated to the establishment of Khalistan, an independent state within the Punjab in India. CSIS had recruited informants inside some of the most militant groups, such as the Dai Khalso, the Babbar Khalso, and the All India Sikh Students Federation, which enjoyed thriving memberships among Canada's large expatriate Punjabi community. However, the need to protect the identity of the CSIS agents and some of the electronic surveillance systems deployed against the suspected plotters, combined with legal errors made when applying for telephone intercept warrants, led to the collapse of the prosecution against those accused of the atrocity, and in August 1987, to the resignation of Ted Finn. All five of his deputies also took early retirement, denuding CSIS of experienced senior intelligence personnel.

AIR INTELLIGENCE AGENCY (AIA). In June 2007, the **U.S.** Air Intelligence Agency at Lackland Air Force Base, Texas, headed by General John Koziol, was renamed the Air Force Intelligence, Surveillance and Reconnaissance Agency. Responsible to the United States Air Combat Command, the new agency was aligned under General David Deptula, the Air Force deputy chief of staff for Intelligence, Surveillance and Reconnaissance (A2) as a field operating agency. The new organization incorporated the 70th Intelligence Wing and the Air Force Cryptologic Office at Fort George G. Meade in Maryland, the National Air and Space Intelligence Center at Wright-Patterson Air Force Base in Ohio, and the Air Force Technical Applications Center at Patrick Air Force Base in Florida.

AIR INTELLIGENCE DIRECTORATE. The title of Great Britain's principal air intelligence organization before and during **World War II**, located in the **Air Ministry**'s London headquarters at Adastral House. *See also* DIRECTOR OF AIR INTELLIGENCE.

AIR MINISTRY. From the creation of the **Royal Air Force** in 1919 and the tri-service amalgamation under the Ministry of Defence in 1964, air intelligence in Great Britain was supervised by the **Air Intelligence Directorate** of the Air Ministry. *See also* DIRECTOR OF AIR INTELLIGENCE.

AIR PIRACY. In the postwar period, the phenomenon of aircraft hijacking was largely limited to eastern Europe, with escapees from totalitarian regimes seizing control of civilian airliners and surrendering upon their arrival in the West, where they were generally well received and were granted political asylum. Similarly, until 1961, a dozen of the skyjackings in the Caribbean were perpetrated by Cubans on domestic flights intent on reaching the **United States**, where invariably the local courts would impound the aircraft in settlement of postrevolution confiscated property claims filed mainly by dispossessed companies.

The first hijacking to **Cuba** took place on 1 May 1961, and in the period up to 31 December 1972 a further 85 American planes were diverted to Havana. The incidents almost became routine, and the vulnerable airlines equipped their pilots with charts of Cuban airfields for use in just such an emergency. Gradually, evidence emerged that Fidel Castro's brother Raul, who had himself been involved in the hijacking of two planes in October 1958 in Oriente province, had organized many of the incidents, and set the sums required for the release and return of the American aircraft.

In this legal vacuum, President John F. Kennedy asked Congress to make various acts amounting to air piracy a felony, and from August 1961 the law enabled the Federal Aviation Administration, the **Central Intelligence Agency**, and the Federal Bureau of Investigation to collect information on the subject.

Modern air terrorism may be said to have begun on 6 September 1970, when a TWA 707 flying from Frankfurt to New York was diverted to Dawson's Field in Jordan and a Swissair DC-8 from Zurich for New York was also seized and forced to land on the same airstrip, but two terrorists, Leila Khaled and Patrick Arguello, on an El-Al 707, flying from Amsterdam to New York, were overpowered. The plane made an emergency landing at Heathrow, where the sole surviving hijacker, Leila Khaled, was detained by the police. She had been carrying a grenade in each cup of her bra, and he had been armed with a pistol and a hand grenade, but the pair had been disarmed by well-trained stewards. A fourth plane, a Pan Am jumbo jet, was flown to Cairo, where it was emptied of passengers and crew and blown up. The next day, a British BOAC jet was hijacked on a flight bound to London from Bahrain. The VC-10 was made to land at Dawson's Field, making a total of three aircraft and adding 115 additional hostages to those already there, surrounded by Popular Front for the Liberation of Palestine (PFLP) guerrillas armed with machine guns and mortars and watched by tanks of an impotent Royal Jordanian Army.

Arguello, the terrorist shot by El-Al sky marshals, turned out to be a Nicaraguan revolutionary and University of California at Los Angeles graduate working on a master's degree in sociology, while his companion was a 24-year-old Palestinian who had already participated in a successful hijacking. The previous August, she had led a group of terrorists who had seized a TWA 707 on a flight from Rome to Tel Aviv, which she had diverted to Damascus. There the passengers had been allowed to disembark and Khaled had been freed, following her unsuccessful attempt to destroy the aircraft. Significantly, the Syrians had retained two of the passengers, both Israelis, and had exchanged them for 13 Syrians in Israeli prisons. She was a dedicated acolyte of Dr. George Habash, the PFLP's Marxist leader, who had learned about air piracy as an instrument of political blackmail and as a military tactic from Raul Castro, the mastermind behind a wave of hijackings in the United States.

With the TWA, BOAC, and Swissair planes emptied of 127 non-Jewish or American women and children, who were taken to three of the major international hotels in Amman, the PFLP's leadership announced its terms for a release of the rest of the hostages. It demanded immediate freedom for Robert Kennedy's assassin Sirhan Sirhan, for Leila Khaled in London, for all Palestinian prisoners in Israeli jails, for three Arabs convicted of an attack on an El-Al 707 at Zurich in February 1969 in which two people were killed, and for three terrorists convicted in Germany of attacking an El-Al bus at Munich airport in February. Thus, there were five governments directly concerned with the negotiations. Only the Israelis refused to participate; the Swiss and the Germans wanted to reach a settlement immediately and independently of the British and Americans. For the British, there were the lives of 21 unaccompanied children who had boarded the VC-10 in Bahrain to return to school. Accordingly, a few days later Leila Khaled, whose offenses had been committed in international airspace, was escorted to Heathrow from her cell in Ealing police station and put on a flight to Beirut to be joined by the other six prisoners from Switzerland and Germany. This served to facilitate the hostages' release in Jordan.

These events, followed by the rescue of hostages taken in Entebbe in June 1976 and Mogadishu in October 1977, led to the introduction of international conventions on airline security and transformed the civil air transport environment. In Britain in 1989, following the transfer of responsibility for counterterrorism to the Security Service, a senior MI5 officer, Harold Dotne-Ditmass, was appointed to co-ordinate measures to improve airport security. A further standard was set by Sir John Wheeler, formerly chairman of the National Criminal Intelligence Service, who undertook several international security surveys, including reports for the British and Australian governments.

The introduction of measures intended to reduce the risk of air piracy, such as the physical separation of all arriving and departing passengers at airports, effectively eliminated the problem, but the recovery of al-Qaeda-sponsored plans in Malaysia in 2000 for a coordinated simultaneous seizure of 10 American airliners by suicide jihadis heralded a new, unanticipated era. Henceforth, concerns about air piracy would be replaced by attempts to thwart sophisticated schemes for flight-trained terrorists to take control of fully fueled aircraft, thus transforming them into instruments of suicide, as outlined in al-Qaeda's scheme codenamed **BOJINKA**. Although several such plots were prevented after 11 September 2001, on that day al-Qaeda succeeded in hijacking four planes and flew three of them into targets in Manhattan and Washington, D.C. *See also* 9/11.

AKULA. Imagery taken by a KH-11 satellite in 1984 of the Komsomolsk shipyard in the Soviet Far East alerted analysts to the existence of the new third-generation nuclear submarine designated as *Akula* by North Atlantic Treaty Organization. Known to the Soviets as the *Karp*, or K-284, the imagery allowed American submarines to be present covertly when it was launched in July 1984 and taken to Bolshoi Kamen, near Vladivostock, for completion. The *Akula* turned out to be astonishingly quiet, with an estimated 2.5 inches of anechoic coating on the hull to reduce noise, making it an exceptionally hard target to detect acoustically.

ALGERIA. During the war of Algerian independence that ended in 1962, French troops were heavily dependent on helicopters, of which 600 were deployed against the guerrillas. However, the insurgents adopted tactics to lure airborne forces into traps, and despite massive air superiority the French were unable to find the necessary countermeasures and suffered heavy losses. The same techniques were later to be passed to the North Vietnamese, enabling them to use them with significant effect against American air power. *See also* VIETNAM WAR.

AL-SHIFA. On 7 August 1998, the U.S. embassies in Nairobi and Dar-es-Sallam were attacked by massive truck bombs, killing 257 and wounding 5,000, including 12 Americans. On President Bill Clinton's orders, the Pentagon executed a retaliatory strike, codenamed INFINITE REACH, against Osama bin Laden's main training facility near Khost in **Afghanistan**, known as the Tarnal Farms, and on a pharmaceutical factory at al-Shifa, outside **Khartoum**, on 20 August. According to the **Central Intelligence Agency**, bin Laden had invested heavily in the Sudan during his four years there, and owned a tannery in the capital. He was also alleged to own the al-Shifa plant, and a covert test of the soil there had revealed the existence of O-ethyl methylphosphonothioic acid (EMPTA), a precursor chemical for VX nerve gas. Seventy-nine Tomahawk cruise missiles were launched from warships and submarines in the Arabian Sea, but because they were to cross Pakistani airspace, advance notice was given to Islamabad and a warning was received by bin Laden, who fled the camp. Up to 20 terrorist trainees were killed in the raid, but bin Laden escaped. The owner of the al-Shifa factory, who said he had only manufactured baby food, was later awarded compensation for his loss, an admitted intelligence failure as he had only manufactured vitamins and food supplements.

ALSOS. The Greek word for "grove," ALSOS was the codename given to a secret study conducted during **World War II** by General Leslie Groves of the Manhattan project to establish whether the Nazis had made any progress in building a nuclear reactor or developing an atomic weapon. ALSOS included a significant air component to collect air samples over suspected sites of Nazi research, in an effort to identify telltale traces of xenon gas and to analyze aerial reconnaissance imagery for the large new buildings that might resemble the huge gaseous diffusion plant at Oak Ridge, Tennessee. Failure to find any airborne radioactive particles over Germany and the absence of any characteristic, large-scale construction of the type associated with the Manhattan project proved that the threat of a Nazi bomb was minimal. ALSOS also included one of the largest aerial photographic operations of the war, in an attempt to identify the huge new windowless buildings associated with nuclear research and, in particular, the gaseous diffusion plant at Oak Ridge, Tennessee, then the largest building in the world, and to locate any likely atomic reactor sited near a source of cold water. The study, headed by Professor Philip Morrison, concluded that the Nazis had not made the visibly massive investment required to achieve fission or a nuclear chain reaction.

ANDERSON, RUDOLF. The **U.S.** Air Force pilot of a **U-2** overflying Cuba's north coast on a photoreconnaissance mission early on the morning of Saturday, 27 October 1962. Major Anderson's plane, designated as Article 343, was shot down by a salvo of Soviet SA-2 Guideline fired by Major Ivan Grechenov from the Banes naval base. The missile detonated above and behind the plane and shrapnel penetrated the cockpit and the pilot's pressure suit at shoulder level.

Rudy Anderson's flight, from McCoy Air Force Base in Florida, was the sixth scheduled for that day, but the five previous missions that morning had been canceled. He had made a previous overflight, Mission 3103 on 15 October, and had flown over 1,000 hours in the U-2 since he had converted to the aircraft in 1957. He was one of the two most experienced 4080th Strategic Air Command (SAC) U-2 pilots based at Laughlin Air Force Base at Del Rio, Texas. He had also trained at Edwards Air Force Base on the **Central Intelligence Agency**'s (CIA) new U-2C version, which was equipped with the SYSTEM-9 intercept warning device and jammer, and the SYSTEM-12 receiver, which emitted a warning when a SAM **radar** locked onto the aircraft.

McCoy had been chosen as a suitable base for the overflights because of its proximity to Cuba, which would allow the aircraft to enter hostile airspace with only 660 gallons of fuel, thereby allowing the lighter plane maximum altitude of 68,000 feet. However, the National Security Agency's (NSA) local intercept platform, the USS *Oxford*, had reported on 15 September that Soviet P-12 SPOON REST emissions, associated with the acquisition radar for SA-2s, had been detected. On 10 October, the NSA revealed that Soviet signal traffic indicated that the recent reorganization and reequipping of Cuba's air defenses had now been completed and therefore posed a new, enhanced threat. CIA pilots would later complain that because the mission planning of the overflights had been surrendered to SAC, the usual precautions of not repeating routes had been abandoned, making it easier for the Cuban air defenses to anticipate incursions. When informed of the loss, President John F. Kennedy considered an immediate retaliation against all the SAM sites in Cuba, but an accidental incursion over the North Pole the same day, by Major **Charles Maltsby**, led to him instead offering an apology to Nikita Khrushchev. All further overflights of Cuba were suspended for several days, until five missions were flown simultaneously in Operation GREEN ARROW. *See also* KOMAKI.

APHRODITE. U.S. Army Air Force codename for a remotely controlled B-17 packed with 20,000 pounds of explosives that was intended to destroy Nazi strongpoints in France in August 1944. The first attempt took off from Fersfield, Norfolk, on 4 August, but crashed at Sudbourne Park in Suffolk before the crew of two could parachute to safety. Eight days later, a second APHRODITE mission, a U.S. Navy Liberator piloted by Lieutenant John Kennedy, exploded over Southwold and killed both crewmen aboard. All further APHRODITE missions were canceled.

AQUACADE. National Security Agency codename for a signals intelligence **satellite** series that became operational in May 1977 as a second generation of the **RHYOLITE** system. *See also* BYEMAN.

ARAB-ISRAELI CONFLICT. The wars fought in the Middle East in 1948, 1956, 1967, and 1973 between **Israel** and her Arab neighbors provided opportunities for Western technology to be tested against Warsaw Pact hardware. Whereas in the **Suez crisis** of October 1956 and **Six Day War** of June 1967 Israel conducted preemptive strikes based upon first-class intelligence that resulted in the destruction of the Arab air forces on the ground, the coordinated surprise attack launched by Jordan, **Syria**, and Egypt on Yom Kippur in October 1973 caught the Israeli Defense Force (IDF) unprepared. Only the emergency airlift of logistics and the supply of air imagery from the **United States** enabled the IDF to repel the Arab offensive. Thereafter, Israel's very survival was largely reliant on an indigenous and American-dependent technological advantage based on the country's ability to monitor its adversary's activities and, where necessary, launching surgical interventions to deny an enemy a potential strategic advantage, as happened in 1981 when Saddam Hussein's nuclear reactor at Osiraq was destroyed in an air raid. *See also* WAR OF ATTRITION.

ARADO-234. The reconnaissance variant of the Ar-234 jet bomber was the Ar-234s, a twin-engined high-performance aircraft with a speed of 500 miles per hour and a range of 1,000 miles. Introduced in February 1944, some 200 would be delivered to the Luftwaffe before the end of the war and a series of missions over England in September 1944 caused considerable alarm among the Allies. Thereafter, all the reconnaissance jets were converted for use as bombers.

AREA 51. Located on the dry Groom Lake in southern Nevada near Las Vegas, Area 51 is the official designation of the Watertown strip, an isolated, heavily guarded airfield where numerous secret aircraft have been tested since the first test flight of the **U-2** in July 1955. The facility enjoys a 26-mile exclusion zone, to prevent being overlooked, and forms part of the 15,000 square miles of ranges and protected airspace managed by Nellis Air Force Base.

ARGON. United States codeword for imagery collected by the **CORONA satellite** system. *See also* LANYARD.

ARGUS. An improved signals intelligence **satellite** introduced in 1975 to replace the **RHYOLITE** system, the Argus was constructed by a **Central Intelligence Agency** contractor, TRW Inc., but in 1976 an employee, **Christopher Boyce**, sold information about it to the KGB.

ARGUS. Canada's principal antisubmarine warfare aircraft, Argus patrols from Nova Scotia provided North Atlantic Treaty Organization cover for the northern Atlantic during the Cold War.

ARMY SECURITY AGENCY (ASA). During the Cold War, the U.S. Army's cryptographic branch conducted airborne collection operations for the National Security Agency with Special Electronic Mission Aircraft based at the 320th ASA Company at Ramstein in Germany, the 138th ASA Company in Orlando, Florida, and the 146th ASA Company at Tageu in South Korea. Equipped with unarmed twin-engined RU-21H Beechcraft, the intercept missions were codenamed **GUARDRAIL**. During the Vietnam War the ASA operated from Hue Phu Bei, mounting missions codenamed LAFFING EAGLE, LEFT FOOT, and LEFT JAB.

ARNISTON. The principal missile test site in South Africa, Arniston was monitored by American satellites when an Israeli Jericho-II was launched in July 1989. Collaboration between the two countries included a probable nuclear test in the atmosphere of an Israeli atomic weapon in 1979.

ARTICLE. A **Central Intelligence Agency** term for the **U-2** reconnaissance aircraft. The U-2 was rarely referred to directly in classified communications, but simply as "article," followed by a three-digit number specific to the particular mission.

ASPIRIN. **Royal Air Force** codename for the transmitters across the country employed to disrupt the **Luftwaffe**'s navigational beams that guided bombers to their targets in England. Some 2,000 personnel of 80 Wing operated 15 ASPIRIN sites, the electronic countermeasures taken to jam the enemy signals codenamed HEADACHE.

AURORA. Codename of a secret **United States** reconnaissance aircraft developed by Lockheed at Burbank, California, as a successor to the **SR-71 Blackbird**. First mentioned in a budget leak, the Aurora is reputed to fly at a speed of between Mach 6 and 7.

AUTOMAT. The **Central Intelligence Agency** codename for the Photographic Intelligence Division, headed by **Art Lundahl**, which was initially accommodated in M Building, a former **World War II** barracks in Washington, D.C. In 1955, HT/AUTOMAT moved to the Que Building, and the staff increased to 13 personnel, and then settled on the top four floors of the Steuart Building, some 50,000 square feet of offices on 5th Street and New York Avenue, over a Ford car dealership and showroom.

AVIATSIYA VOENNO MORSKOVE FLOTA (AVMF). The Soviet Naval Air Service conducted electronic and photoreconnaissance operations against the West throughout the Cold War. *See also* SOVIET UNION.

– B –

BABINGTON-SMITH, CONSTANCE. Flying Officer Constance Babington-Smith was the photo interpreter based at **Medmenham** during **World War II** credited with being the first to identify a V-2 rocket in imagery taken by a **Royal Air Force** aerial reconnaissance mission over **Peenemünde**. After the war, she wrote an account of her work, *Evidence in Camera*, in which she described the process of photographic interpretation.

BABYFACE. American codename for an abortive U-2 mission from Bodo in **Norway** scheduled for September 1958 but canceled because of technical problems with both the aircraft delivered to the base.

BAEDEKER RAIDS. In the spring of 1942, the **Luftwaffe** launched a series of surprise air raids against poorly defended English provincial centers, starting with Exeter in April, followed by Bath, Norwich, York, and Canterbury. Because these market cities were not military targets, the logic behind the German strategy eluded air intelligence analysts who noted only that all were listed in the popular *Baedeker* tourist guide.

BALDWIN, STANLEY. In May 1935, Prime Minister Stanley Baldwin admitted to the House of Commons that the figures he had given earlier in the month for the **Luftwaffe**'s strength had been entirely wrong. He had been forced to make the admission by the Secret Intelligence Service chief, Admiral Sir Hugh Sinclair, who had threatened to resign unless the correction had been made. Sinclair's complaint had resulted in an enquiry conducted by a Cabinet subcommittee chaired by the secretary of state for air, Sir Philip Cunliffe-Lister, and comprising the President of the Board of Trade

Lord Runciman, the Postmaster-General Sir Kingsley Wood and Lord Londonderry, the former minister for air. Also present when Sinclair presented his evidence were the chief of the air staff, Sir Edward Ellington, the **Royal Air Force**'s director of operations and intelligence, Air Vice Marshal Christopher Courtney, and the director of air intelligence, Archie Boyle. Sinclair was supported by the head of air section, Fred Winterbotham, and Desmond Morton, and his view had prevailed, prompting Baldwin to make the retraction.

BALLOONS. The first use of hot-air balloons, in the 18th century, were for the collection of intelligence, although in subsequent years tethered balloons were deployed for artillery spotting and eventually for photography. In more modern times, it was used as a platform, codenamed **FILBERT**, to deceive enemy **radar** during the **D-Day** landings, and then as vehicles for remote **GOPHER** cameras, released in Europe and intended to drift over the **Soviet Union**.

Ballooning dates back to 1783, when the Montgolfier brothers first flew, and within the decade a balloon corps had been formed in France to exploit the military applications. Two years later, in 1795, Captain Jean Marie Coutelle was the first soldier to come under fire while airborne, while making observations over many hours during the Battle of Fleurus in Belgium. Napoleon understood the balloon's value and in 1798, a Companie d'Aérostiers, created four years earlier, was sent to Egypt.

Until 1856, soldiers going aloft in balloons were dependent on their eyesight, but the French conducted experiments in aerial photography, the first of which ended in disappointment. However, in 1858 Felix Tourachon carried a darkroom into the air on a balloon to process images on glass plates, thereby establishing the camera as an essential component of air reconnaissance, and in 1866 photographs were taken of Boston, Massachusetts. This breakthrough amounted to airborne espionage, as the meteorologist Thaddeus Lowe discovered in 1861, when he was arrested as a Union spy when he landed accidentally in South Carolina in the *Eagle*. The Confederates were also exploiting balloons, and in 1862 Professor Lowe's balloon, the *Intrepid*, was deployed during the Battle of Fair Oaks.

In Europe, balloons were used during the Franco-Prussian War in 1870 to fly agents and documents out of besieged Paris. Over the next

10 years, balloons became widely accepted as part of the military arsenal. In 1884, the British Army in Bechuanaland was equipped with them, and a year later the Sudan Expedition used observation balloons. By 1890, the Royal Engineers introduced a Balloon Section, and this would play an active role in Natal during the Boer War. In the **United States**, the army established a balloon unit at Fort Myer, Virginia, in 1908.

BAY OF PIGS. One of the largest air operations ever conducted by the **Central Intelligence Agency** (CIA) was to provide air cover over the Bay of Pigs (Bahia de Cohnos) during Operation **ZAPATA**, the invasion by a force of Cuban émigrés, Brigade 2506, in April 1961. The aircraft, resembling Fidel Castro's obsolete B-26 bombers and Hawker Sea Furies, were painted in Cuban Air Force colors and were flown from a CIA-constructed airstrip at Puerto Cabezas on Nicaragua's Caribbean coast. To enhance the Cuban émigré aircrew, the CIA recruited 80 additional pilots, navigators, and armorers from the Alabama Air National Guard, one of the last American military units with B-26 experience. The landings were to begin with a parachute drop of 172 troops from six C-46s and a C-54, to be followed by Operation PLUTO, the assault ships carrying six battalions of infantry supported by five M-41 tanks, hitting the beaches.

The 1,400 soldiers of Brigade 5706 had been trained at a CIA camp in Guatemala designated as Rayo at Retalhuleu, while the air component had assembled at Puerto Barrios, codenamed TRAX, prior to moving down to Nicaragua for embarkation. Their original landing area was the port of Trinidad, but this would be changed in the final weeks to the Bahia de Cochinos. The original plan, prepared during the Eisenhower administration, called for three air raids by 16 B-26 medium bombers before the invasion to destroy Castro's air force of six B-26 bombers, five Lockheed T-33 jet fighters, and five Hawker Sea Furies. Castro's inventory also included two F-47s and two F-61s that were not airworthy, three C-47 transports, a Catalina, and a few small spotter planes. The CIA's plan also anticipated that the invaders' aircraft would be escorted by fighters, and there was a time imperative because 300 Cuban pilots had been sent to flight school in Czechoslovakia for conversion to MiG-15s, and it was uncertain when the first of the jets would be assembled from their crates and made operational.

However, the CIA's plan, prepared by Colonel Jack Hawkins, William ("Rip") Robertson, and Gerry Droller (alias "Frank Bender"), would be largely rewritten by the Kennedy White House, which canceled the last two preemptive air raids, halved the bombers on the first strike, and banned the fighter escorts, thus handing the Cuban Air Force complete air superiority. At dawn on 15 April, eight B-26s attacked the airfields at Campo Libertad and San Antonio de los Bahos, and Antonio Maceo Airport at Santiago de Cuba, destroying a Cuban DC-3, a Lodestar, two B-26s, and a couple of fighters. Later, Castro would claim that the plane wrecks at Campo Liberdad had only been plywood decoy dummies. On the day of the invasion, a total of 13 combat sorties were flown, and two Cuban B-26s and two Sea Furies were shot down by ground fire. However, Cuban aircraft quickly sank a supply freighter, the *Rio Excondido*, and the troopship *Houston*.

Altogether, four CIA aircrew were killed: Thomas ("Pete") Ray, navigator Leo Baker, Major Riley Shamburger, and navigator Wade Gray. The Cuban casualties were navigator Eddie Gonzales, Captain Matias Farias, and Captain Raul Vianello, whose two B-26 bombers crash-landed in Cuba after having been hit by T-33 fighters; and Captain Oswaldo Piedra, navigator Joe Fernandez, Captain José Alberto Crespo, and navigator Lorenzo Perro Lorenzo, whose B-26s came down in the sea after encounters with Cuban Sea Furies. Captain Crispin Garcia and navigator Juan Gonzales were killed when their B-26 ran out of fuel 50 miles from the runway in Nicaragua. The B-26s, with their tail gun-turrets removed, had proved extremely vulnerable to the Cuban fighters, and as a result had failed in their two objectives, to prevent Castro's reinforcements with T-34 tanks from reaching Giron, and to establish an air bridge to TRAX, 500 miles away, so the ground troops could be resupplied. Several damaged planes, unable to make the return flight home, limped onto the runway on the British colony of Grand Cayman, whence their aircrew were evacuated discreetly by the CIA. During the four days of fighting, 36 missions were flown from Nicaragua and 14 aircrew died, including five from Castro's air force. The four Americans, all killed on 19 April, were shot down over Cuba during a period when President John F. Kennedy had reluctantly agreed to an hour's air cover provided by **U.S.** Navy A-4 Skyhawks from the carrier USS *Essex*. Unfortunately, the one-hour time difference between Central American

time, when the CIA missions began, and Eastern Standard Time in
Washington, D.C., were unnoticed by the flight planners, so the CIA
aircrew were unprotected and fell prey to the T-33s.

The Bay of Pigs defeat, which resulted in almost 1,200 of the invaders being taken into captivity, led to the departure from the CIA
of **Richard Bissell** and then in December of his Director of Central
Intelligence, Allen Dulles. Thereafter, the CIA took the blame for a
massive failure, although the postmortem report of June 1961 concluded that the original plan had enjoyed a better than fifty-fifty
chance of success. Unmentioned was the belief held by the principal
CIA planners that a separate operation to assassinate Castro would
have had a significant impact on ZAPATA's outcome.

BERBERA. In June 1975, the U.S. Department of Defense released
U-2 pictures of a large Soviet bunker complex outside Berbera, on
Somalia's north coast, opposite Aden. The photographs, published in
preference to compromising satellite imagery, proved the Red Banner
Fleet operating in the Indian Ocean had acquired an extensive stor-
age facility to replenish warships with missiles.

BIG BEN. Royal Air Force codename for **ELINT** flight flown in 1944
to detect the signals mistakenly believed to have guided German V-2
missiles to their targets. In fact, the **V-weapons** were not radio-
controlled.

BIG BIRD. A second generation American photoreconnaissance
satellite system designated as KH-11. The first Big Bird was 64
feet long, 10 feet in diameter, and weighed 29,260 pounds; it was
launched a year late and $1 billion over budget from Vandenberg
Air Force Base on 15 June 1971 into a sun-synchronous orbit that
lasted 54 days. Altogether, a dozen Big Birds were put into orbit
until July 1978, and they played a significant role in detecting Soviet violations of the Strategic Arms Limitation Talks (SALT)
treaties that were intended to cap the number of nuclear warheads
and delivery systems in the possession of the **United States** and
the **Soviet Union.** The huge investment in the KH-11 led some in
the intelligence community to complain that it had starved other
projects of funding.

BIG SAFARI. The Strategic Air Command codename for the Peacetime Airborne Reconnaissance Program that conducted **ELINT** collection flights along the periphery of the **Soviet Union.**

BIG TEAM. Codename of the **U.S.** Air Force classified contract for the construction of 10 RC-135 Boeings in 1964.

BIRD DOG. The Cessna two-seat observation aircraft was developed from the commercial Model 170 in 1949 and used by the **U.S.** Air Force, Army, and Marines for artillery spotting, front-line communications, medical evacuation, and pilot training. In Vietnam, the slow, unarmed Bird Dogs were used by forward air controllers to reconnoiter targets, and in Laos they were used by the Central Intelligence Agency to direct ground-attack aircraft onto Vietcong positions. The French also used them as observation aircraft during Algeria's war of independence.

BISMARCK. On the morning of 27 May 1941, HMS *Rodney, Dorsetshire,* and *King George V* closed in on the stricken *Bismarck* and sank the German pocket battleship and her crew of 2,000 with a series of lethal volleys, followed by a final torpedo. The previous day, the *Bismarck*'s rudders had been disabled by a torpedo during an attack by 15 Fairey Swordfish of the *Ark Royal*, and she could only steam in circles, making her a vulnerable target. The question of precisely how the *Bismarck* had been discovered in the Atlantic, 700 miles off the French coast, having skillfully eluded the **radar** contact with her Royal Navy shadows, and having sunk the battle-cruiser HMS *Hood*, remains a matter of debate. Certainly she was spotted at 1030 on 26 May by a patrolling **Royal Air Force** Coastal Command Catalina from Lough Erne, but that discovery may have been a cover for a cryptographic breakthrough that had compromised Admiral Lutjen's decision to head not for the open sea or back to Norway, but to the French port of Brest. Many who worked at Bletchley Park and knew of the signals that had indicated the *Bismarck*'s objective remain sure that the Catalina's encounter was not entirely fortuitous, and merely a cover for the code breakers. Signals intelligence had revealed on 24 May that wireless control of the *Bismarck* had been changed from Wilhelmshaven to Paris, a good indication she was heading for

France, and that conclusion had been confirmed by a wireless message on a Luftwaffe circuit, encrypted in the RED Enigma key from the Luftwaffe's chief of staff in Athens, who had enquired about his nephew serving on board. The reply was that the *Bismarck* was heading for the west coast of France.

Admiral Sir James Somerville may have already concluded, without the help of signals intelligence, that his adversary was heading for the Bay of Biscay, and the intercepts confirming his judgment may have arrived too late to influence him, but it is certain that the Catalina was briefed on where to patrol based on the Enigma information and the aircraft was seen and engaged briefly by the *Bismarck*. The Catalina's mission was unusual in that it was an extra reconnaissance, and had been ordered personally by Sir Frederick Bowhill, Coastal Command's air officer commander-in-chief, a very senior officer with access to the ULTRA source. Thus, by intention or otherwise, the Germans were led to believe that the battle cruiser's position had been compromised by a plane and not a signal. But was Bowhill responsible for "a shrewd guess" as the historian Patrick Beesly suggested, or a calculated ruse?

BISSELL, RICHARD. Educated at Groton, Yale, and the London School of Economics, Richard M. Bissell had taught economics at the Massachusetts Institute of Technology before joining the **Central Intelligence Agency** (CIA) in 1954 as chief of the Development Projects staff. Four years later, the Director of Central Intelligence Allen Dulles named him deputy director for plans, the head of the CIA's Clandestine Service. Although replaced by Richard Helms following the Bay of Pigs debacle in April 1961, Bissell is credited with having encouraged the innovative use of high-flying reconnaissance aircraft, such as the **U-2** and **SR-71** to penetrate the Soviet Union and the People's Republic of China, and the development of satellites. He died in February 1994.

BITING. British codename for a raid on a German coastal **radar** station at Bruneval, near Le Havre, on 27 February 1942. A force of 119 paratroops was dropped near the isolated cliff-top site, which had been the subject of several photographic reconnaissance missions. The operation resulted in the capture of a German radar operator and the removal of a **WURZBURG** antenna, receiver, amplifier, and modulator. The equipment was returned to England by boat where it was examined by experts. As a result of the raid, the Germans fortified their other radar sites with characteristic rings of barbed wire, making them much easier to identify from the air.

BLACKBIRD. The **SR-71** Blackbird flew at 90,000 feet at Mach 3 and went into operation in 1966 at Beale Air Force Base, near Sacramento, California, headquarters of the 9th Strategic Reconnaissance Wing. Two aircraft were permanently rotated to **Royal Air Force** (RAF) Mildenhall in Suffolk, England, and flew missions across Europe and operated from RAF Akrotiri in Cyprus. Immensely thirsty, the plane required refueling every 90 minutes, a maneuver undertaken by a tanker aircraft, accompanied by a backup to provide a margin of safety.

The Blackbird remained in service for 24 years, and none of the 29 aircraft delivered to the **U.S.** Air Force was lost to hostile fire, although more than 1,000 missiles were fired at them during a total of 3,551 operational missions. The aircraft, which was never equipped with a downlink, was designed to outrun Soviet surface to air missiles and flew over North Korea and Vietnam, but was never deployed over the Soviet Union or the People's Republic of China.

BLACK BUCK. The most complex bombing mission ever flown by the **Royal Air Force**, BLACK BUCK was the codename for a raid undertaken by a Vulcan B-2 operating from Ascension on 1 May 1982 to destroy the Argentine-occupied airfield at Port Stanley in the Falkland Islands. The ageing bomber from 101 Squadron Strike Command, its nuclear bomb bay having been converted to accommodate conventional weapons, flew the marathon 8,000-mile, 15-hour round-trip supported by 11 Victor K2 tankers, each loaded with 100,000 pounds of fuel. After five refuelings on the outward journey, the single plane flown by Flight-Lieutenant Martin Withers, which was actually a backup for the original Vulcan from 50 Squadron that had abandoned the mission because of a pressurization problem, had dropped 21 1,000-pound bombs over the target from an altitude of 10,000 feet, well out of range of the French Roland and the British Tiger Cat missiles on the ground. By the time the Argentine AN/TPS-44 radar, manned by the 601st Anti-Aircraft Regiment on Sapper Hill, had identified the lone intruder, the Vulcan was on its journey home, its sophisticated electronic countermeasures, including the U.S. AN/ALQ-101 jammers carried in pods borrowed from Buccaneers, had defeated the Skyguard **radar** that controlled the eight lethal 35mm twin-barreled Oerlikons defending the airstrip.

A photographic reconnaissance flown from HMS *Hermes* shortly after dawn showed a series of craters, 50 yards apart, across the airfield, with one on the tarmac, and accordingly the mission had been judged a partial success. In reality, the runway was still operational, potholed only in appearance through the skillful use of camouflage by the Argentines, who constructed some false craters to deceive the British cameras. However, this successful deception was not to be discovered until the surrender in June 1982. The consolation was that the mission represented an implicit threat to Buenos Aires, demonstrating that the Argentine mainland was within the RAF's reach. *See also* FALKLANDS WAR.

BLACK CROW. U.S. Air Force codename for an airborne electronic radiation detector perfected during the **Vietnam War** that, when tuned to Soviet-built vehicle ignition systems, could detect camouflaged enemy trucks moving down the Ho Chi Minh trail.

BLACKJACK. On 14 December 1981, *Aviation Week and Space Technology* published unauthorized **KH-11** imagery of the new Soviet Blackjack intercontinental bomber reportedly taken over Ramenskoye military airfield on 25 November 1981. The supersonic aircraft, with a range of 7,300 miles and a maximum speed of Mach 2, was pictured parked beside two Tu-144 Concordskis, and represented the first ever publication of KH-11 imagery, even if it had been deliberately degraded to prevent an accurate assessment of the **satellite**'s resolution, which was 5.46 at its apogee.

BLIND APPROACH TRAINING AND DEVELOPMENT UNIT (BATDU). The cover-name for the **Royal Air Force** intelligence unit established in 1940 to investigate the enemy's secret beam navigation systems. It was later renamed the Wireless Intelligence Development Unit.

BLOUNT, CHARLES. Appointed **director of Air Intelligence** at the Air Ministry in London in 1930, Sir Charles Blount was educated at Harrow and Sandhurst and was a pioneer of the collection of intelligence by aircraft and established AI-4 at **Royal Air Force** Waddington. He died in October 1940, aged 47, and was succeeded by Archie Boyle.

BLUE DIVER. The **Royal Air Force** (RAF) codename for a highly classified **radar** jamming device installed in Great Britain's V-bombers, but compromised by a technician, Nicholas Prager, who had been based at RAF Wittering in 1956. Originally Czech-born, Prager had also served at the radar development unit at Finningley, near Doncaster, but had left the RAF in August 1961 to join English Electric. He had been identified as a spy by a Czech defector, Josef Frolik, and was arrested in January 1971. He was charged with breaches of the Official Secrets Act and of having betrayed details of the RED STEER countermeasures system. In his defense, Prager said he had been entrapped by his wife, a Czech agent, and he was sentenced to 12 years' imprisonment.

BLUE SKY. Air Force Security Service codename for an airborne intelligence collection program conducted by the 1st Radio Squadron Mobile (RSM) in modified C-46s during the **Korean War**. Having deployed from Johnson Air Force Base near Tokyo to Pyongyang in November 1950, the 1st RSM gave F-86 pilots a significant advantage over their MiG-15 adversaries by providing early warning of enemy air operations, leading to a kill ratio of 13:1.

BODYLINE. British air intelligence codename for the coordination of scientific information relating to Nazi secret weapons in April 1943 that resulted in the appointment of the **CROSSBOW** subcommittee of the Joint Intelligence Committee in November 1943. The BODY-LINE experts found it hard to reach a consensus because of the conflicting evidence that came in from so many contradictory sources, including agent reports, **prisoner of war** interrogations, radio intercepts of downrange plotting in the Baltic, Enigma decrypts, refugee information, photographic reconnaissance, and diplomatic reporting. There was so much material that some BODYLINE members argued that the entire issue could only be a deception campaign and a huge bluff because of the apparent lack of secrecy surrounding the project. Ultimately it became clear that BODYLINE had failed to distinguish between four separate but parallel plans, involving the **A-4** rocket, the Fi-105 flying bomb, the Hochdruckpumpe gun intended for installation at **Mimoyecques**, and the WASSERFALL antiaircraft missile. BODYLINE was also handicapped by its reluctance to accept that the Germans had developed a liquid fuel capable of achieving better results than solid rocket fuel. *See also* V-WEAPONS; WORLD WAR II.

BOEING 767-300 ER. In September 2002, Chinese technicians discovered 27 listening devices installed in a Boeing 767-300ER that had been ordered by the China Aviation Supplies Import and Export Corporation as President Jiang Zemin's personal aircraft and had been delivered the previous month. The miniaturized, satellite-controlled equipment had been installed while the aircraft was undergoing a $15 million custom refit in San Antonio, supervised by 75 Chinese security officials. The investigation into how the Chinese found the sophisticated hardware, so quickly retrieved from the presidential bathroom and bedroom, led to a leak enquiry that would implicate a Los Angeles-based agent of the Ministry of State Security, Katrina Leung. The mole hunt, codenamed PARLOR MAID by the Federal Bureau of Investigation (FBI), would conclude that Leung had compromised her FBI handlers and passed classified information to Beijing.

BOJINKA. The codename, meaning "loud noise" in Serbo-Croat, adopted by al-Qaeda in 1995 for a plan to place bombs on 11 aircraft in the Far East destined for the **United States**. Masterminded by Ramzi Yousef, a Pakistani from Quetta already identified by the Federal Bureau of Investigation as responsible for the February 1993 car bomb attack on New York's World Trade Center, the plot was to detonate all the devices simultaneously, thereby causing unprecedented chaos to the international airline industry. BOJINKA was exposed when a fire in an empty Manila apartment in January 1995 revealed explosives and incriminating computer disks. Yousef's fingerprints were found on several items, including a bomb-making manual; his confederate Abdul Hakim Murad, arrested at the scene, agreed to cooperate and he described Yousef as a veteran of the war in Bosnia.

After fleeing New York to Thailand in 1993, Yousef had moved to Manila and in December 1994 had left a bomb under a seat on a Philippine Airlines plane that had killed a Japanese tourist. Yousef was later arrested in Islamabad, having been betrayed by a recruit, a South African subordinate unhappy at being required to place a bomb on a United Airlines flight, and was extradited to New York where he was convicted of his involvement in the 1993 car-bomb attack.

Under interrogation, Murad described how he had been trained to fly a plane into the headquarters of the **Central Intelligence Agency** outside Washington, D.C., and had discussed plans to crash into a nuclear power plant somewhere in the United States.

The computer disks that revealed the BOJINKA plot were studied by intelligence analysts in several countries but, because of the complexity of the audacious scheme, none grasped that the plan was the work of a terrorist organization and was not state-sponsored. *See also* 9/11.

BOMBER GAP. Following the surprise detonation of the first Soviet atomic bomb in 1949, the **Central Intelligence Agency** (CIA) issued a report in 1950, *Estimate of the Effect of the Soviet Possession of the Atomic Bomb Upon the Security of the United States and Upon the Probability of Direct Soviet Action*, which predicted the Soviets would possess 100 atomic weapons by 1953 and double that figure within a further two years, with sufficient Tu-4 bombers to deliver them.

In May 1955, the CIA's National Intelligence Estimate predicted that by 1959 the Red Air Force would possess 600 long-range bombers capable of reaching the **United States** and that half of them would be Myasischev Mya-4 Molot Bisons or Tupolov Tu-95 Bears. Based on this assessment, President Dwight D. Eisenhower authorized a large investment in B-52s to close what became known as the "bomber gap." A Senate subcommittee chaired by Stuart Symington held hearings on the subject in April 1956, but it would be years before it was publicly acknowledged that poor intelligence had resulted in a massive exaggeration of Soviet bomber strengths. Imagery from the **U-2** quickly provided compelling, but not conclusive evidence of the true Soviet strengths, and the American estimates were reduced accordingly. In fact, only 150 Bisons had been built by 1959, not the 900 predicted by U.S. Air Force analysts. *See also* ESTIMATES OF SOVIET AIR STRENGTH.

BOSSARD, FRANK. Betrayed by the GRU's Dmitri Polyakov, Frank Bossard was arrested on 15 March 1965 as he left the hotel room in Bloomsbury where he had spent his lunch hour photographing secret documents he had removed from his post in the Guided Weapons Research and Development Division of the **Air Ministry**. Bossard had joined the **Royal Air Force** in December 1940 and in December 1951 had been posted to the scientific and technical intelligence branch in Germany. Later, he was attached to the British embassy in Bonn, and was then transferred to the Air Ministry. On 10 May 1965, Bossard was sentenced to 20 years' imprisonment.

BOYCE, CHRISTOPHER. The son of a Federal Bureau of Investigation special agent, Christopher Boyce worked for TRW Inc. in California between July 1974 and December 1976 and had access to highly classified **satellite** manuals. He stole dozens of secret documents, removed from a secure communications vault, and handed them to a drug addict, Daulton Lee, who sold them to the KGB in Mexico City. In January 1977, Lee was arrested by the Mexican police and found to be in possession of classified data. Under interrogation by the FBI, Boyce admitted having compromised the **RHYOLITE** and **ARGUS** satellite systems and in April 1977 was convicted of espionage and sentenced to 40 years' imprisonment. He escaped in January 1980 and remained on the run, robbing banks until he was recaptured in August the following year. In April 1982, he received a further 20 years for 16 bank robberies.

BRAVO, RAFAEL. A security guard employed by British Aerospace, Rafael Bravo was arrested in 2002 and convicted of having attempted to pass classified information concerning **radar** systems to an MI5 officer masquerading as a Russian intelligence officer. He was sentenced to 11 years' imprisonment.

BROTHERS TO THE RESCUE (BTTR). A group of anti-Castro Cuban émigrés based in Miami, Brothers to the Rescue not only flew air-sea rescue patrols in the Caribbean to alert the **U.S.** Coastguard to refugees fleeing the regime in unseaworthy, homemade boats, but flew missions over Havana to drop propaganda leaflets. After several warnings about violating Cuban airspace, two MiG interceptors shot down a pair of unarmed BTTR civilian planes on 24 February 1996 over international waters as they returned to the United States. All four aircrew were killed and the bodies of Armando Alexandre Jr., Carlos Costa, Mario de la Pena, and Pablo Morales were never recovered. The incident took on a greater significance when it emerged that the previous day, Admiral Eugene Carroll had been interviewed by a senior Defense Intelligence Agency analyst, **Ana Montes**, and that the retired naval officer had passed on a warning about the likelihood of Cuban retaliation for the BTTR incursions. After she was arrested in September 2001, she revealed that she had spied for the Cuban Direction General de Inteligencia for the previous 16 years, leaving the suspicion that the BTTR episode had been orchestrated by her.

BRUGIONI, DINO A. Having flown more than 60 missions over Europe during **World War II**, Dino Brugioni joined the **Central Intelligence Agency** (CIA) in 1948 as an intelligence analyst specializing in Soviet industrial installations. When the **National Photographic Interpretation Center** was established in 1955, he was one of the 12 senior officers to manage it, and during the **Cuban missile crisis** he was chief of the section responsible for collating the all-source intelligence for the photo interpreters. Brugioni was also responsible for undertaking a study of the imagery collected during World War II of the Auschwitz-Birkenau concentration camp in Poland. *See also* LUNDAHL, ART.

BYEMAN. The **United States** intelligence community generic codename for a highly classified category of special compartmented intelligence emanating from all aerial intelligence sources, and ascribed its own cryptonyms to individual systems, so the **U-2** became IDEALIST, the **SR-71** was **OXCART**, and the **KH-11** was KENNAN. *See also* KEYHOLE.

– C –

C-130. The signals intelligence variant of the Hercules transport aircraft was the C-130 A-II and the C-130 B-II that were flown by the 7406th

Combat Support Squadron from Rhein-Main during the Cold War. Codenamed SUN VALLEY, the aircraft flew signals intelligence collection flights along the Soviet border from Norway to Turkey. On 2 September 1958, a flight from Incirlik was shot down by four MiG-17 Frescos, with the loss of all 17 crew, when it accidentally strayed over Armenia. On 21 March 1973, another plane, flying from Hellinikon, Greece, was attacked by Libyan Mirages over the Mediterranean. *See also* LOPATKOV, VIKTOR.

CANBERRA. The first Canberra PR-3 aircraft, using a converted B-2 airframe, were flown operationally by No. 540 Squadron in 1952 from **Royal Air Force Wyton**. The twin-jet bomber, manufactured by English Electric, could fly above 50,000 feet and was later built under license by Glen Martin, designated as the B-57. The high-altitude PR-9 variant flew from July 1955 and was introduced into service in July 1958 by 39 and 58 Squadrons at Wyton. In October 1983, three former 39 Squadron PR-9s were sold to Chile after they had participated in the **Falklands** conflict.

CANYON. National Security Agency codename for a series of seven signals intelligence satellites first launched in 1968, designed to intercept Soviet microwave communications.

CASEY JONES. Allied codename for a joint Anglo-American aerial mapping project conducted after 1945, intended to provide an accurate map of the whole of Europe.

CENTRAL IMAGERY OFFICE (CIO). Created in May 1992, the Central Imagery Office was established to work in parallel with the **National Reconnaissance Office** to provide overhead photographic imagery to the Department of Defense and combat units and to assess future requirements. The CIO was subsumed into the **National Imagery and Mapping Agency** in October 1996.

CENTRAL INTELLIGENCE AGENCY (CIA). Created in 1947, the Central Intelligence Agency came to rely on aerial reconnaissance systems to provide the Directorate of Intelligence analysts with the information required to develop accurate assessments of Soviet strengths during the Cold War. The CIA was responsible for commissioning the design of advanced high-altitude aircraft, including the **U-2** and **SR-71**, and staffing the **National Reconnaissance Office.**

Although the CIA relied on the **U.S.** Air Force to provide the launchers and ground-stations for its satellite programs, it retained control over the procurement, contacting, and management of the actual systems. The CIA was also responsible for security, which was breached by one of its own officers, William Kampiles in 1978, and by Andrew Daulton, an employee of a major CIA contactor, TRW Inc., which handled satellite communications.

The paucity of sources within the Soviet Bloc left the CIA heavily reliant on what was termed "national technical means," a euphemism for overhead reconnaissance, although the recruitment of an avionics engineer, **Adolf Tolkachev**, in 1976 gave the agency an unprecedented advantage. Similarly, information from another human source, Colonel Oleg Penkovsky, had proved critical during the **Cuban missile crisis** and enabled the CIA to accurately interpret overhead imagery of suspected Soviet military bases, and to reassess the strategic threat posed by the Kremlin.

Because of its heavy reliance on satellite and other airborne collection systems, the CIA was weak in predicting the introduction and assessing the performance of new Warsaw Pact weapons, leaving the task largely to Defense Intelligence Agency (DIA) analysts. Working in parallel with the CIA, the DIA was supported by a network of service attachés posted to diplomatic missions overseas and benefited from liaison relationships that provided access to hardware acquired in proxy conflicts against Egypt, **Syria**, **Vietnam**, and Angola.

At the end of the Cold War, both the CIA and the DIA were the almost reluctant recipients of all kinds of military hardware stolen by disaffected Warsaw Pact military personnel, leaving both organizations in possession of a wealth of matèriel, ranging from small arms to entire rocket batteries and their radars. *See also* AIR AMERICA; AIR ASIA.

CHALET. Codename for a third-generation U.S. signals intelligence **satellite** system, designed to intercept Soviet telemetry and introduced in June 1978. Altogether, five satellites were placed into orbit.

When the codename was compromised in 1979, it was replaced with **VORTEX**. *See also* BYEMAN; RHYOLITE.

CHICKADEE. The American codename for an intelligence report from Colonel Oleg Penkovsky in June 1961 that led to a reassessment by Howard Stoertz of the draft National Intelligence Estimate (NIE) that predicted up to 400 Soviet ICMB launchers by mid-1964. The revised estimate capped the number at 250. The NIE released on 21 September 1961, designated as 11-8/1-61, reduced the immediate prediction to less than 35 missiles. It stated, "New information, providing a much firmer base for estimates on Soviet long-range ballistic missiles, has caused a sharp downward revision in our estimate of present Soviet **Inter-Continental Ballistic Missile** (ICBM) but strongly supports our estimate of medium range missile strength. We now estimate that the present Soviet ICBM strength is in the range of 10–25 launchers from which missiles can be fired against the U.S. and that this force will not increase markedly during the months immediately ahead."

CHINA, PEOPLES' REPUBLIC OF (PRC). A target of overhead surveillance by the **United States** and **Taiwan** since 1948, the PRC's only nuclear test site at Lop Nur is so remote that it can only be monitored effectively by overflights and **satellite** passes. Other targets include the missile test center at Shuangchenzi, the SLBM launch facility in the Bohai Gulf, south of Huludao; the IRBM launch site at Changxing, the gaseous diffusion plant at Lanzhou, and the space center at Chongqing. Overflights also concentrated on the 1st Submarine Flotilla headquarters at Quingdao, the bomber factory at Harbin, and the laser research laboratories at Changcun.

Incursions into mainland China by the SR-71 were terminated in 1971, as part of Dr. Henry Kissinger's agreement with Beijing, but flights by pilotless aircraft continued, despite a heavy rate of attrition. Between 1964 and 1969, the New China News Agency reported that 19 such **drones** had been shot down.

The most aggressive aerial reconnaissance of China was conducted by Taiwan, which lost up to nine **U-2**s, three RB-57s, and two RF-101s over the mainland. Their operations were pioneered by Dr. Ray Cline, the **Central Intelligence Agency** (CIA) station chief in

Taipei between 1957 and 1962, and later the CIA's director of intelligence. During his posting to Taipei, Cline supervised a program of leaflet drops over the mainland offering rewards for defectors with military information, and this resulted in the unexpected arrival of a PRC pilot in his obsolete MiG-15 fighter. *See also* CHINESE EMBASSY BOMBING.

CHINA, REPUBLIC OF. *See* TAIWAN.

CHINESE EMBASSY BOMBING. On 7 May 1999, the new Chinese embassy in Belgrade received a direct hit from a precision bomb dropped by the **U.S.** Air Force during the bombing campaign conducted by the North Atlantic Treaty Organization. The building had been erroneously identified as a military target, the Yugoslav Federal Directorate of Supply and Procurement, and an investigation into the blunder was conducted by Britt Snider, the **Central Intelligence Agency**'s (CIA) inspector general. He discovered that a CIA contract officer had relied upon an out-of-date street map to locate the building, and had used a parallel street to work out the exact street address. A further review of the target list, intended to highlight hospitals, churches, and diplomatic premises, had failed to spot the mistake and a warning from an analyst familiar with the city had gone unheeded. The correct site, a warehouse suspected of holding missiles parts destined for Iraq and Libya, was located 300 yards away, and the error was spotted by a CIA analyst who made a call to the U.S. Department of Defense Task Force in Naples, Italy, suggesting the coordinates were wrong. He gave a second, follow-up warning, but by then the aircraft had been dispatched and it was too late to correct the data.

As a result, the director of central intelligence, George Tenet, fired the contract employee and reprimanded six others in the management chain, making them ineligible for promotion or financial rewards for a year, while commending the lone analyst. The U.S. government issued an apology to Beijing and compensated the family of the three Chinese diplomats killed in the accident, and the 20 others injured, but the damage to Sino-American relations proved considerable.

CHRISTIE, MALCOLM. The former air attaché at the British embassy in Berlin between 1927 and 1930, Group Captain Christie developed his own sources in Germany and concentrated on the **Luftwaffe**. He supplied accurate assessments of the Nazi bomber fleet, and recruited an informant inside the German air ministry he referred to only as "**X**." Christie's reports were circulated in Whitehall by **Lord Vansittant**, the government's chief diplomatic adviser.

CIENFUEGOS. The discovery in the middle of September 1970 of imagery indicating that the Soviets were constructing a nuclear submarine base at Cienfuegos in **Cuba** prompted a political confrontation, with President Richard Nixon alleging that the Kremlin had broken undertakings given in October 1962 by Nikita Khrushchev to end the **Cuban missile crisis**. In September 1970, the Soviets confirmed their commitment not to station nuclear weapons on the island, and the base project was abandoned, although they won acceptance of the deployment of reconnaissance and antisubmarine warfare variants of Tu-95 *Bears* to Cuba.

CIVIL AIR TRANSPORT (CAT). Created in January 1947 in China, and staffed by veterans of the Office of Strategic Services (OSS) Detachment 101, led by the legendary General Claire L. Chennault of the Flying Tigers, CAT was an ostensibly civilian airline of a dozen C-47s that played a significant role during the Chinese civil war, initially in support of Chiang Kai-shek's troops, and then in support of American-sponsored guerrillas operating independently of the Nationalists. When Chiang Kai-shek was forced to withdraw to Taiwan, CAT followed him there and established itself as the region's largest airline, linking Taipei to other countries by scheduled and charter flights.

In August 1950, the company was incorporated in Delaware as the Pacific Corporation, a proprietary company of the **Central Intelligence Agency** (CIA), and undertook clandestine missions over mainland China. In 1954, CAT resupplied the French garrison at **Dien Bien Phu**, and later ran clandestine flights into North Vietnam, Tibet, Indonesia, and Laos. In 1959, 30 of CAT's aircraft were absorbed into another CIA proprietary, **Air America**, but the Chinese Nationalists were unwilling to allow CAT to be dissolved because China Air Lines was insufficiently experienced to take over CAT's domestic and international routes. Instead, CAT continued to fly until 1968, when a CAT 727 crashed near Taipei airport, killing 21 passengers. As a result of demonstrations in Taiwan against the American-owned airline, CAT passed its international business on to China Air Lines. *See also* TROPIC.

CLEF. National Security Agency codename for a signals intelligence intercept site at the **radar** station at Wakkanai, in the far north of Hokkaido, just 27 miles from Sakhalin Island, operated by Japanese personnel, which recorded the voice traffic of the Soviet fighter pilots who attacked **KAL 007** in September 1983. Opened covertly in 1982, CLEF acted as a relay for the 6820th Electronic Security Group at **Misawa**.

COBRA BALL. U.S. Air Force codename for signals intelligence collection flights outside Soviet airspace during the Cold War by **ELINT** aircraft monitoring air defense emissions and missile test telemetry for the Defense Special Missile and Aeronautics Center at Fort Meade. On 16 March 1981, an RC-135 on a COBRA BALL mission crash-landed on Shemya Island, killing six of the crew after a mission to Kamchatka.

COBRA DANE. The **U.S.** Air Force codename for a phased array radar system constructed on Shemya Island in Alaska, with a capability of monitoring up to 200 satellites and up to 300 warheads and detecting potentially hostile missiles at a range of 2,000 miles.

COCOM. The abbreviation of the Coordinating Committee on Multilateral Export Controls, administered since 1949 from an unmarked building next to the U.S. embassy in Paris, operated bans on three trade categories—industrial, military, and atomic energy—and extended the embargo beyond the Warsaw Pact countries to Vietnam, North Korea, Mongolia, Albania, and China, with an additional list of suspected countries known as "diverters." Although a far from ideal mechanism for restricting exports to the Soviet Bloc, because the European membership in particular was keen to promote trade, CoCom proved highly effective until it was dismantled in 1994, with individual states strengthening the regime under American pressure.

COLD WAR. From 1945 until the collapse of the Soviet Bloc in 1991, air intelligence played a pivotal role during the Cold War, principally because it proved to be one of the most reliable sources of information from inside the Iron Curtain. With a paucity of human and open sources and the inability of foreign travelers to visit the cities and regions of greatest interest to Western analysts, intelligence staffs came to rely on defector debriefings at refugee centers in Austria and Germany and on intercepted signals. While the latter fulfilled a useful early-warning function and assisted in the development of creating a comprehensive order-of-battle for the Warsaw Pact forces, only air intelligence could positively confirm the exact location of strategically important sites and monitor activities in what became known as denied areas.

Initially, Western air intelligence depended on **ferret** incursions into hostile airspace, but the introduction of the **U-2** provided the very first long-range high-altitude aerial reconnaissance platform over the Eastern Bloc, at least until May 1960, when the **Central Intelligence Agency** was forced to abandon those missions in favor of satellites. In addition, air missions provided signals interception opportunities where there was a lack of suitable ground stations, and these flights continued in the Black Sea and the Pacific throughout the Cold War.

Air intelligence would have a profound impact on the Cold War, with several of the moments of greatest tension being caused by incidents perceived to have been related to collection efforts. The loss of **F. Gary Powers'** U-2 in May 1960 undermined relations between President Dwight D. Eisenhower and Nikita Khrushchev, just as the destruction of KAL 007 in September 1983 was seen by President Ronald Reagan as an act of unprovoked aggression. The catalyst for the **Cuban missile crisis** in October 1960 was a U-2 reconnaissance flight that captured imagery of Soviet surface-to-air missile sites, and President Richard Nixon nearly ordered a retaliatory attack in April 1969 when an EC-121 was shot down by North Korean MiGs.

While less dependent on air intelligence than their adversaries, because of the numerous alternative sources of information available to them, from both open and clandestine sources, the Soviets flew long-range air reconnaissance missions across the globe throughout the Cold War, mainly in an effort to monitor Western naval exercises. Soviet doctrine suggested that any surprise attack on the Warsaw Pact countries would occur under cover of ostensibly routine maneuvers, so overflights were made to establish patterns of potentially hostile activity that could be monitored.

While the Cold War was occasionally fought in guerrilla campaigns by surrogates, the principal characteristic of the period was the lack of actual confrontation between the protagonists on land, even if Berlin in particular became a focus for tension and submarines regularly played dangerous games at sea. In contrast, 252 U.S. aircrew died in encounters with Soviet fighters between 1950 and 1970, a statistic that demonstrates the realities of the Cold War in the air.

COLOMBO AIRPORT. On 24 July 2001, Tamil Tiger rebels attacked Katanayake Airport in Sri Lanka with mortars and suicide bombers and destroyed eight military aircraft, including a pair of Kfir fighters, a MiG-27 and a helicopter, and six airliners, including two A340s and a A330 Airbuse, amounting half of Air Sri Lanka's fleet.

Altogether, 21 people died in the attack that crippled the island's tourism even if the airport was reopened the following day. The devastating attack amounted to a significant failure of intelligence on the part of the Sri Lankan authorities, who had no advance warning of the separatists' plan.

COMBINED SERVICES DETAILED INTERROGATION CENTRE (CSDIC). From September 1943, British air intelligence personnel supervised the interrogation of all captured enemy aircrew. Dedicated Combined Services Detailed Interrogation Centres were established at Cairo and Algiers to process the prisoners. Forward units were later deployed to Sicily, Italy, and northwest Europe, and this particular source of information proved exceptionally valuable. *See also* PRISONERS OF WAR.

COMINT. The acronym for communications intelligence, covering the disciplines of the interception and analysis of communications, including voice and signal channels.

COMMITTEE ON IMAGERY REQUIREMENTS AND EXPLOITATION (COMIREX). A subcommittee of the **U.S.** National Foreign Intelligence Board, COMIREX was created in July 1967,

replacing the **Committee on Overhead Reconnaissance** to coordinate the intelligence community's imagery requirements. In May
1992, COMIREX was absorbed into the **Central Imagery Office**.

**COMMITTEE ON OVERHEAD RECONNAISSANCE (CO-
MOR).** Originally a subcommittee of the **U.S.** National Foreign Intelligence Board, COMOR was replaced by the **Committee on Imagery Requirements and Exploitation** in July 1967.

COMPASS ARROW. U.S. Air Force codename for a project to develop an unmanned **Ryan** AQM-91A reconnaissance aircraft for missions into high-risk denied airspace. The **drone**, with a 48-foot
wingspan, was eventually abandoned,

CONCENTRATION CAMPS. After the liberation of the German
concentration camps at the end of **World War II**, a controversy arose
as to why the Allies had failed to bomb some of them, and especially
Auschwitz-Birkenau, which came into range of Allied bombers based
in Italy in September 1944. The Polish government-in-exile reportedly first raised the issue of an air raid on this target in August 1944,
to assist in a breakout from the three local camps, but the request was
turned down. The declassification of relevant enemy decrypts in October 1996 showed that from August 1941, the Allies had become
aware of genocide on the Russian front and in 1942 and 1943 intercepted daily prisoner and execution returns from Dachau, Mau-
thausen, Guben, Buchenwald, Flossenberg, Auschwitz, Hinzert,
Niederhagen, Lublin, Stutthof, and Debica, addressed to SS Brigade-
führer Gluecks at Oranienberg. These Enigma messages ceased in
February 1943 as a security precaution, but none ever referred to
deaths by gas, or to extermination camps. The daily toll usually referred to typhus and spotted fever as the principal cause of death,
with hangings and shootings also mentioned. With a fluctuating population of over 20,000, Auschwitz-Birkenau was by far the largest
collection of prisoners, being mainly Poles and Jews, and when the
first reports of mass killings there reached London they were so incredible, with air pressure being cited as the means of execution, that
they were disbelieved. Photographic reconnaissance imagery showed

Auschwitz to have grown to be one of the largest conurbations in Poland, and any air raid undoubtedly would have exacted a terrible price among the prisoners, so none were ever launched. The alternative, of temporarily cutting the railway lines from the air, was rejected as a wasteful diversion from the priority targets of crippling the enemy's industrial output and thereby bringing the conflict to a swifter conclusion.

CONTINENTAL AIR SERVICES (CAS). A **Central Intelligence Agency** (CIA) proprietary, CAS operated in Laos in parallel with **Air America**. CAS's chief pilot was the legendary Ed Dearborn, a CIA contractor who effectively had created the Congolese Air Force in 1960 to resist the secessionist rebels.

CORONA. In 1956, the **United States** embarked on a secret project, codenamed CORONA, to replace the **U-2** reconnaissance aircraft with a photographic **satellite** system. After a dozen launch failures, the first successful flight occurred in February 1960, described as a weather satellite. The very first batch of pictures included 64 Soviet airfields and 26 SAM sites that hitherto had been undetected, and effectively dispelled the **missile gap** myth. From 1963, the program was headed by the director of the **Central Intelligence Agency**'s Science and Technology Division, Albert ("Bud") Wheelon.

By the time the program ended in May 1972, 95 satellites had been launched, and 26 missions failed, in a total of 146 attempts, at a cost of $820 million. In 12 years, 800,000 images had been captured of 600 million square miles of the earth's surface, of which 1.65 million were inside the **Soviet Union.** Classified as **TALENT-KEYHOLE**, the imagery had been processed by 1,500 technicians at the **National Photographic Interpretation Center.**

Although the CORONA series provided vastly more imagery than the U-2, the satellites were hard to maneuver, operated in a polar orbit only, and could not provide stereo pictures. The CORONA satellites mapped much of the Eastern Bloc, the People's Republic of China, and the Middle East, and the declassified imagery has now been released to the INMOS facility at Brookings, in South Dakota. *See also* BYEMAN.

CORONA. British codename for a **World War II** operation that broadcast spoof ground control instructions to enemy bombers conducting air raids over England.

COSMOS 954. In January 1978, a Soviet signals intelligence **satellite**, Cosmos 954, malfunctioned and crashed into Canada's Northwest Territory. Powered by a Romashka miniature nuclear reactor containing 110 pounds of enriched uranium, Cosmos 954 was launched from Tyuratam on 18 September 1977 and placed into orbit 150 miles above the earth. At a speed of 15,000 miles per hour, the satellite completed a full orbit every 88 minutes and was intended to have a virtually unlimited life. When the orbit became erratic in December 1977, precautions codenamed Operation MORNING LIGHT were taken in the **United States** and Canada in anticipation of an uncontrolled reentry, and the satellite impacted on the 350-mile-long frozen Great Slave Lake, a desolate area between the settlements of Fort Smith and Fort Resolution, and the town of Yellowknife. As the satellite disintegrated in midair, contamination in the form of microgram particles of the atomic core was spread over 200 square miles, prompting a massive cleanup operation that recovered only microscopic radioactive fragments.

COVENTRY RAID. The **Luftwaffe** attack on the Midlands manufacturing center of Coventry on the full moon of 14 November 1940 by 449 bombers that dropped 46 tons of incendiaries, 394 tons of high-explosives, and 127 parachute mines lasted 10 hours and left 400 inhabitants dead and 800 injured. In 1974, following the disclosure of British cryptographic success against the Luftwaffe's Enigma ciphers, a myth developed suggesting that the **Royal Air Force** had advance knowledge of the target, but Prime Minister Winston Churchill had deliberately sacrificed the city to protect the ULTRA secret. In reality, 80 Wing had set up countermeasures, to bend the **X-Gerät** navigation beams, but the jamming transmitters had been set accidentally to the wrong frequency modulation and therefore failed to interfere with the bombers.

CRAIL. The **Royal Air Force** station at Crail, in a remote corner of Scotland, provided postwar Russian language tuition to a generation of linguists, intercept operators, interrogators, and interpreters who were to undertake intelligence duties during the Cold War.

CRATEOLOGY. The science of determining the content of a wooden cargo crate is known as crateology, and during the **Cuban missile crisis** American photo interpreters developed the skill of making accurate measurements of crates lashed to the decks of Soviet freighters. Although no warheads were ever spotted, scrutiny of the *Omsk* and *Poltava* timber-carriers unloading at Mariel showed boxes matching the dimensions of the Sopka R-12 MRBM, designated by the North Atlantic Treaty Organization as the Sandal.

In October 1984, American crateologists incorrectly identified cargo aboard the Bulgarian freighter *Bakuriania* as MiG-21 fighters bound for **Nicaragua**; they turned out to be four patrol boats and a pair of helicopters.

CREEK MISTY. U.S. Air Force codename for signals intelligence missions flown by RC-130A-II aircraft from Tempelhof, Berlin, and Rhein-Main in West Germany. On 2 September 1958, one of these planes was shot down over Armenia by five MiGs.

CRESTED ICE. Codename for the joint **United States** and Danish operation to recover plutonium debris deposited on the sea ice near Thule Air Force Base in Greenland in January 1965 following the accidental loss of a B-52 bomber carrying four nuclear weapons. The plane developed an electrical fire, forcing the crew of six to bail out, and the aircraft crashed onto the ice.

CROSSBOW. The British codename for a **World War II** Joint Intelligence Committee subcommittee chaired by Duncan Sandys that from November 1943 assessed intelligence reports of the secret weapon threatened by Adolf Hitler. CROSSBOW examined messages from agents in France and Poland and aerial reconnaissance photographs to predict the development of the **V-weapons** that were deployed operationally in 1944.

CROSSBOW proved controversial because the photographic imagery from **Peenemünde** never provided conclusive proof of the existence of rocket research, and the estimates of the V-2 were highly speculative when British experts failed to agree about a likely propulsion system. On the mistaken assumption that the rocket was dependent on solid fuel, the weight estimates varied from 20 to 100 tons, with a warhead of between two and eight tons. The experts also suggested a two-stage rocket, whereas the Germans had perfected a liquid oxygen and alcohol mixture to fuel a single-stage missile. The absence of any obvious launch sites in northern France also undermined the scientists' argument that a massive rocket offensive was imminent. Ultimately, CROSSBOW sifted through 159 reports from Secret Intelligence Service agents, 35 prisoner of war interrogations, 37 reports from diplomatic missions, and seven enemy diplomatic decrypts to assess the scale of the threat. In addition, CROSSBOW received information from CORNCRAKE, the Schutzstaffel communications link between Peenemünde and the test range at Blizna in Poland, from the Polish resistance that monitored the flights at Blizna, and from two British scientists who traveled to Sweden to inspect the wreckage of an **A-4** that had overshot the range. *See also* BODYLINE; SONNIE.

CUBA. Since the 1959 revolution that replaced President Fulgencio Batista with Fidel Castro, Cuba has been the subject of the most intensive air reconnaissance, and from 5 August 1962, when the first **U-2** overflight took place, the island's entire 111,000 square kilometers have been photographed. Air intelligence betrayed the first indications of the deployment of Soviet antiaircraft missile batteries, and this proved the catalyst for the **Cuban missile crisis** of October 1962, which was resolved a month later with an agreement that would sustain a Communist regime for the next 45 years in return for the removal of all offensive weapons. Tension rose again in September 1970 when further air reconnaissance revealed the construction of a nuclear submarine base at **Cienfuegos**, but a crisis was averted when President Richard Nixon prevailed upon the Kremlin to abandon the plan. *See also* BAY OF PIGS; BROTHERS TO THE RESCUE; MONTES, ANA.

CUBAN MISSILE CRISIS. On 14 October 1962, Colonel Steve Heyser flew his **U-2** over the San Cristobal area and in six minutes took 928 photographs that revealed the existence of four mobile

SS-4 Sandal erector-launchers in a grove of palm trees. The SS-4 medium range ballistic missile, of which 42 would be deployed in Cuba, had a range of 1,020 miles and was armed with a three-megaton warhead. According to photographs taken during the annual May Day parade in Red Square, the SS-4, known to the Soviets as the R-12, was 67 feet in length. This single overflight remains one of the most signification milestones in air intelligence history as it eloquently refuted the Special National Intelligence Estimate 85-3-62, *The Military Build-Up in Cuba*, issued only a month earlier, which had rejected the possibility that Soviet strategic weapons might be sited on the island. The paper had argued that no sane leader would contemplate such a hazardous scheme.

Heyser's flight on 14 October had been preceded by others that had been less productive. The very first had taken place on 5 August, and had been followed by another on 31 August, having been much delayed because of bad weather, which revealed a SA-2 site. The next mission was scheduled for 5 September, but in the meantime there was an accidental incursion into Soviet airspace, for only nine minutes, by a U-2 on an air-sampling assignment on 30 August. When the next Cuban overflight took place as planned, more SA-2s were found. Then, on 9 September, a Taiwanese U-2 was lost over mainland China, an incident that had a significant impact on the **Central Intelligence Agency** (CIA) and prompted the national security adviser, McGeorge Bundy, to cancel the follow-up mission. Eventually, under pressure from the CIA, Bundy agreed to a compromise. There would be four further flights in September, of which two would remain in international airspace, undertaken on 26 and 29 September, and the other two each would be permitted to make a single quick dash in-and-out of the island's airspace over an area of central and eastern Cuba. Critically, these last two missions were not completed until 5 and 7 October, and this was the window of opportunity that allowed the Soviets to deliver their weapons to San Cristobal on 17–18 September undetected. Neither flight detected any weapons.

The period leading up to Heyser's flight on 14 October became known within those indoctrinated into the secrets of the missile crisis as the "photo gap" because of the political implications of the White House vacillations and restrictions that had left the vital San Cristobal area untouched for 45 days. The CIA had argued that the characteristic trapezoidal configuration of the SA-2 launch sites were unmistakable and must have been built to protect some other, really important, installation. The administration, however, had balked at the CIA's estimate of the odds of losing a U-2 over Cuba as "one-in-six," but once Heyser's pictures had been examined President John F. Kennedy gave his blanket approval to unrestricted U-2 overflights, and 20 missions were completed in the next five days, providing a total mosaic of the entire island.

Further low-level reconnaissance flights by Navy F8U-1P Crusader jets disclosed two MRBM sites near Sagua la Grande, four SS-5 Skean IRBM fixed launchers (with eight R-14 missiles each) near Remedios and Guanajay, and a radar and communications center at Camaguey, all defended by 16 SAM batteries. By the end of the month, a total of 24 SS-4 MRBMs were found at six sites (La Coloma, Santa Lucia, Bahia Honda, San Diego de los Banos, San Cristobal, and Los Palacios), and 18 IRBMs, with a range of 2,200 miles, at four sites (Nuevitas, Mariel, Santa Cruz de Norte, and Matanzas) were identified. In addition, Ilyushin-28 medium-range light bombers and MiG-21 fighters had been spotted on the airfields of Holguin and San Julian. Following the initial U-2 flights, more than 400 reconnaissance missions were flown over Cuba during the crisis, principally by RF-101 Voodoos of the 363rd Tactical Reconnaissance Wing based at Homestead, Crusaders from the Navy's Light Photographic Squadron 62, and the Marines' Light Photographic Squadron VMC-32 from Boca Chica, Key West, flying at 600 miles per hour at an altitude of 500 feet. At such low levels, the aircraft were hard to hit from the ground and produced spectacular imagery.

Following tense negotiations between the Kremlin and the White House, all the missiles were dismantled and shipped back to the **Soviet Union**. In exchange, 30 recently installed but obsolete Jupiter MRBMs were withdrawn from Cigliano and Giolle del Colle in Italy, 15 from Izmir in Turkey, and a squadron of Thors from Great Britain. Undetected throughout the crisis were 12 Luna short-range tactical nuclear weapons, designated as Frog by the North Atlantic Treaty Organization, which had been hidden in caves near Santa Cruz del Norte, apparently intended for coastal defense in the event of an American invasion of the island.

Although the crisis is often portrayed as a moment when the superpower protagonists came closest to a nuclear exchange, no imagery ever disclosed the existence of any nuclear warheads in Cuba. The warheads had been shipped from Severomorsk in September 1962 aboard the *Indigirki* and *Aleksandrovsk*. The *Indigirki*'s cargo included 80 warheads for the Styx SS-N-2 antiship missiles carried by the 12 *Komar* class gunboats, six 8- to 12-kiloton freefall bombs for the Ilyushin-28 bombers already delivered to the San Julián airbase, and 12 Luna warheads. The *Aleksandrovsk* carried 24 R-14 warheads for the IRBMs, but none were offloaded at La Isabela. Although the voyages of both freighters were monitored by air reconnaissance patrols, the precise nature of their cargos remained unknown.

During the crisis, tension was increased by several incidents, including the loss of Major **Rudolf Anderson**'s U-2 over Banes on 27 October, and an accidental incursion over Siberia on the same day by another U-2, flown by Major **Charles Maltsby**. On the previous day, an Atlas **inter-continental ballistic missile** (ICBM) had been test-fired from Vandenberg Air Force Base to the Kwajalein range in the Marshall Islands.

Hostilities were almost initiated following the accidental intervention of a **U.S.** Navy P2V Neptune on 26 October, 380 miles southeast of Bermuda, which dropped incendiaries over the B-59, a Foxtrot-class long-range diesel attack submarine of the Red Banner Northern Fleet that had been forced to the surface by grenades dropped by the USS *Cory*. Misunderstanding the Neptune's tactics, which had been intended to activate the aircraft's photoelectric camera lenses, the B-59 immediately altered course and opened her two forward torpedo hatches. Fortunately, the *Cory* signaled an apology to the submarine, which promptly resumed its course.

Contrary to popular myth, no Soviet ICBM came close to being launched during the crisis, and according to National Security Agency intercepts, the only Soviet troops placed on alert in the Warsaw Pact were in Berlin. Communications traffic also showed that no reserves were mobilized, and none of the railroad contingency plans for emergency missile and troop transport (always reliable indicators) were implemented. *See also* KAMA; LUNDAHL, ART.

CUB-B. North Atlantic Treaty Organization designation of the Antonov An-12 long-range bomber converted by the Soviet Naval Air Service to conduct electronic intelligence collection missions during the **Cold War**.

– D –

D-21. The **U.S.** Air Force designation of an unmanned, high-altitude reconnaissance **drone** that was intended to be launched from a B-52H bomber. Codenamed **SENIOR BOWL**, four flights were made over China from Beale Air Force Base between 1969 and 1971 but the project was abandoned because of the political risk of sending the large aircraft, 43 feet long with a wingspan of 19 feet, over hostile territory with no prospect of recovery. One D-21 failed to self-destruct and eventually crashed in Siberia at the limit of its 3,500-mile range at 95,000 feet.

DAMOCLES. Israeli codename for a clandestine operation intended to penetrate and sabotage the Egyptian missile development program. In July 1962, President Abdel Gamal Nasser announced the successful test-firings of the Al-Zafir (Victory), with a range of 175 miles and the Al-Kabir (Conqueror) with a range of 350 miles, and took the salute during a military parade that included 20 rockets. These weapons had been designed and built by up to 100 German scientists and technicians, many of them veterans of **Peenemünde** and the Wehrmacht's V-2 project, and recruited by General Mohammed Khalil, formerly Nasser's chief of Air Intelligence. The Israelis penetrated the German émigré community in Cairo with an agent, Wolfgang Lotz, who was himself of German parentage, and learned that work on the Egyptian missiles had been conducted under cover of a recently built Messerschmitt airframe and engine factory near Heliopolis. Having previously served in the British Army's Jewish Brigade, and as an interrogator of PoWs during the North African campaign and an Israeli Defense Force officer, Lotz claims to have served in the Afrika Korps' 115th Division and later to have made his fortune in Australia were believed by visitors to his stud farm near Gezira, many of whom were German compatriots working for Khalil.

Another source, Otto Joklik, who was an Austrian scientist, reported that Khalil planned to build a conventional warhead filled with strontium 90 and cobalt 60, which upon detonation would cause widespread radioactive contamination. However, Joklik's reports were disbelieved by some of the government's scientific advisers in Tel Aviv, and the controversy over his reliability led to a high-level political crisis in the cabinet.

Having identified many of the German employees, a campaign of intimidation conducted in Germany and Egypt proved ineffective, so letter bombs were mailed to selected senior staff, resulting in the death of five of the personnel. Although these incidents could not be linked directly to Mossad, DAMOCLES became a political embarrassment in March 1963 when the Swiss Bundespolizei arrested an Israeli agent, Joseph Ben-Gal, in Basel as he tried to persuade Heidi Görke, the daughter of a leading German rocketry expert, to warn her father that, for his own safety, he should leave Egypt immediately. Also implicated in an apparently bungled attempt on the life of an electrical engineer, Dr. Hans Kleinwachter, in Lorrach, DAMOCLES was terminated, but the publicity given to the role of the German scientists led to their withdrawal from the Egyptian missile project. As for Lotz, he was arrested in January 1965 after his wireless transmitter had been traced by Soviet radio direction finders, and he was sentenced in July 1965 to life imprisonment, his role as an Israeli spy undiscovered. Following the **Six Day War** in 1967 he was released in exchange for 500 PoWs, including nine Egyptian generals.

DARKSTAR. The fourth generation of the **U.S. unmanned aerial vehicle**, after the **Predator** and **Global Hawk**, the Darkstar is a sophisticated reconnaissance platform that was deployed in support of coalition operations in Iraq and Afghanistan.

D-DAY. In anticipation of the Allied invasion of Europe, the 2nd Tactical Air Force was created in March 1944 and included four photographic reconnaissance squadrons, consisting of 18 aircraft in each, mainly Mosquito XVIs (with a range of 2,090 miles) and Spitfire XIs (with a range of 1,290 miles without drop tanks). They flew intensive operations before and during the landings and then concentrated on German positions and **V-weapon** installations in northern France.

DEFENSE ADVANCED RESEARCH PROJECTS AGENCY (DARPA). Established by the **United States** in 1958, DARPA has undertaken highly sophisticated projects, applying modern technology to military requirements, and has been responsible for pioneering the development of unarmed airborne vehicles. These aircraft range in size from small executive jets to miniaturized devices, **micro air vehicles** (MAV) with a six-inch wingspan weighing less than two ounces. The AeroVironment Black Widow was developed from 1986, part of a $30 million budget intended to develop an MAV with a range of 10 kilometers, a speed of 65 miles per hour, and a duration of two hours.

DEFENSE AIRBORNE RECONNAISSANCE OFFICE (DARO). The **United States** agency responsible for the management of advanced **unmanned aerial vehicles**.

DESERT STORM. The liberation of Kuwait in February 1991 from Iraq's occupation, codenamed Operation DESERT STORM, resulted in a prolonged opportunity to test Western military technology against Soviet-supplied hardware. *See also* PERSIAN GULF WARS.

DIEN BIEN PHU. The battle for the French fortress at Dien Bien Phu in July 1954 was deliberately calculated by the commander-in-chief of Indochina, General Henri Navarre. He recognized that the airfield was the strategic obstacle to a full-scale Communist invasion of Laos from northern Vietnam, but the two-month siege resulted in a massive defeat and the surrender of the entire garrison, of whom only half survived captivity. The debacle marked the beginning of the end of France's bitter but futile Indochina War.

French intelligence reports, based mainly on air reconnaissance, accurately identified the size of the surrounding forces as 49,000 men, including 33,000 combatants, and as the enemy possessed not a single aircraft, Navarre's plan called for a massive conventional confrontation under the protection of complete air superiority of 275 aircraft. The plan began to go wrong when the Vietminh penetrated the largest and most heavily fortified French airbase in the region, at Cat-Bi outside Haiphong, and destroyed 18 transport aircraft. In a coordinated attack, saboteurs achieved similar success at Hanoi's Gia-Lam airfield. The garrison of 15,094 men required constant replenishment by air, but heavy ground fire from the surrounding hills turned the Dien Bien Phu valley into *les pièges* (the traps) and the losses were huge: 48 planes shot down, 14 destroyed on the ground, and a further 167 damaged. During the entire war, the French lost 650 military aircrew, and a further 70 civilian pilots. The garrison required an airdrop of 200 tons a day, but the French depended on the C-47, with their narrow side doors that could only deliver 2.5 tons, and to meet the requirement had to pass over the drop zone 12 times. Fourteen **Civil Air Transport** pilots contracted by the **Central Intelligence Agency** also participated in the 500-kilometer air bridge with C-119s capable of delivering 6 tons of supplies in one pass, but on some days it was impossible to approach the drop zone, and occasionally the valuable cargoes would be dropped accidentally to the enemy.

Numerous lessons were learned at Dien Bien Phu, one of which was the impotence of air superiority in a jungle environment where the guerrillas were not dependent on mechanized transport and kept to concealed paths and bridges, against which the B-26s were ineffective. One analysis concluded that to destroy a camouflaged bridge required an average of 70 tons of high explosive, and at no point during the siege did the French ever manage to close the strategic Route 41 that led to the town. While air reconnaissance proved accurate in assessing the enemy's strength in manpower, it failed to spot the Russian multitube rocket launchers that proved the basis for the final assault. The defeat led to a French withdrawal from Indochina and helped establish a Communist insurgency across the rest of the region. *See also* VIETNAM WAR.

DIRECTOR OF AIR INTELLIGENCE. A post created at the Air Ministry in 1930 with the appointment of Sir **Charles Blount**, his successors were Archie Boyle, **Charles Medhurst** (1941–1942), and Frank Inglis (1942–1945).

DIRTY BIRD. In 1957, Lockheed engineers developed a material, codenamed WALLPAPER, which contained tiny electronic circuits designed to absorb **radar** signals in the 65- to 85-megahertz range and reduce the risk of reflection. When applied to **U-2** surfaces, the fiberglass coating, which was a honeycomb seven millimeters thick, had the effect of making the aircraft known as DIRTY BIRDS almost invisible to Soviet air defenses. WALLPAPER's disadvantage was that it tended to absorb heat, making the notoriously delicate U-2 even harder to fly, and on 2 April 1958, a Lockheed test pilot, Bob Sieker, was killed in just such an accident in Nevada. DIRTY BIRDs flew a total of seven Soviet overflights, but WALLPAPER was discontinued after Soviet protests about a mission completed successfully over Siberia on 1 March 1958 demonstrated that the early stealth technology had not been perfected.

DISCOVERER. The official name of the first **U.S. satellite** project that concealed three separate systems: the first to collect imagery and transmit it to ground stations by radio, the second to eject recoverable capsules containing exposed film, and the third, the Missile Alarm Defense System (MIDAS), known originally as SENTRY, designed to detect the flare of Soviet ballistic missile launches.

The Discoverer was 19 feet long (but was later elongated to 23 feet), five feet in diameter, and weighed 8,500 pounds, including a battery and 7,000 pounds of liquid fuel and oxygen to maneuver the satellite once it had been launched into orbit by a booster rocket.

Although the first Discoverer satellites were launched on Thor Agena-B rockets by the United States in 1958, flight failures prevented any imagery being produced until Discoverer 13 in August 1961, when the film capsule was recovered from the Pacific 330 miles northwest of Honolulu by the USS *Haiti Victory*, allowing analysts to conclude that there were only between 10 and 14 Soviet **inter-continental ballistic missile** (ICBM) launch sites. Eight days later, a capsule ejected from Discoverer 14, designated as Mission 9009, became the first capsule to be recovered in the air, by a C-119 Flying Boxcar on the third pass at the parachute. The resulting imagery boasted a resolution of 12 inches, allowing photo interpreters to distinguish between Zim and Podeba cars in Moscow's Red Square. The 3,600 feet of film weighed 20 pounds and covered 1.5 million square miles of the Soviet Union, more than all the imagery captured during 24 **U-2** flights.

Discoverer 29, launched on 30 August 1961, flew over Plesetsk, 500 miles northeast of Moscow, to confirm that it was the first Soviet ICBM launch site. During the remainder of the year, a further five launches were made in the Discoverer series, Discoverer 30 to Discoverer 34.

Seven ground stations were constructed to control the satellites, at New Boston, New Hampshire; Vandenberg Air Force Base, California; Kodiak Island, Alaska; Oahu, Hawaii; Kuneitra in Ethiopia; and Mahé in the Seychelles.

DISTANT EARLY WARNING (DEW). In 1954, approval was given for a chain of linked **radar** stations located from Alaska to Greenland intended to provide between two and six hours' warning of an attack by **Soviet** bombers on the **United States of America**.

DIVELEY, DUANE W. On 22 June 2005, Major Duane W. Diveley was killed when his **U-2** crashed on the approach to the main runway at al Dafra airbase outside Abu Dhabi. A member of the 380th Air Expeditionary Wing, he had just completed a reconnaissance mission over Afghanistan.

DIYARBAKUR. A small village outside the Turkish Black Sea resort of Samsun was the location of a large American **radar** station that became operational in 1955 to monitor Soviet missile tests at Kapustin Yar. In May 1957, Diyarbakur detected the first Soviet intercontinental ballistic missile launch, the same month as the Jupiter IRBM was successfully fired in the **United States**. *See also* MISSILE GAP.

DOMINO. British codename for the electronic countermeasure for the German **Y-Gerät** night navigation apparatus. Powerful transmitters, located at Beacon Hill, outside Salisbury, and one using the television antenna mast at Alexandra Palace in south London, broadcast pulses on the same frequencies as those selected by the enemy to guide bombers to their targets. DOMINO commenced in February 1941. On 3 May 1941, three Heinkel bombers were shot down during a raid on Liverpool and examination of the Y-Gerät equipment recovered from the aircraft resulted three weeks later in BENJAMIN, an improved version of DOMINO. *See also* WORLD WAR II.

DOUBLE CLICK CORPORATION. A **Central Intelligence Agency** proprietary founded in Miami in 1959 that supplied pilots to fly the unmarked ground-attack aircraft that supported the April 1960 **Bay of Pigs** invasion of **Cuba**. All four American pilots killed in combat over the landing area were employees of the Double Click Corporation.

DRONES. *See* UNMANNED AERIAL VEHICLE.

DUMBO. British designation of the Soviet RUS-2 early warning **radar** that had been copied from **World War II** equipment originally supplied by the Allies. In 1951, ELINT operators of the 91st Strategic Reconnaissance Squadron detected the telltale signals of the RUS-2 in **North Korea**.

– E –

EAGLE CLAW. The codename for the planned rescue of 53 American hostages held by Iranian revolutionary guards in the U.S. embassy compound, 14 buildings set in 27 acres, in Tehran in April 1980. Overhead **KH-11** imagery played a crucial role in the preparations of the operation that originally had been codenamed Operation RICE BOWL. The objective was to transport a team of Green Berets from Fort Bragg, North Carolina, via Frankfurt to Qena in Egypt. At the appointed hour, they would be flown in six C-130s to Masirah, a British airbase off the coast of Oman in the Persian Gulf, where they would refuel and make ready for a flight to a secret landing strip codenamed DESERT ONE, in an isolated location 265 nautical miles from Tehran. There, the Delta Force troops would rendezvous with eight Sikorsky Sea Stallion helicopters launched from the USS *Nimitz*, cruising in the Arabian Sea, and fly in them to DESERT TWO, a wadi in a mountainous area just 65 miles southeast of the capital. The troops would then transfer into cars and vans already procured by CIA personnel and drive into Tehran to seize the compound the following day. Because satellite imagery had shown that the Revolutionary Guards had taken the precaution of erecting poles in the compound to deter a helicopter-borne attack, the hostages and their rescuers would gather at the nearby Amjadieh soccer stadium where they would be picked up by the Sea Stallions, refueled at

DESERT ONE, to be flown to a remote airfield at Manzariyeh, some 35 miles south, where C-141 Starlifters would be waiting to complete the extraction, escorted by U.S. Navy fighters. To cover the entire evacuation, AC-130 gunships armed with Gatling guns were to circle overhead and disperse any opposition. The complex scheme began to fail when, because of mechanical problems, only five of the helicopters reached DESERT ONE, and the operation was aborted. As the aircraft prepared to leave, a helicopter's rotors hit a fully fueled C-130, causing an instant conflagration that killed eight crewmen. When the Iranians eventually reached DESERT ONE, they recovered from the smoldering wreckage a treasure trove of intelligence material, including large quantities of KH-11 imagery that had been distributed to the troops, each marked with details of the original plan. Eager to gain every ounce of propaganda advantage from the humiliating fiasco, the revolutionary guards published a compendium of the captured material, including the highly classified imagery.

EC-121. On 14 April 1969, an unarmed EC-121M reconnaissance aircraft, a variant of the Lockheed 749 Constellation operated by the **U.S.** Navy's Reconnaissance Squadron VQ-1, flying from Atsugi to Osan on a BEGGAR SHADOW signals intelligence mission, was shot down over the Sea of Japan by **North Korean** MiG-21s armed with Atoll infrared missiles, with the loss of the crew of 31. When protesting the attack, President Richard Nixon complained that the aircraft had been operating in international airspace and disclosed that the North Koreans had known this because it had been possible to monitor the data on their **radar** displays.

Only narrowly persuaded not to launch a retaliatory attack on North Korea, Nixon ordered an air raid on Base Area 353, a North Vietnamese stronghold three miles inside the Cambodian border. The assembly area had been bombed already on 18 March but Nixon was infuriated by the loss of the EC-121. He had been critical of his predecessor's failure to respond with force when the North Koreans had seized the *Pueblo* in January 1968 and intended the operation to be a clear warning to all the Communist regimes in the region.

Only two bodies were recovered from the sea by the USS *Tucker*, although the Soviet destroyer, the *Vdokhnovenie*, found some debris. *See also* VIETNAM WAR.

EC-130. In September 1958, a **U.S.** Air Force EC-130 was shot down by MiG interceptors over Armenia, with the loss of all 17 crew. The U.S. administration claimed the aircraft had flown off-course due to a navigational error but two years later two National Security Agency employees, Bernon Mitchell and William Martin, defected to Moscow and held a press conference at which they claimed the EC-130 had been engaged in an intelligence collection mission.

EL DORADO CANYON. The American codename for a coordinated air raid in April 1986, mounted in retaliation for a terrorist attack on the La Belle nightclub in Berlin on five targets in Libya: the dozen MiG-23s and a wing of Mil-8 Hip helicopters on Benina airfield; terrorist training camps at Murat Sidi Bilal; nine Il-76 transports at Tripoli's military airport and naval base; the Jamahiriyah Guard barracks at Benghazi; and Mu'ammar Gadhafi's command bunker in his 200-acre compound at Bab al-Azizyah.

Conscious of the losses sustained by U.S. fighters in the December 1983 daylight engagement over **Syria**, the decision was taken to launch a night attack with A-6Es flown off the carriers *Coral Sea* and *America*, F-111Fs based at Lakenheath, Suffolk, and EF-111As from Upper Heyford, Oxfordshire. The F-111Fs, equipped with Paveway II Mark-84 2,000-pound bombs and 500-pound Snakeye bombs, could deliver their ordinance with tremendous precision using a laser target designation system, but they were vulnerable to one of the world's most sophisticated ground defenses, consisting of SA-2 Guidelines, SA-3 Goas, SA-6 Gainful, SA-8 Gecko missiles, French Crotale missiles, and ZSU-23/4 **radar**-controlled antiaircraft guns.

Altogether, 100 aircraft gathered over the Mediterranean for a three-stage raid that lasted 12 minutes and cost the life of one F-111A pilot. The first stage was saturation of the Libyan radar systems by electronic warfare planes, followed by strikes with high-speed anti-radiation (HARM) and Shrike missiles to eliminate the ground defense radars. Sixteen HARMS and eight Shrikes were fired over Tripoli, and 20 HARMS and four Shrikes were launched on Benghazi, effectively blinding the Libyans. Finally, the strike aircraft flew in at low level and completed their missions.

EL DORADO CANYON was considered a success, although in retaliation, the Libyan leader ordered the sabotage of **Pan Am Flight**

103 in December 1988, killing 259 people, and in September 1989 destroyed UTA 772 over Niger, with the loss of 171 passengers and crew. *See also* GULF OF SIDRA INCIDENT.

ELINT. The acronym applied to electronic intelligence, a source covering the spectrum of **radar** and other noncommunication emissions.

ENIGMA. The machine cipher system adopted by the German armed forces for all high-grade Morse communications, the Enigma proved vulnerable to Allied cryptographers. The **Luftwaffe**'s general key, RED, was one of the first to be solved. Others included PRIMROSE (the Luftwaffe's ground organization in Italy), LOCUST (liaison between Kliegerkorps II and the Wehrmacht), and MAYFLY (used by Fliegerkorps XIV, the Luftwaffe's transport branch). Together this decrypted traffic offered a large, accurate, and continuing insight into the enemy's air operations across the whole of Europe.

EQUINE. The **Central Intelligence Agency** codename for the unit within the Photographic Intelligence Division created to process imagery from a new source, the **U-2**, in 1956.

EROS. The first Israeli civilian photoreconnaissance satellite, manufactured by Israel Aircraft Industries, the Eros A-1 was launched in December 2000 by a Russian Start rocket to supply imagery with six-foot resolution to commercial clients. A second generation of satellites, designed Eros-B, is planned to offer better quality imagery, benefiting from **OFEQ** technology. *See also* TECHSTAR.

ERPROBUNGSTELLE. The experimental branch of the Federal German Republic's **Luftwaffe**, the Erprobungstelle 61, based at Oberfaffenhofen near Munich, was equipped with three former **Royal Air Force** Canberra B-2s from September 1966 to undertake signals interception missions. In 1974, they were transferred to the Deutsche Anstalt für Luft und Raumfart at Eggebeck.

ESCADRON ELECTRONIQUE 51. Known within the French Air Force at Aubrac, the signals intelligence squadron based at Evreux was equipped in 1978 with DC-8 aircraft.

ESTIMATES OF NAZI AIR STRENGTH. The issue of prewar estimates of the **Luftwaffe**'s strength was politically sensitive, as the British government had failed to rearm in anticipation of Nazi aggression, an error that had cost the air minister, **Lord Londonderry**, his Cabinet post. The controversy was exacerbated by Rex Fletcher, a senior Secret Intelligence Service officer, and since 1935 the Labour Member of Parliament for Nuneaton. In 1938, he published *The Air Defence of Britain*, a critical analysis of comparative European air strengths, in which he asserted that the Luftwaffe possessed a total of between 5,200 and 5,500 frontline and reserve aircraft. This contrasted with SIS's own classified assessment of 2,640 German planes, predicting a rise to 4,320 in 1939, with the monthly production escalating from 550 to 700. After **World War II**, the true position was established from a study of captured enemy documents and the interrogation of prisoners, and the actual figures had been 3,000 frontline aircraft in 1938 and 3,647 in 1939, showing SIS's statistics to have been rather more accurate than Fletcher's interpretation.

ESTIMATES OF SOVIET AIR STRENGTH. From 1921, when Western intelligence agencies began attempting to compile statistics on Soviet air strength, the task proved daunting because of the total lack of official information provided on a topic considered by the Kremlin to be a state secret. American, British, French, Polish, and Yugoslav attachés posted in Moscow and Riga over the next two decades made considerable efforts to collect accurate figures but they were handicapped by deliberate attempts to mislead them and a paucity of contacts with access to the data. What became evident early was the willingness of the Soviets to steal aeronautical technology, as was reported in 1937, following the realization that the Vultee V-11 attack bomber, built under license, had been enhanced with stolen designs.

Open sources, such as newspaper articles, provided a very wide range of figures for analysts to study. In December 1936, the *Daily Telegraph* reported a Soviet air fleet of 4,500, of which only 2,000 were modern planes. It predicted a potential annual production capacity of 10,000 to 12,000 if the assembly plants improved efficiency and claimed that the Kremlin planned to increase this rate to 24,000 a year by 1938. A German newspaper in February 1937 claimed an annual production of 1,500 planes in 1932, 3,100 in 1934, 5,000 in 1936, a target of 8,000 in 1937, and 12,000 to 15,000 by 1940.

In 1939, the military commentator Sir Basil Liddell Hart was quoted as accepting the claim of Pierre Cot, then the French aviation minister, that the Soviet Air Force was the most powerful in the world, with 200,000 trained pilots. However, estimates ranged from 8,210 aircraft, supplied by the U.S. military attaché in Moscow, to 10,450, made by his counterpart in Riga. The British suggested 6,900, of which only 4,600 were fit for front-line operations. A more comprehensive American analysis completed in August 1940 included an incomplete list of airframe, aero-engine, and propeller factories and claimed production figures of 500 airframes a month, 1,800 engines a month, and 1,500 propellers. The discrepancies were to be exacerbated during the Winter War with Finland, when the American attaché in Moscow estimated a total production of 500 aircraft a month, but suggested that despite a Soviet air superiority of 10 to one, about half the strength deployed in combat had been destroyed, amounting to 600 aircraft. The attaché in Helsinki credited the Soviets with a total strength of 10,000 to 12,000 aircraft. The true position remained obscure, even after Josef Stalin had made a plea for British aid in 1942 and had negotiated massive support from the Roosevelt administration. No consistent statistics have ever been produced, and the suspicion remains that the Kremlin's secrecy was intended to encourage underestimates of Soviet air strength.

EVERGREEN AIRLINES. A **Central Intelligence Agency** (CIA) proprietary company, Evergreen Airlines undertook clandestine missions for the CIA's Directorate of Operations.

EY-8. A Chinese turboprop aircraft built to a Russian design and deployed on air reconnaissance duties.

– F –

F-117. U.S. Air Force designation of the **Stealth** tactical fighter-bomber deployed operationally in 1984 but not publicly acknowledged until 1988. Designed to be undetectable by enemy radar, the F-117 took part in Operation DESERT STORM in 1991. *See also* PERSIAN GULF WAR.

FALKLANDS WAR. During the campaign conducted in the south Atlantic following the Argentine invasion of the Falklands in April 1982, the **Royal Air Force** flew two long-range bomber missions from Ascension to block the occupation forces from using the runway at Port Stanley airfield. Both operations were unsuccessful, although deception measures taken by the Argentines persuaded air photographic interpreters that the craters had made the runway unusable. In fact, Argentine C-130 aircraft continued to make night landings to resupply the local garrison up until the day of the final surrender in June 1982.

At the beginning of the conflict, three PR-9 Canberras of 39 Squadron were supplied to Chile to monitor communications inside Argentina. They were formally handed over to the Chilean Air Force in October 1982 and one crashed in March 1983. *See also* BLACK BUCK; MIKADO.

FAR EAST COMBINED BUREAU (FECB). The prewar British intelligence organization in the Far East, based at Singapore and Hong Kong, was tri-service with Group Captain Chappell representing Air Intelligence.

FAREWELL. Central Intelligence Agency codename for Colonel Vladimir Vetrov, a Line T KGB officer who had collected scientific and technical information in Montreal and Paris until he volunteered to act as a mole for the French Direction de la Surveillance du Territoire (DST). His reports were circulated inside the North Atlantic Treaty Organization (NATO) under the codename KUDO, and they included evidence that the Soviets had acquired blueprints of the **radar** systems fitted to the F-14, F-15, and F-18 fighters.

Vetrov revealed the true scale of effort devoted to Soviet technology theft, in blatant violation of the **CoCOM** restrictions on the export of strategic materiel, from his position at the heart of Directorate T, the scientific branch of the KGB's First Chief Directorate. He was run under the supervision of Yves Bonnet of the DST, having spent five years at the KGB's *rezidentura* in Paris. When approached initially by the DST, Vetrov had rejected the "pitch" in a way that appeared to leave the door open. Later, when posted to the Soviet Trade Delegation in Montreal in 1978, he had been approached by the Royal Canadian Mounted Police's Security Service, but on this occasion his less than emphatic rejection had been betrayed by a mole, Gilles Brunet. Vetrov became the focus of a counterintelligence investigation conducted by a KGB expert dispatched from Moscow that, although judged inconclusive, resulted in his withdrawal from Canada in 1979.

Infuriated by his treatment, Vetrov had subsequently approached the French military attaché in Moscow and had volunteered to document the Kremlin's covert procurement program, thus revealing the true purpose of the innocuously titled Military Industrial Commission (VPK) that coordinated the KGB and GRU's new focus on technical data with an economic significance. He passed the VPK's annual reports for 1979 and 1980, which made astonishing reading, asserting that the organization had saved billions of rubles, had acquired shortcuts from thousands of Western research projects, and had supplied key knowledge and hardware in 5,000 military categories to numerous Soviet schemes.

FAREWELL's material, which amounted to 4,000 documents, was supplied until November 1982, when the hard-drinking Vetrov was charged with the murder of his mistress and another colleague with whom she was also having an affair. He revealed that the Soviet RYAD computer was actually a counterfeit IBM 370 and that the radars of the F-14, F-15, and F-18 had been copied and fitted to Soviet fighters. According to a DIA report circulated in 1980, before Vetrov had come into play, 70 percent of Warsaw Pact weapons were reliant on components from the West.

FARNBOROUGH. The principal aeronautical research facility in Great Britain, the Royal Aircraft Establishment at Farnborough was penetrated by a Soviet espionage organization in October 1937 when Major Wilfred Vernon was convicted of unauthorized possession of classified information. Formerly an Air Ministry official, Vernon had commanded a Royal Naval Air Service Squadron during **World War I** and in 1923 had been appointed chief draftsman of the Bristol Aeroplane Company. At the time of his arrest, MI5 did not realize he had been an active Soviet spy for some years, and accepted his assertion that he had overlooked the documents he had brought home from Farnborough, where he had worked since 1925.

In 1945, Vernon was elected to the House of Commons as the member of Parliament for Dulwich but when he lost his seat in 1952, he was reinterviewed by MI5 and admitted his previous involvement with the GRU.

FEDDEN, ROY. The designer of the Bristol aero engine, Roy Fedden was invited in July 1937 to visit the Messerschmitt aircraft factory, where he inspected the Me-109 fighter and the Me-110 twin-engined bomber. His reports to Whitehall drastically altered British estimates of the Luftwaffe's strength and capability. *See also* ESTIMATES OF NAZI AIR STRENGTH.

FEED-BACK. The **Central Intelligence Agency** codename for a series of studies conducted by the RAND Corporation between 1952 and 1953 on designs for reconnaissance satellites. The final document, *An Analysis of the Potential of an Unconventional Reconnaissance Method* was produced in March 1954 by Dr. Arnon Katz, the chief physicist at the **U.S.** Air Force's Aerial Reconnaissance Laboratory at Wright-Patterson Air Base at Dayton, Ohio, since 1940.

FERRET FLIGHTS. The tactic of deploying a reconnaissance aircraft along the end of Soviet airspace, and occasionally making incursions to provoke the local air defenses into switching on their **radar** and scrambling interceptors, was conducted by aircraft known as "ferrets." The first ferret mission was flown in May 1943 against a Japanese radar site on Kiska Island in the Aleutians. Between May and September 1943, the 16th Reconnaissance Squadron flew 184 missions in the Mediterranean and identified 450 enemy radar stations.

Fi-103. The German designation of a Fiesler pilotless aircraft developed at **Peenemünde** and perfected in mid-1943, driven by a pulsejet with a speed of 375 miles per hour and a range of 150 miles. Referred to deliberately deceptively as the FZG-76, implying that it was a Flakzielgerät, an antiaircraft target **drone**, the flying bomb was ordered into production by Reichmarschal Hermann Göring with a target of 60 a month in September 1943, rising to 300 a month in October, reaching a total arsenal of 5,000 by the end of 1943, to be built at the Volkswagen factory in Fallersleben. When Adolf Hitler was briefed on the Fi-103, he ordered 30,000 to be completed by 30 October 1943, the date he chose for the airborne offensive on England. The plan anticipated 64 "ski-ramp" catapult launch sites in northern France, oriented toward their targets, supplied by eight protected stores containing 250 weapons each. Significantly, Hitler's directive rescinded an earlier one making tank production the Reich's first priority, with the effect of moving 1,500 skilled technicians from military fabrication to missile manufacture.

Allied bombing of the launch sites and other locations associated with the weapons delayed the expected offensive of 500 flying bombs until 12–13 June 1944, when a total of 10 missiles were fired at London. Five crashed immediately on takeoff and only four reached England. Three days later, there was a second attack, with 244 weapons launched from 55 catapults. Of the 144 that crossed the English coast, 73 reached London. *See also* BODYLINE; CROSSBOW; V-WEAPONS.

FILBERT. British codename for a 29-foot naval **balloon** containing a large **radar** reflector that emulated the echo of a 10,000-ton ship. Fourteen FILBERTs were deployed from naval launches during the **D-Day** deception schemes to draw the enemy's attention away from Normandy and toward an area north of Le Havre, giving the impression of a ghost fleet.

FIREDOG. British codename for antiterrorism operations conducted during the Malaya Emergency by Mosquito PR-34s from 81 Squadron **Royal Air Force**.

FITZWILLIAM. Codename of an Anglo-American high-altitude air-sampling operation conducted throughout the Cold War by WB-29s equipped with filters to detect fissionable material from the **Soviet Union**. Four long-range Weather Reconnaissance Squadrons (the 518th based on Guam, the 275th at Eielson Air Force Base in Alaska, the 374th at Travis Air Force Base in California, and the 373rd at Kindley Field, Bermuda) collected radioactive dust in the northern hemisphere. Analysis was undertaken from 1948 at Hickam Field, Oahu (a laboratory that later moved to Berkeley, California), and in Boston. The British component, operated in 1949 from bases in Scotland and Gibraltar, were codenamed BISMUTH and NOCTURNAL, respectively. *See also* MOGUL.

FLEMING, PETER. One of the most imaginative British intelligence officers of **World War II**, Peter Fleming had established a reputation as an author and explorer when he was posted to India in 1942 to supervise deception operations in southeast Asia. One of his contributions was the distribution of dead carrier pigeons from Allied aircraft over enemy-held territory, the birds having been fitted with small canisters containing deliberately misleading messages. The objective was for the pigeons to be found by Japanese troops who would treat the information as authentic and report their finds to the intelligence branch, the Kempetai.

FLEURUS. On 26 June 1794, the French General Moriot went aloft in a hydrogen balloon to watch his Austrian adversaries during the Battle of Fleurus.

FLIGHT 1474. Created by the **Royal Air Force** in 1942, Flight 1474 was equipped with Wellingtons that flew the first **ELINT** flights. The unit was redesignated as 192 Squadron in January 1943, and was amalgamated with 1483 Flight in January 1944. At the end of the war the unit was transformed into the Central Signals Establishment at **Watton**.

FLYGVAPNET. Swedish airborne signals intelligence platforms have been active in the Baltic since the end of **World War II**. In June 1952, a Dakota DC-3 disappeared with the loss of all eight crew while on a joint reconnaissance mission for the British and American agencies. A few days later, MiG fighters shot down a Convair Catalina near the island of Hüumand while searching for survivors. As well as flying Dakotas, the Flygvapnet was equipped with Vickers Varsity aircraft and in 1960 the Swedish Air Force purchased two Canberra T11 signals intelligence aircraft that were based at Malmslätt. In 1971, they were replaced by a pair of former Scandinavian Airline System (SAS) Tp85 Caravelles.

On 23 May 1980, a Saab-Scania SF-357 Viggen, one of a squadron of photoreconnaissance aircraft based at Norrköping, Ronneby, and Lulea took pictures of the Soviet nuclear battle cruiser *Kirov* as it emerged from Baltic Yard 189 in Leningrad.

FOCKE-WOLF 190. The introduction of the Focke-Wolf 190 fighter by the **Luftwaffe** in late 1941 proved a turning point in Allied air intelligence because it was the first aircraft of the conflict not to have been in service before the war. Hitherto, the Germans had relied on the Messerschmitt-109, Me-110, Junkers-97, Ju-88, and the Heinkel-111, and had simply made improvements to their existing aircraft, but the FW-190 was an entirely new, innovative model with a high-performance, heavy armor and sophisticated weaponry. Air Intelligence was unable to assess the plane's characteristics until June 1942, when one force-landed in Wales, providing the Air Ministry with an opportunity to examine it in detail. *See also* AI-2(g).

FOREIGN TECHNOLOGY DIVISION (FTD). A component of the **U.S.** Air Force's Systems Command and headquartered at Wright Patterson Air Force Base in Ohio, the FTD collects and analyzes information about foreign air forces. The FTB also supervises exercises from a secret base in Nevada in which foreign aircraft simulate conflict against American planes to train pilots in aerial combat. Such drills are intended to improve dog-fighting skills and expose weaknesses. However, only direct confrontations in Vietnam, between Phantoms and MiG-17s, revealed the advantage of the smaller, slower, less maneuverable Soviet fighter that was equipped with a cannon, whereas the F-4 carried only missiles.

Following the 1973 Yom Kippur War, FTD personnel visited the Egyptian airbase at Fayid on the Suez Canal that had been captured by the Israelis and removed SA-2 **Guideline**, SA-3 Goa and shoulder-launched SA-7 *Strella* missile systems, an SA-6 **Gainful** transporter-erector-launcher, and its STRAIGHT FLUSH control radar. Also removed were KNIFE REST, SPOON REST, and BAR LUCKY early-warning **radar** systems, FAN SONG and LOW BLOW missile control radars, and a ZSU 23-4 tracked antiaircraft battery and its GUN DISH control radar. All were subsequently tested at the FTD's classified range out west.

FORT GEORGE G. MEADE. Headquarters of the U.S. National Security Agency, Fort George G. Meade, near Baltimore, Maryland, accommodates the 6940th Electronic Security Wing, 6947th and 1994th Electronic Security Squadron, and all components of the **U.S.** Air Force's Electronic Security Command that, at the height of the **Cold War**, maintained 23 ground stations across the globe.

FOXBAT. The North Atlantic Treaty Organization designation of the **Soviet** Mach-3 high-altitude MiG-25 fighter. The aircraft was studied by Western aviation analysts in September 1976 following the defection of Lieutenant Viktor Belenko, who flew into Hakodate airfield. Although the design and finish of the Foxbat-A appeared surprisingly primitive, it was easy to service and was found to contain advanced avionics. The aircraft was eventually returned to the Soviets, 67 days after it had arrived, the FOXFIRE (Smertch-A) airborne intercept **radar**, IFF, and data link systems having been examined, and one engine removed for study by metallurgists.

First seen at the Domodedovo air show on 9 July 1967, when four of the preproduction aircraft were shown to the public, a reconnaissance variant of the Foxbat was delivered to Egypt in March 1971 and was monitored at a speed of Mach 3.2 at 73,000 feet. On 10 October, two of the four MiG-25Rs flew the length of Israel over the Mediterranean and easily evaded the Phantom F-4Es equipped with Sparrow missiles sent to intercept them. Further flights by Soviet pilots, over Israeli positions in the Sinai, followed on 6 November 1971, 20 March 1972, and 16 May 1972. The planes were withdrawn in July 1972, when President Anwar Sadat ordered the expulsion of all Soviet personnel from Egypt.

On the first occasion the MiG-25 was engaged in combat, on 27 June 1979, a flight of Syrian fighters attempted to intercept Israeli Phantoms over **Lebanon**. When they did so, they were attacked by their escort of F-15 Eagles equipped with Sidewinders, and five of the Syrian MiG-25s were shot down. *See also* FOREIGN TECHNOLOGY DIVISION.

FRANTIC. The **U.S.** Army Air Force codename for the establishment of American bomber bases in the Soviet Union in 1943, Operation FRANTIC resulted in the delayed occupation in 1944 of airfields at

Poltava, Mirgorod, and Piryatin to refuel and rearm heavy bombers that had undertaken missions over Nazi Germany, initially by the 15th Air Force in Italy. Altogether, 2,207 sorties were flown to or from Soviet bases. FRANTIC became an operational and political embarrassment when the Soviets exercised a veto over the selection of enemy targets, with the implication that certain strategically important industrial plants, such as aero engine factories, should be saved for eventual seizure intact by the Red Army. An undefended Luftwaffe air raid on Poltava in June 1944, which lasted over an hour, resulted in the loss of 60 B-17 bombers of the 45th Combat Bombardment Wing of the 8th Air Force, and the death of two aircrew, leading to suspicion that the Soviets had colluded in the attack and definitely had prevented the Americans from taking defensive measures. Mustangs of the 4th and 352nd Fighter Groups, based at Piryatin, were refused permission to intercept the enemy. When Poltava came to be closed in June 1945, the Soviets refused to allow the removal of the remaining aircraft or the destruction of radar equipment.

FRAUENKNECHT, ALFRED. A Swiss aero engineer, Alfred Frauenknecht was paid $200,000 to supply his Israeli contacts, starting with Colonel Dov Sion of the Israeli embassy in Paris, with blueprints of the Mirage III jet fighter in 1968. He was arrested in 1969 and sentenced in April 1971 to four and a half years' imprisonment, but after his appeal was released after a year. The blueprints were used by the Israeli Bureau of Scientific Liaison (LAKAM) to improve the Nesher jet fighter and to develop the Kfir interceptor, which was unveiled in April 1975.

FRESSANGES, FRANCIS. Director of Air Intelligence at the Air Ministry from 1952 to 1954, Air Vice Marshal Francis Fressanges had commanded a squadron of flying boats during the Battle of the Atlantic and after **World War II** was appointed director of operations at the Air Ministry. He retired in 1957 as commander-in-chief of the Far East Air Force and died in October 1975, aged 73.

FREYA. The German codename for an early-warning **radar** system first spotted at Lannion in France in July 1940. The codename referred to the Nordic goddess of beauty and love, whose husband could see for 100 miles. By October 1941, aircraft from 109 Squadron had helped identify 27 FREYA sites between Cherbourg and Bodo in Norway.

FUGO. Japanese codename for the release of bomb-carrying **balloons** into the Pacific jet stream, intended to detonate upon landing in California. The operation succeeded only in diverting **U.S.** Army Air Force fighters deployed to intercept and destroy the balloons.

FULCRUM. The North Atlantic Treaty Organization designation of the MiG-29, first spotted by a **satellite** in 1977, which entered service in 1985 as an all-weather interceptor equipped with look-down shoot-down **radar**, to replace the MiG-21, MiG-23, and MiG-27. In February 1984, a Department of Defense budget document accidentally included the imagery, taken overhead from an altitude of 100 to 150 miles, together with a photograph of the Su-27 Flanker, and when these pictures were broadcast by CBS News in late February 1984 they were the very first satellite imagery ever publicly disclosed.

FX. The German abbreviation of Funk X-Gerät ("radio apparatus X"), the designation of the PC-1400 radio-guided free-fall bomb that in September 1944 sank the new Italian battleship *Roma* and severely damaged the *Italia*. The armor-piercing high-explosive bomb could be guided onto its target by an operator in the Dornier-217 bomber, so it would detonate with great accuracy. The innovation took the Allies entirely by surprise although signals intelligence had revealed earlier references to aircraft of the 111/KG100 in the Mediterranean being equipped with FX, which required especially tight security, but the significance of the messages had gone unnoticed. When the **Luftwaffe** abandoned the airfield at Foggia, several bombers with the guidance equipment were recovered, allowing the Allies to take countermeasures. *See also* GUIDED MISSILES.

– G –

GAINFUL. The North Atlantic Treaty Organization designation of the Soviet-built SA-6 mobile surface-to-air missile, with three mounted on a half-track. A small rocket powered by a two-phase engine, it left a very short, six-second exhaust plume when fired, making it difficult to detect from the air. The first SA-6 batteries were not photographed until the summer of 1972, when Israeli Phantoms from Ramat David spotted three batteries between Damascus and the Golan Heights.

GAMBIT. Between July 1963 and June 1967, the **United States** launched a total of 36 GAMBIT reconnaissance **satellites** intended to provide **imagery** of Soviet **inter-continental ballistic missile** deployments. Two capsules from each satellite, containing the exposed film, were jettisoned over the Pacific where they were intercepted by specially equipped aircraft. The second-generation GAMBIT and KH-8 satellite lasted 18 years and concluded with a final launch in April 1984, a flight that lasted 118 days. Altogether, there were 50 successful launches, and in June 1984 the first KH-9 HEXAGON satellite went into orbit. *See also* SOVIET UNION.

GERHARDT, DIETER. A Soviet spy codenamed FELIX, Commander Dieter Gerhardt of the South African Navy was arrested at his New York hotel in January 1983 and convicted of treason and sentenced to life imprisonment. His Swiss wife, Ruth Johr, was sentenced to 10 years' imprisonment. Gerhardt confessed that he had spied for the GRU since 1960 and had provided his handlers with many tens of thousands of classified documents. In particular, he had supplied details of the weapons systems he had been trained on while serving on various attachments with the Royal Navy, including the Seacat and Sea Sparrow missiles. During his career, which had begun when he had graduated from the Simonstown Naval Academy in 1956, he had attended an electronic warfare course in England at HMS *Collingwood*, and had served on HMS *Tenby*, a Type 12 frigate. He also admitted compromising a secret March 1975 report relating to the Israeli **Jericho** missile and an agreement reached in November 1974 in which the South Africans had purchased eight of them and undertook to fit them with their own atomic warheads. He also disclosed other details of South Africa's nuclear plans, including free-fall weapons for the Buccaneer aircraft.

Gerhardt was released from prison in August 1992 and moved to Switzerland to join his wife.

GERMAN AIR SECTION. In 1936, the Government Code and Cipher School (GC&CS) introduced an Air Section to exploit **Luftwaffe** traffic intercepted at West Kingsdown and Cheadle. Headed by Joshua Cooper, a graduate of Brasenose College, Oxford, and King's College, London, the section liaised closely with the Air Ministry and succeeded in reading low-level enemy wireless traffic. By September 1940, the Air Section had begun to break some Enigma traffic. Cooper, who had been taught cryptography by the czar's code breakers Ernst and Felix Fetterlein, both Russian refugees from the 1917 Revolution, was later succeeded by (Sir) Eric Jones and Professor Arthur Humphreys.

The German Air Section, accommodated first in Bletchley Park's library and then in F Block, achieved considerable success against the Luftwaffe's three-letter RHN code known as Rhino, which was intended to abbreviate longer messages. The entire hand-cipher had been reconstructed from codebooks recovered from downed enemy aircraft in France in 1940 and from straightforward deduction. In breaking the Luftwaffe's Enigma traffic, the code breakers received considerable assistance from signals transmitted from Staaken, the Luftwaffe airfield in East Berlin that provided a daily Ju-52 shuttle service to the Fuhrer's headquarters at Rastenburg. These messages often contained the names of senior officers, such as General Freytag von Loringhoven, Adolf Hitler's Luftwaffe adjutant, and General Wolfgang Martini, the Luftwaffe's signals chief, which had to be spelled out in full, thereby helping the Allied cryptographers who accumulated a card index of personalities likely to appear in the texts.

GERMANY. The appointment by Adolf Hitler in January 1933 of Hermann Göring as his air minister heralded the development of a new air ministry, established in Berlin's Bendlerstrasse, and a modern **Luftwaffe**, even if initially its creation was concealed behind an expansion of Lufthansa's civil air fleet, with training exercises conducted in the Soviet Union, because of restrictions imposed by the Treaty of Versailles. Having negotiated permission at the disarmament talks at Geneva for an air force of 500 fighter and reconnaissance aircraft, with no mention of bombers, and the covert training of an initial cadre of 800 pilots at the Glider Research Institute at Jüterbog, Germany's rearmament gained pace. It was directed by a new air staff based at a vast headquarters on the Leipzigerstrasse, with an underground control center at Potsdam. Two million construction workers were engaged in building airfields and other support facilities, and by the end of 1935 the Luftwaffe had grown to 1,900 modern front-line aircraft supplied by 14 factories.

The new Luftwaffe's deployment in the Spanish civil war gave the aircrews valuable combat experience and amounted to some 5,000 men and 200 aircraft, including a squadron of bombers from KG 88 at Greifswald. Germany's support for General Francisco Franco's forces against the republican government enabled the Luftwaffe to practice the transportation of troops, air to ground coordination, and aerial bombardment techniques, all of which would become characteristics of the blitzkrieg strategy later used during the Polish campaign, which lasted just three weeks; the Luftwaffe deployed 1,939 aircraft and lost only 285.

While the Luftwaffe adopted a policy of deliberately understating its production statistics and future plans, it benefited in 1936 from the **Royal Air Force**'s accurate declarations to the air attaché in London, General Wenninger, of 1,022 bombers and 420 fighters by the end of 1938, with some reserves and some squadrons based overseas. In contrast, the Luftwaffe would grow, before mobilization in 1939, to 20,000 aircrew manning 1,176 bombers, 408 twin-engined fighters, 772 single-engined fighters, and 552 Ju-52 transports, amounting to the world's largest and most powerful air force, backed by a vast, modern, and well-equipped aviation industry.

German intelligence analysts in 1938 estimated that the French Air Force consisted of 640 bombers, of which all but 120 were obsolete, and they correctly predicted that France's air defenses would be no match for the modern Luftwaffe. However, after initial successes in the first year of **World War II**, German air intelligence concentrated on the collection of target information from the Abwehr's air branch, which would prove unreliable, partly because of enemy deception, but mainly through poor photo-imagery analysis caused by a reluctance to use stereoscopic viewers that would have added texture to objects that turned out to be deception ruses, such as rubber tanks, cardboard aircraft, and balsa-wood landing craft. German susceptibility to such techniques, exacerbated by a lack of air superiority in any theater, made the Reich's air intelligence counterproductive.

GLIMMER. British codename for a **D-Day** deception scheme perpetrated by Stirlings of 218 Squadron that distributed **WINDOW** in the English Channel off Boulogne to simulate the existence of an air armada. *See also* WORLD WAR II.

GLOBAL HAWK. An **unmanned aerial vehicle** developed by the **U.S. Defense Advanced Research Projects Agency** and manufactured by Northrop Grumman in San Diego, the Global Hawk is a high-altitude reconnaissance platform the size of an executive jet with a wingspan of 116 feet. With a range of 10,000 miles and an endurance of up to 40 hours at 65,000 feet, each aircraft costs $40 million. Equipped with a variety of sensors, the aircraft's operations are controlled from Beale Air Force Base in southern California, with the imagery processed at the National Guard's 152nd Intelligence Squadron at Reno, Nevada. The Global Hawk proved highly effective during Operation IRAQI FREEDOM when it flew on 18 consecutive days, controlled by personnel of the 11th Reconnaissance Squadron, based at Indian Springs Auxiliary Airfield. Missions in Iraq have been controlled by the Combined Operations Center at the Prince Sultan Air Force Base in Saudi Arabia.

GODDARD, VICTOR. The deputy director of Air Intelligence between 1938 and 1939, Air Marshal Sir Victor Goddard undertook a detailed study of the Condor Legion's tactics during the Spanish civil war and concluded that in any future conflict, the **Luftwaffe**'s primary role would be of in support of ground troops, not in undertaking the long-range strategic bombing task anticipated by other air intelligence experts. Goddard had relied on the analysis of intercepted Luftwaffe wireless traffic, monitored military exercises, and recognition that German bombers possessed neither the payload nor the fuel to attack British cities in strength.

Born in February 1897, Goddard was educated at Osborne, Dartmouth, and Jesus College, Cambridge, and Imperial College, London, before joining the Royal Naval Air Service and then the Royal Flying Corps. He wrote several books, including *Skies to Dunkirk*, and died in January 1987.

GOERTZ, HERMAN. In November 1935, an Abwehr spy was discovered living in Stanley Road, Broadstairs, a quiet seaside resort in

Kent. He had rented a bungalow in September, but had left without paying the rent, so his landlady, Mrs. Florence Johnson, had called the police. A search of the house revealed that her tenant, 45-year-old Dr. Herman Goertz, had left a mass of incriminating espionage paraphernalia, including sketches of local airfields, such as the nearby Royal Air Force (RAF) station at Manston, and a map with every RAF base marked on it. A diary listed:

> Aug 29 1935 Mildenhall; Aug 31 Duxford; Sept 1 Mildenhall; Sept 2 Hunstanton; Sept 3 Feltwell; Sept 5 and 6 London; Sept 7 Hatfield; Sept 10 Martlesham; Sept 11 Broadstairs, Ramsgate; Sept 12 Broadstairs; Sept 13 Mildenhall; Sept 19 Broadstairs.

Unaware of the excitement he had caused in his absence, Goertz returned in November from a trip to the continent and was arrested as he landed at Harwich. He was charged with breaches of the Official Secrets Act. Under interrogation, he revealed that he had served in the German Air Force and had flown 30 missions during **World War I** as an observer.

At his Old Bailey trial in March the following year, Goertz was sentenced to four years' imprisonment at Maidstone jail. The case was the only prewar German espionage trial in England, and was a considerable embarrassment to the German government.

GOPHER. In 1950, the **Central Intelligence Agency** initiated a project to fly huge helium-filled **balloons** across the Soviet Union, capturing imagery in cameras stowed in gondolas. The operations, launched from West Germany, Scotland, and Turkey, and later codenamed GRANDSON and GENETRIX, depended on recovering the equipment once the flight had been completed, but were abandoned in March 1956. Altogether, 516 balloons had been launched, of which 399 took photographs, but only 44 were recovered over the Pacific by C-119 transports.

GOVERNMENT COMMUNICATIONS HEADQUARTERS (GCHQ). The principal British signals intelligence organization, GCHQ had tasked **Royal Air Force** (RAF) collection platforms to intercept all types of electronic transmissions, across the spectrum from radar to voice channels. Throughout the **Cold War**, GCHQ relied upon the RAF's Signals Directorate to provide the data required for signals analysis at its headquarters located at Eastcote, Middlesex, and, since 1953, at three sites in the city of Cheltenham, Gloucestershire. *See also* GERMAN AIR SECTION.

GOWADIA, NOSHIR S. A naturalized U.S. citizen originally from India, 61-year-old Noshir Gowadia was arrested in October 2005 at his home in Haiku, Hawaii, by the Federal Bureau of Investigation and charged with having sold classified information to **China** about the B-2 Spirit **stealth** bomber for $110,000. An avionics engineer who had played a key role in the development of the B-2 and an acknowledged expert on infrared signature suppression, Gowadia was later charged with having attempted to sell information relating to advanced Cruise missiles to unnamed individuals in **Israel**, **Germany**, and Switzerland. Between November 1968 and April 1986, Gowadia worked for Northrop Grumman and he later became a contractor at the Los Alamos National Laboratories in New Mexico. His trial was scheduled to begin in April 2009.

GRAF ZEPPELIN. In March and August 1939, the airship LZ 130 *Graf Zeppelin* flew reconnaissance flights at 1,000 feet along the east coast of England and took a close interest in the radar sites at Bawdsey and Canewdon on instructions from General Wolfgang Martini, the **Luftwaffe**'s signals chief. Its final mission, on 2 August 1939, lasted 48 hours and traveled 2,000 miles from its base at Frankfurt am Main.

GREAT BRITAIN. Air intelligence was not recognized as a separate intelligence branch until 1930, when the Secret Intelligence Service (SIS) created an air intelligence section, designated as Section II, and the Air Ministry appointed a director of intelligence, Air Commodore **Charles Blount**. Treasury parsimony meant that very limited resources were allocated to air intelligence, leaving Blount and his SIS counterpart, Wing-Commander **Fred Winterbotham**, assisted by Squadron-Leader John Perkins, to operate in virtual isolation, acting as analysts rather than collectors of intelligence and using their own initiative to develop an aerial reconnaissance capability by employing Sidney Cotton. An attempt to acquire a complete order-of-battle for the Luftwaffe failed when an agent recommended by SIS's head of station in Berlin, Frank Foley, sold John Perkins information in Zurich for £10,000 that turned out to be worthless.

Upon the outbreak of **World War II**, the need for reliable air intelligence forced the **Royal Air Force** to create an air reconnaissance capability at **Wyton**, the airfield in Cambridgeshire that would remain the RAF's center of air intelligence throughout the remainder of the war and the **Cold War**.

GUARDRAIL. The National Security Agency codename for an airborne signals intelligence intercept system developed at a disused Nike missile base at Gruenstadt in Germany in 1971 and then deployed in **Vietnam** and later in Korea and Iraq. GUARDRAIL-1 consisted of a flight of up to three Beechcraft light aircraft that relayed the intercepted signals traffic to Integrated Processing Facilities, 40-foot mobile trailers parked on the ground in which up to 18 operators monitored the signals remotely.

GUELLICH, GUSTAV. An **Abwehr** agent based in New York, Gustav Guellich was instructed in 1936 by the German military attaché in Washington, D.C., General Friedrich von Boetticher, to collect information about tests conducted by the American rocket pioneer Robert H. Goddard, who in the 4 January 1936 edition of *Science News Letter* reported a successful launch of his Nell missile over 7,400 feet at Roswell, New Mexico.

GUIDED MISSILES. The first remote-controlled radio-guided missile was the Heinkel Hs-293 that was used to attack Allied warships in the Bay of Biscay in September 1943. Although the weapon had been referred to in the **Oslo Report** in 1939, Allied air intelligence had been unprepared for the near miss on HMS *Bideford*, the damage to HMCS *Athabaskan*, and the loss of HMS *Elgin*. **Prisoner of war** interrogations revealed that the Hs-293 was launched from a specially adapted Heinkel-177 and that the missile was then guided onto the target by a radio signals from the bomber that was obliged to continue its course and fly at considerably less than its maximum speed, making it vulnerable to antiaircraft fire, thus allowing Air Intelligence to circulate ships with possible countermeasures. Designed as an antiship missiles, neither the Hs-293 nor the Fritz-X proved either reliable or popular, and technicians had insufficient time before the end of the war to perfect them.

In the postwar era, all the major military powers attempted to develop guided weapons and research possible countermeasures, a competition that became the focus of rival air intelligence agencies. Western manufacturers found limited opportunities to either find export markets overseas for their advanced weapons or to test them under combat conditions, and entire series, such as the British air defense Bloodhound, were never fired in anger. In contrast, the Soviet SA-2 **Guideline** was distributed widely to **Syria**, Egypt, China, and North Korea, and successive improvements proved effective and cheap to construct.

GUIDELINE. The North Atlantic Treaty Organization designation of the Soviet-built SA-2 antiaircraft missile that was first spotted at the 1957 May Day parade in Moscow. Weighing more than two tons, the 30-foot long missile carried a warhead containing 280 pounds of explosives that detonated on contact with or in proximity to a target. The SA-2 was a primitive weapon that could reach a target 20 miles away, at a maximum altitude of 11 miles, at a speed of Mach 3.5. It was powered by a solid-propellant booster and a kerosene-based second-stage sustainer, and was guided toward its target by a P-12 SPOON REST acquisition radar. However, it was ineffective under 3,000 feet and although radar-guided, it was unwieldy and could easily be outmaneuvered. The SA-2, deployed in batteries of six launchers, formed the basis of air defenses in the Warsaw Pact countries, **China**, Egypt, **Syria**, **Cuba**, **Afghanistan**, and **Vietnam** but was vulnerable to low-level attack where the sites were not protected by SA-3 missiles, which could destroy planes as low as 300 feet, and antiaircraft artillery. These combinations were developed following numerous Israeli Phantom F-4 attacks on SA-2 sites along the Suez Canal during the **War of Attrition**.

The SA-2 formed the foundation of the **Voiska Protivovozdushnoi Oborony**, the Soviet air defense system, and some 2,000 sites were eventually identified. Initially, potential targets were tracked by the P-14 TALL KING radar, which was replaced by the P-8 KNIFE REST and P-12 SPOON REST target acquisition radars. Western **ferret flights** were flown throughout the **Cold War** to test the limits of these systems and monitor response times. Improved SA-2s, with an extended range of up to 25 miles, were responsible for bringing down U-2s flown by **F. Gary Powers** in May 1960 and **Rudolf Anderson** in October 1962, and an undisclosed number of others over mainland China. *See also* SOVIET UNION.

GUILD. The North Atlantic Treaty Organization designation of the SA-1 Soviet surface-to-air missile that was vehicle-mounted and fired vertically. *Guild* sites were built about 12 miles apart in two circles, 25 and 45 miles from Moscow, toward the end of 1955. Constructed in a distinctive herringbone fashion of parallel roads, the launch sites were easy to spot from overhead, and the first **U-2** overflight of the Soviet Union, in July 1956, had as one of its objectives the collection of SA-1 imagery. *See also* SOVIET UNION.

GULF OF SIDRA INCIDENT. On 23 March 1986, the U.S. 6th Fleet carriers *Saratoga* and *America* entered the Gulf of Sidra and waters claimed by Libya's mercurial leader, Colonel Mu'ammar Gadhafi. The deliberate incursion, codenamed Operation PRAIRIE FIRE, had been planned for months and elaborate preparations had been made for a confrontation involving some of the most sophisticated aircraft and air defenses on the planet. For example, a flight of EA-6B Prowler electronic countermeasures aircraft of the Tactical Electronic Warfare Squadron (VAQ) 135 were flown to the USS *Coral Sea* from their base at Whidbey Island, Washington, to neutralize any Libyan radar. The Libyan Arab Air Force boasted MiG-25 Foxbats, MiG-23 Floggers, Su-22 Fitters, Mirage Vs, and Mirage F-1s.

When the operation began the Libyans responded by firing two SA-5 Gammon missiles from a battery near Surt at a pair of F-14 Tomcats. The fighters, protected by circling Hawkeye surveillance platforms, easily detected the Soviet FOUR SQUARE radar as it locked on to the targets at a range of 80 miles and evaded the missiles. The following day, after the 161-foot *Waheen*, a Libyan missile boat armed with Italian Ottomat antiship missiles, had been destroyed, the Surt radar site was also disabled by a high-speed antiradiation missile (HARM). Two other Soviet-built *Nanuchka*-class corvettes were also engaged, and the *Ean Mara* was sunk by a Harpoon missile fired by an A-6E from the *Saratoga*.

In the aftermath of the humiliating defeat, the Libyan intelligence agency arranged a series of terrorist attacks in Europe, including the bombing of TWA Flight 870 as it landed in Athens and an attack on the La Belle discotheque in Berlin.

In a second incident, on 4 January 1989, a pair of Libyan MiG-23 Floggers were engaged head-on by two **U.S.** Navy F-14 Tomcats as they headed for a task force of the 6th Fleet sailing in the same disputed area. The combat lasted seven and a half minutes, and both Libyan jets were shot down into the Mediterranean. *See also* EL DORADO CANYON.

– H –

HABBANIYA. The principal **Royal Air Force** base in Iraq, Habbaniya also accommodated the wartime Combined Intelligence Centre Iraq, the focus of regional security and intelligence operations that, given the topography, was heavily dependent on air reconnaissance. After the war, Habbaniya was home to No. 13 Squadron's Mosquitoes, which undertook overflights of the southern **Soviet Union** until the introduction of the MiG-15 jet fighter in 1948. During the Israeli war of independence in 1948, 13 Squadron lost four PR Spitfires and 213 Squadron lost a Tempest to Israeli fighters while on missions over the combat zone.

HAINAN INCIDENT. On 1 April 2001, a **U.S.** Navy EP3V Orion ARIES II (Airborne Reconnaissance Integrated Electronic System) II aircraft, one of 12 of the Fleet Reconnaissance Squadron (VQ-1) at Kadena on Okinawa, made an emergency landing at Lingshui on the Chinese island of Hainan after it had been in a collision with one of two Navy F-8 twinjet Finback II interceptors. Wang Wei, the pilot of the MiG-21 variant, ejected but his body was never recovered.

Based at the Naval Air Station Whidbey Island, Washington, VQ-1 was the U.S. Navy's largest squadron, with 75 officers and 350 other ranks, and flew from detachments deployed to Misawa on Honshu, Manama in Bahrain, Rota in Spain, Crete, and on counternarcotics flights from Manta in Ecuador. With a flight duration of 10 hours, the EP3Vs undertook routine signals intelligence intercept missions, but the flight in April would experience harassment in international airspace from one of the Chinese pilots.

The crew of 24, which included three women, attempted to destroy the signals intelligence intercept and LINK-11 STORY BOOK secure communications equipment aboard, but were taken into custody before they could complete the task. They were released after 11 days and the plane was dismantled and in July loaded onto a giant Antonov An-124 leased cargo aircraft when the Chinese refused to allow it to be repaired and flown out to the Lockheed-Martin factory in Marietta, Georgia. The EP3V's pilot, Lieutenant Shane Osborn, who would be decorated with the Distinguished Flying Cross, was flown out with his crew on a chartered Continental 737 to Anderson Air Force Base on Guam, and then transferred on a C-17 to Hickam Air Force Base on Hawaii for debriefing. *See also* CHINA, PEOPLE'S REPUBLIC OF.

HAMBURG. Between 24 July and 1 August 1943, the **Royal Air Force** flew four devastating raids on Hamburg that flattened 80 percent of the city and provided the Air Ministry's air intelligence branch with information with which to assess the impact and influence of the air war. Some service Enigma channels indicated that all military leave in the area had been canceled, and the local Japanese vice-consul submitted graphic reports, using the compromised diplomatic cipher, on the scale of the bomb damage. Other decrypts referred to the evacuation of the civilian population, the dispersal of the region's industry, and even mentioned panic in Berlin. The resulting assessments gave credence to the controversial argument that carpet-bombing could undermine morale to the point of causing the regime to collapse, a view that would later prove to be unjustified. *See also* GERMANY; WORLD WAR II.

HEADACHE. British **World War II** generic codename for the countermeasures taken to bend the navigational beams used by **Luftwaffe** bombers.

HEAVY GREEN. The National Security Agency codename for **Lima Site** 85, a clandestine TSQ-81 radar station located on the summit of Phou Pha Thi, a mountain strategically located 12 miles inside Laos.

The facility, established in March 1966, monitored air movements over Hanoi, intercepted North Vietnamese communications traffic, and played a key role in the ROLLING THUNDER bombing campaign. It was overrun by North Vietnamese commandos on 10 March 1968 and 11 U.S. personnel were reported killed or missing. The last two technicians to be rescued by an **Air America** helicopter were Willie Husband and Richard Etchberger. Soon afterward the site was bombed by American aircraft to eliminate any evidence of HEAVY GREEN's existence.

Shortly before the commando assault, two North Vietnamese Air Force Soviet-built AN-2 biplanes attacked Site 85, dropping mortar bombs from the observer's cockpit. By chance, an unarmed Air America UH-1 flew onto the scene while on a separate ammunition delivery mission, and the crewman Glenn Woods used an AK-47 to shoot at the biplanes, causing both to crash, the first time that a rotor-wing aircraft had attacked and destroyed a pair of fixed-wing planes.

HÉLIOS. French codename for a surveillance satellite introduced in 1994.

HERCULES. On 30 January 2005, a **Royal Air Force** Special Duties C-130 Hercules was shot down 20 miles north of Baghdad with the loss of the pilot, Flight Lieutenant David Stead, and his crew of nine while on a 40-mile low-level flight to Balad. Five of the crew were from 47 (Special Duties) Squadron, which routinely flies on operations in support of the Special Air Service regiment. A video released by al-Qaeda claimed responsibility for the attack and a Ministry of Defence investigation concluded that the aircraft had indeed been shot down by insurgent ground-fire that hit a wing fuel tank. The board of inquiry was unable to determine whether the ground fire included a missile, possibly a shoulder-fired SAM-7 Strela, or even a Kornet antitank missile.

HERITAGE. National Reconnaissance Office codename for an infrared sensor deployed in satellites to detect short-burning, high acceleration flares of Soviet antiballistic missile systems.

HERMES. United States Army Ordinance Department codename for a contract given to the General Electric Corporation in early 1945 to develop a high-altitude rocket modeled on the **A-4**.

HIGH ALTITUDE SAMPLING PROGRAM (HASP). In 1948, British and American aircraft were deployed to collect air samples that were analyzed for the presence of radioactive particles, which indicated recent atmospheric testing of Soviet nuclear devices. The first of three U-2 aircraft assigned to these missions in England arrived at **Royal Air Force** Upper Heyford in August 1962. *See also* FITZWILLIAM.

HIMLI, MAHMOUD. The pilot of an Egyptian Yak trainer, Captain Mahmoud Himli defected to Israel in his aircraft in 1964, apparently in protest of his country's support of rebels in the Yemen and its use of poison gas against the royalists. He was resettled in Argentina but was traced by the Mukhabarat after he had sent an indiscreet postcard to his mother, lured from a Buenos Aires nightclub by an attractive Mukhabarat agent, and returned by ship to Egypt where he was tried for treason and executed by a firing squad.

HIROSHIMA. The U.S. Army Air Force attack on Hiroshima at 0915 on the morning of Monday, 6 August 1945, was the first time an atomic weapon had been dropped in anger, and a further attack, on the port of Nagasaki on Kyushu three days later, persuaded the Japanese cabinet on 14 August to agree to an unconditional surrender.

The decision to use the atom bomb against Japan had been made by President Franklin D. Roosevelt and Winston Churchill in September 1944, although the precise target, of a highly populated industrial center, was not confirmed until the end of May 1945, when the secretary of state, Henry Stimson, chaired a meeting of the Interim Committee, a seven-member advisory group appointed by President Harry Truman. The Interim Committee, conscious that there was to be a single test at Alamogordo, New Mexico, in July, which would leave just two weapons available for the attack on Japan, with the possibility of a third a few weeks later, had been warned that an assault on Japan's mainland would result in between half a million and a million Allied casualties, and a larger, unknown number of Japanese dead.

Air intelligence played a central role in the selection of Hiroshima on Honshu as the first target, and the plutonium implosion weapon detonated on time, the equivalent of 20,000 tons of TNT, at an altitude of 1,800 feet after it had been dropped by a B-29 flown from Tinian by 29-year-old Captain Paul Tibbets. There were an estimated 100,000 deaths in Hiroshima and a further 40,000 at Nagasaki.

Because so few people had been indoctrinated into the secret of the Manhattan project there was considerable doubt about whether either the first spherical "Fat Man" bomb, or the second device, a cylindrical gun-method uranium weapon, would work. The third bomb was stored in Utah, and the Japanese capitulation made its transfer to the Pacific unnecessary.

HOME RUN. Codename for a surveillance operation conducted between March and May 1956 over Siberia, consisting of 156 missions flown from Thule in Greenland by 16 RB-47 photographic reconnaissance aircraft and five RB-47H electronic intelligence collectors. The final mission was flown in daylight at 40,000 feet by six RB-47s, which crossed the Soviet coast at Ambarchik and exited at Anadyr on the Bering Straits before landing at Eielson Air Force Base in Alaska.

HOT SHOP. The **Central Intelligence Agency** codename for a series of **U-2** and RB-57D flights conducted in June 1959 from Incirlik along the Soviet border with Iran to collect telemetry signals transmitted from **SS-6** test launches at **Tyuratam** and Kapustin Yar.

– I –

IGLOO WHITE. American codeword for an aerial surveillance operation conducted during the **Vietnam War** on the Ho Chi Minh trail, the principal supply route from North Vietnam to the combat zone in the south. Because the rainforest canopy was too dense to allow conventional techniques, IGLOO WHITE included drops from aircraft of thousands of remote movement sensors that transmitted information indicating the movement of troops and matèriel.

ILYUSHIN-20. Designated as the Coot-A by the North Atlantic Treaty Organization, the Il-20 was the reconnaissance variant of the Il-18D four-engined airliner. *See also* SOVIET UNION.

ILYUSHIN-38. Designated as May by the North Atlantic Treaty Organization, the Il-38 is a modification of the Il-18 Coot civil airliner that entered service in 1968 and conducted AMVF maritime reconnaissance missions and antisubmarine warfare. In November 1978, a detachment was posted permanently to the Al-Hajj airbase in Aden. *See also* SOVIET UNION.

INDIA. In August 1981, 106 Squadron at Uttar Pradesh replaced its dozen Canberra reconnaissance aircraft with eight MiG-25R Foxbat-Bs so as to safely penetrate Pakistani airspace defended by F-16 interceptors.

INDONESIA. A **Central Intelligence Agency** (CIA) plan to assist Indonesian rebels to overthrow the pro-Soviet President Achmed Sukarno in 1958 was abandoned following the capture of a CIA pilot, Allen Pope, whose B-26 was shot down while on a raid over Jakarta. Although the State Department denied all knowledge of the operation, Pope, a veteran of the **Korean War** and the **Dien Bien Phu** airdrops, was found to be carrying documents identifying him as an employee of **Civil Air Transport**, a CIA proprietary. In an effort to improve relations with the regime, and obtain Pope's release, an embargo on the export of weapons to Indonesia was lifted, and the sale of 37,000 tons of American rice was approved, but Pope was not released from prison until 1962, when he went to work for **Southern Air Transport**.

INDUSTRIAL INTELLIGENCE CENTRE (IIC). Headed by Desmond Morton, the IIC collected information about the size and performance of the German air industry prior to the outbreak of **World War II**. Working closely with the **Air Ministry**, the IIC produced 12 reports between March 1934 and July 1939 on Nazi air rearmament. The IIC monitored individual factories through visits made by British aeronautical engineers, who enjoyed good access until 1938. In addition, the air attaché at the British embassy in Berlin used his own private aircraft to make his own observations.

INGLIS, FRANK. The **director of intelligence** at the Air Ministry between 1942 and 1945, Frank Inglis was born in June 1899 and was educated at Rigby and Sandhurst before he transferred to the **Royal Air Force** in 1925 and graduated from Cranwell. He retired in 1952 and died in September 1969.

INTER-CONTINENTAL BALLISTIC MISSILE (ICBM). Compiling accurate assessment of Soviet missile strengths remained a key Western air intelligence objective throughout the **Cold War**, but after the **missile gap** was proved in 1962 to have been a fallacy, considerable resources were devoted to the development of better collection systems. *See also* SOVIET UNION.

INTERMOUNTAIN AVIATION. A proprietary company owned by the **Central Intelligence Agency** (CIA), Intermountain Aviation was based at Marana, a privately owned airfield, formerly a **World War II** landing strip, near Tucson, Arizona, and played a key role in the training of Tibetan rebels, loyal to the Dalai Lama, who were infiltrated back into their homeland to resist the Chinese occupation that had been imposed in 1951. In 1959, a widespread revolt against the Chinese began spontaneously, but was encouraged by Khamba tribesmen trained by CIA at Camp Hale in Colorado, and returned to the mountain hideouts by Intermountain Aviation.

Ostensibly engaged in pilot training, parachute jumping, and the maintenance and restoration of military aircraft, Intermountain Aviation became the focus of an official complaint to the United Nations in 1965 when it was identified as the vendor in the sale of 20 B-26 bombers that had been delivered by pilots contracted by Aero Associates to Portugal in breach of an international embargo.

IRAN. In 1975, the Imperial Iranian Air Force purchased 80 F-14 Tomcats to replace its F-4E Phantoms, and undertook "live-firing exercises" of the Phoenix air-to-air missiles, which promptly terminated the regular Soviet overflights by MiG-25 Foxbats from across the Caspian Sea.

Since the 1979 revolution, Iran has been obliged to procure defense equipment from other sources and has acquired weapons, including missiles, from North Korea. One motive for Iran's effort to improve the country's air defenses has been its concealed, and then declared, development of nuclear weapons, at the existing reactor at Bushehr on the Gulf, at the Natanz storage and enrichment facility, and at the heavy water factory at Arak. In addition, Iran runs a reactor in Tehran, with subsidiary facilities at Karaz and Mo'allam Kalaych and a processing laboratory at Isfahan, and mines uranium at Saghand. Other sensitive locations associated with the Iranian nuclear industry are at Fasa and Dakhovin in the south, Chala and Neka on the Caspian Sea, Bonab and Tabriz in the northwest, and at Tabas, close to the Afghan border. All these sites, which have received equipment and advice from Pakistan's Dr. A. Q. Khan, are the subject of occasional international inspection but constant aerial surveillance. To protect these sites from a preemptive strike by Israeli F-15 Strike Eagles, Iran acquired the Tor-M1 antibomb missile from Russia in December 2005. *See also* SINAH-1.

IRAN-IRAQ WAR. The invasion of Iran in September 1980 by Iraq resulted in a conflict that lasted eight years and enabled Western analysts to study the operational performance of Soviet military technology. Iraq deployed the Frog-7 short-range surface-to-surface missile, with a range of 44 miles, and fired many Scud-B IRBMs. Highly inaccurate because they had been designed to carry nuclear warheads, the Scud-Bs were of minimal military significance until they were fired against Iranian cities, including Dizful, Abwaz, and Khurramabad. Because Tehran was 120 miles beyond the Scud-B's range, it was modified to produce the Al-Hussein, which was first fired in August 1987 and reached Qom and Tehran. During the conflict, the U.S. satellite ground station at Nurrungar in Australia detected a total of 153 IRBM launches from Iraq.

IRAQ WAR. The Allied invasion of Iraq in March 2003 to remove Saddam Hussein from power, codenamed Operation IRAQI FREEDOM, was planned on the basis of Iraq's air defenses being eliminated in the first few hours of the conflict and that intelligence had provided an accurate assessment of the enemy's ability to react and perhaps to retaliate with weapons of mass destruction (WMD). The legal status of the conflict was the right to preemptive strike in anticipation of a threatened attack, and policy makers were dependent upon intelligence to provide information about the nature of the threat and the coalition's ability to execute an effective plan to liberate the country from a tyrant whose very existence had a destabilizing effect on the region.

Air intelligence played a significant role in the identification of Iraqi targets and the provision of tactical support once the offensive had begun. However, imagery analysis in the months before the conflict would prove controversial as it failed to offer corroboration for intelligence gleaned from human sources that revealed details of Iraq's WMD programs. In particular, two Allied intelligence agencies raised doubts in 2001 concerning reports from CURVEBALL, an Iraqi defector resettled in Germany who claimed to have participated in a biological weapons project at Djerf al-Naddaf, where he had been a witness to an accident. His detailed descriptions of mobile chemical laboratories were contradicted by the air analysts, who pointed out that CURVEBALL's account, which would be mentioned by Secretary of State Colin Powell when he addressed the United Nations in February 2003, was inconsistent with the imagery. By April 2002, CURVEBALL had been assessed as a fabricator, by which time Allied troops had occupied Iraq but had failed to uncover any stocks of WMD, despite a search of 946 suspect sites.

Since no WMD were found in Iraq, suspicions were raised that perhaps they had been buried or smuggled into **Syria**, but no imagery was found to support either explanation, although numerous sealed containers were spotted on their way to Damascus. Those that were intercepted and searched were found to contain the regime's wealth, looted from Baghdad shortly before the coalition occupied the city. Once Saddam's forces had surrendered, a dysfunctional resistance campaign was started by a Baathist underground, which would later escalate into a major, urban-oriented guerrilla insurgency backed by Iran and Syria and consisting of indigenous criminal gangs, foreign jihadists, and religious zealots. Whereas air intelligence had made a very large contribution to the successful prosecution of IRAQI FREEDOM, the new technology proved impotent in combating roadside bombs made from improvised explosives, or distinguishing insurgents from the rest of the community, especially in built-up areas.

ISRAEL. Denied the opportunity to collect information on its principal adversaries in the Arab world through personnel protected with diplomatic immunity, Israeli intelligence agencies have been dependent on agents to recruit sources and gain access to technology. At the trial in Cairo in 1962 of Jack Thomas, an Egyptian of Armenian extraction, the prosecutors alleged that he was a Mossad agent who had attempted to recruit an army officer, Hanna Karolos. In fact, Karolos had reported the incident and when Thomas was arrested he was accused of having tried to persuade several Egyptian pilots to defect to Cyprus or Israel with their MiG jet fighters. Israeli efforts to attract defectors later succeeded when **Mahmoud Himli** and then **Munir Redfa** flew their planes to Tel Aviv.

In the absence of alternative sources of information, air intelligence has played a pivotal role in Israel's collection efforts, a lesson learned by her Arab neighbors in 1973, when routine aerial reconnaissance and signals interception failed to give adequate advance warning of a surprise attack over the Yom Kippur holiday. In 1956 and 1967, the **Arab-Israeli** conflicts had been characterized by impressively efficient preemptive strikes intended to eliminate the enemy's air forces, hard lessons learned at considerable cost by Jordan, **Syria**, and Egypt.

Even before the Yom Kippur War, Israel had made a strategic decision to reduce the country's reliance on embargo-sensitive foreign sources of critical matèriel, and this had been reflected in the recruitment of **Alfred Frauenknecht** by the Israeli Bureau of Scientific Liaison (LAKAM) in 1968 to improve supply information about the French Mirage fighter, knowledge that assisted in the development of the Kfir interceptor, which was unveiled in April 1975. Similarly, LAKAM acted as a convenient intermediary when **Jonathan Pollard** began hemorrhaging **satellite** imagery to the Israeli embassy in Washington, D.C., in 1981. Recognition of Israel's special needs, its semipermanent war footing and determination not to caught unawares, has led a considerable investment in atomic weapons and an indigenous aerospace industry that has produced the **OFEQ** reconnaissance satellite and the Mastiff **unmanned aerial vehicle**.

Conscious of the proximity of extremist organizations in the Palestinian enclaves, where the Israelis found it hard to conduct clandestine surveillance on the ground, UAVs have provided an invaluable airborne eye to maintain a watch on suspects and their hideouts, and to provide the information required to deploy accurate helicopter-launched assassination operations aimed at eliminating terrorist leaders.

Israel's neighbors, wholly dependent on external sources for weapons and technology, and devoid of an indigenous industry comparable to the investment made in electronics, avionics, and aerospace in Tel Aviv's equivalent of Silicon Valley, have been disadvantaged by relatively obsolescent Warsaw Pact hardware and poorly served by Mukhabarats that have failed to penetrate their target's unique strength of combined religion, race, and nationality, making the Israeli intelligence community exceptionally difficult to compromise.

– J –

JAPANESE NAVAL MISSION. Much of the Allied air intelligence on Nazi Germany was derived from messages sent by the Japanese naval attaché in Berlin and the head of the Japanese Naval Mission, Vice Admiral Abe, whose cipher was solved by the British in the spring of 1943. This channel conveyed significant information about the technical specifications of German aircraft and aeronautical developments to Tokyo, including tactics and production plans of aircraft such as the Messerschmitt-262 jet fighter, which were of intense interest to the Allies.

JEREMIAH REPORT. Following the surprise test by the Indian government of an atomic weapon at Pokharan on 8 May 1998, retired Admiral David E. Jeremiah, a former deputy chairman of the joint chiefs of staff, undertook a review of the information available to the U.S. intelligence community. Jeremiah identified numerous reasons for the lapse, pointing out that only one senior analyst had been responsible for monitoring imagery of the site in Rajastan, and that two **KH-11**s, and two **LACROSSE** radar satellites had been recently assigned to other, more pressing targets. Assisted by 10 photo interpreters, who examined all the imagery available immediately prior to the test, Jeremiah concluded that there had been insufficient coordination between the various analytical disciplines and that Indian preparations should have been spotted earlier.

JERICHO. The **Royal Air Force** (RAF) codename for an attack on Amiens Prison on 18 February 1944 to free 120 prisoners condemned to death for resistance activities. Altogether, the jail contained 700 prisoners, of whom about half were "political" detainees and at the request of Dominique Ponchardier, leader of the local *reseau*, the Secret Intelligence Service prepared a plan to free them. Twelve *resistants* had been shot by a German firing squad in December, and further executions were anticipated imminently. Initially codenamed RENOVATE, the operation was planed at 140 Wing RAF at Hunsdon in Hertfortshire and a total of 18 de Havilland Mosquitoes, six each drawn from 21, 464 (Royal Australian Air Force), and 487 (Royal New Zealand Air Force) Squadrons were selected for the low-level raid, supported by an escort of 12 Typhoons from 198 Squadron at Westhampnett. Led by Group Captain Percy Pickard DSO, the aircraft were intended to destroy part of the prison's perimeter wall, which was 20 feet high and four feet thick, thus enabling the inmates to escape.

Although a snowstorm prevented all the aircraft from reaching a rendezvous over Littlehampton the main force reached Amiens and created four gaps in the perimeter wall. They also destroyed the guard annexes and damaged the block in which most of the target prisoners were confined, allowing 487 to escape, of whom 255 remained free despite threats of reprisals from the Gestapo against their families. Four aircrew perished, including Pickard, and 110 French civilians were also killed in the raid, either by the bombs or machine-gunned as they attempted to escape. In addition, 20 Germans were killed and 70 wounded.

JERICHO-II. In May 1987, American satellites detected the test launch of the Jericho-II, an Israeli ICBM fired from Palmikhim, near Yavne, which splashed down near Crete. Another was fired in September 1989, which impacted 800 miles away in the Mediterranean, 250 miles north of Benghazi.

JOCKEY. Air intelligence codename for a committee established at the Air Ministry in June 1943, which met weekly until the end of **World War II**, to advise on the reduction of the enemy's production of fighter aircraft. In September 1943, JOCKEY estimated German strength at 780 single-engined aircraft and 740 twin-engined nightfighters, with a monthly production level of 2,700 to be doubled, and the assembly plants placed underground. Records examined after the war showed that the actual figures for October 1943 were 964 single-engined fighters, and 682 twin-engined aircraft. JOCKEY achieved considerable accuracy and studied all sources of intelligence to achieve its statistics. *See also* ESTIMATES OF NAZI AIR STRENGTH.

JOE-1. Anglo-American codename for the first Soviet atomic weapons test, conducted on 29 August 1949, also referred to as VERMONT. Traces of barium, cerium, and molybdenum associated with a pluto-nium implosion detonation was detected at 18,000 feet by a **FITZWILLIAM** high-altitude air sampling WB-29 of the 375th Weather Reconnaissance Squadron based at Misawa in Japan, and the results were confirmed on 1 September by a further flight to the coast of the Kamchatka Peninsula from Eielson Air Force Base, and deliv-ered to the Data Analysis Center on G Street, Washington, D.C. A fur-ther flight, of the 514th Weather Reconnaissance Squadron on 5 Sep-tember from Guam to Yokota collected 1,000 counts per minute on an air filter, an equally anomalous increase in ruthenium, yttrium, cerium, and silver was recorded at ground-level in Alaska, and rain-water analyzed at Kodiak was found to contain large quantities of bomb debris.

The information was shared with Dr. Wilfred Mann, the scientific attaché at the British embassy in Washington, who used the Secret In-telligence Service channel to London, provided by the local station commander Peter Dwyer, to inform the chief, Sir Stewart Menzies, who in turn passed the news to Prime Minister Clement Attlee. Pres-ident Harry S. Truman made the official announcement on 23 Sep-tember, taking the Kremlin by surprise as the Soviet atomic weapons development program, codenamed BORODINO, had been con-ducted in conditions of exceptional secrecy, and the actual test, code-named PERVAYA MOLNIYA, had also been tightly held. The Sovi-ets were eventually informed of the source of the leak by Dwyer's replacement in Washington, D.C., Kim Philby, who was indoctri-nated into the classified remote-sampling project by Dr. Mann, who was unaware of his colleague's role as a NKVD spy.

JOHNSON, CLARENCE (KELLY). The Lockheed aeronautical en-gineer responsible for designing the **U-2** and **SR-71** reconnaissance aircraft, Kelly Johnson graduated from the University of Michigan in 1933 and in 1952 was appointed chief engineer at the Advanced Development Projects facility in Burbank, California, the site known as the **Skunk Works**, where dozens of secret projects were created. He retired in 1975 and died in 1990.

JOINT RECONNAISSANCE CENTER (JRC). Established in 1960, following the loss of **Gary Powers'** **U-2**, the Joint Reconnaissance Center was located in the Pentagon and coordinated all American military reconnaissance flights.

JOINT RECONNAISSANCE COMMITTEE (JRC). Technically a subcommittee of the U.S. Joint Chiefs of Staff, the JRC retains overall responsibility for all technical collection projects conducted by air. The existence of the JRC was first disclosed by a **Central Intelligence Agency** retiree, Victor Marchetti, who had spent 14 years in the agency, and John D. Marks in their controversial study *The CIA and the Cult of Intelligence*, released in 1974 after a lengthy legal battle to prevent publication of certain sensitive passages containing classified information.

JOINT RECONNAISSANCE SCHEDULE. Every aerial intelligence collection mission undertaken by **U.S.** personnel is contained in a submission known as the Joint Reconnaissance schedule, which is submitted to White House policy makers for approval. The objective is to identify politically risky missions and prevent embarrassment to the administration should a flight coincide with some sensitive event. Following the loss of a U.S. Navy EC-121 in international waters in 1969 after it had been attacked by North Korean MiGs, a review was undertaken of all potentially dangerous flights, and a regular patrol off the coast of Albania was canceled because it took advantage of the proximity of the Greek island of Corfu to the Albanian coastline, and brought the route taken by the aircraft too close to hostile air defenses.

JONES, R. V. Appointed chief scientific adviser to the Air Ministry in 1940, Reg Jones was a graduate of Wadham College, Oxford, who had worked at the Culham Laboratories before joining a team of scientists working on the development of radar at Bawdsey Manor and moving on to the infrared research at the Admiralty Research Laboratory at Teddington. In September 1939, he was posted to the Air Ministry's Directorate of Scientific Research, which was evacuated to Harrogate, but after preparing a report on German secret weapons he was recruited by Fred Winterbotham into SIS's air branch, designated as Section III, and transferred to Bletchley Park, where he worked alongside Squadron-Leader Courtleigh Nasmith Shaw.

Appointed the Air Ministry's assistant director of scientific intelligence, Jones would play a key role in assessing the authenticity of the Oslo Report and developing countermeasures for the Luftwaffe's night navigation systems. At the end of the war, he was elected professor of natural philosophy at Aberdeen University, and he remained there until his death in December 1997.

JUMPSEAT. Codename of a **National Reconnaissance Office** classified signals intelligence **satellite** system developed in 1971 to intercept traffic from Soviet spacecraft in *Molniya* orbits, and to monitor microwave transmissions from Soviet phased-array radars. *See also* BYEMAN.

JUST CAUSE. Codename of the 1989 invasion of Panama to arrest General Manuel Noriega, in which 23 American soldiers were killed. Some evidence emerged after the invasion that the Panama Defense Forces may have received advance warning of the operation, perhaps from the Cuban Direcion General de Inteligencia, which received information from the large signals intelligence site at Lourdes, and from the Defense Intelligence Agency spy **Ana Montes**.

– K –

K-19. The K-19 framing camera, manufactured by Fairchild, was the standard equipment for aerial photography during **World War II** and was replaced by the K-21 mapping camera. They boasted a focal length of 24 to 40 inches and produced the best imagery until the introduction of Edwin Land's equipment, designed for use on the **U-2**.

KABKAN. The U.S. National Security Agency intercept station located at Kabkan, 65 kilometers east of Meshed in Iran, was abandoned in February 1979 following the fall of the Shah. Codenamed TACKS-MAN-2, the site was close to the Soviet frontier and 1,000 kilometers southwest of the missile test facility at **Tyuratam**. *See also* SOVIET UNION.

KAL 007. On 31 August 1983, a Korean Airlines Boeing 747, on flight from New York to Seoul, was shot down over the Sea of Japan by two AA-3 Anab missiles fired by Major Vassili Kasmin, the pilot of a Sukhoi-15 Flagon based at Dolinsk after the jumbo jet had strayed into Soviet airspace over Sakhalin Island. All 269 passengers and crew were killed and the incident was denounced as a deliberate atrocity, although some commentators claimed that the airliner had been fulfilling a covert intelligence collection role. When the plane's "black box" flight recorder was finally surrendered by the Russian government in 1990 it emerged that the Korean flight-deck crew had accidentally entered the incorrect coordinates into the navigational system, leading the plane to stray from its intended route to Seoul.

Initially, the Kremlin had denied that the flight data and cockpit voice recorders had been recovered, but a GRU defector, Vyacheslav Baranov, revealed this information to his **Central Intelligence Agency** handlers in 1985. As a former pilot, Baranov had kept an interest in aviation matters and had been shocked that the Soviet government had pretended the black box had not been found.

Before being shot down, KAL 007 had overflown Sakhalin Island, and had come close to several military facilities, including the Su-15 airfield at Doninsk-Siokol, a MiG-23 airfield at Smirnykh, and the submarine base at Petropavlovsk. Apologists for the Soviets claimed that the Boeing had been on a covert reconnaissance mission, and that the aircraft had been mistaken for an RC-135 on a **RIVET JOINT** mission. Release by the State Department of tapes made of the exchanges between Kasmin and his ground controller, including the chilling message "the target is destroyed," eliminated the possibility that the Soviets could claim the incident had been an unfortunate accident. *See also* SOVIET UNION.

KAL 902. On 20 April 1978, Soviet Su-15 Flagon fighters intercepted and shot down Korean Airlines flight 902 from Paris to Seoul with 97 passengers and 13 crew aboard while over the Barents Sea. The Boeing 707 crash-landed on a frozen lake near Kem, a fishing village on the White Sea, two passengers having been killed and 13 injured during the attack.

KAMA. The Soviet codename for the naval component of Operation ANADYR, the deployment of large amounts of military aid to **Cuba** in 1962. KAMA was intended to consist of seven Golf strategic missile submarines and four Foxtrot attack submarines of the 69th Submarine Brigade of the 4th Red Banner, Order of Ushakov, Submarine Squadron, all to be based permanently at Mariel as the 20th Special Submarine Squadron. The flotilla of four Foxtrots, which were really modified Type XXI Kriegsmarine U-boats, sailed at the end of September 1962 from **Polyarny**, having first been equipped with two nuclear-tipped, 533-millimeter torpedoes with 15-kiloton warheads each, in addition to the usual 21 conventional weapons carried aboard.

The submarines B-4 *Chelyabinskaya Komsomolets*, B-36, B-59, and B-130 were first detected by P2V Neptune long-range maritime reconnaissance aircraft patrolling the Iceland-Faroes-Shetland gap, operating from the Naval Air Station Keflavik, and British Shackletons from Rosyth. They were then monitored in the Caribbean by Orion P3 ASW aircraft based at Jacksonville, Florida, and Sea King helicopters from the carriers USS *Essex* and *Randolph*, all equipped with SSQ-23 passive sonar buoys. On 27 October, the B-59 was forced to the surface 300 miles south of Bermuda by grenades from the USS *Cory*, after being tracked for 12 hours, and was escorted out of the declared quarantine area by the destroyer USS *Waller*. On 31 October, the B-36 was forced to surface 300 miles north of Puerto Rico by the destroyer USS *Charles B. Cecil* after being tracked by P2V Neptunes of Patrol Squadron 56, based at Jacksonville, Florida, for 34 hours. On the same day, the B-130 surfaced beside the destroyer USS *Blandy* 300 miles northeast of the Caicos Passage, having sustained damage to all three diesel engines. The B-130 took three weeks to limp home to Polyarny on the surface, assisted in the Barents Sea by the rescue tug *Pamir*. Finally, the B-4, the last to be detected, 100 miles south of Jamaica, was tracked by Neptunes, Orions, and aircraft off the carrier USS *Independence* but avoided being forced to the surface. In addition, a further Zulu and Foxtrot were monitored in the north Atlantic as they returned to their bases. *See also* CUBAN MISSILE CRISIS.

KAMFGRUPPE 200 (KG-200). The **Luftwaffe** designation of the German squadron equipped during **World War II** with captured Allied aircraft, KG-200.

KAPUSTIN YAR. When news of this first Soviet missile test site on the Volga in the Ukraine, southeast of Moscow, filtered out in 1952 following reports from returning German rocket technicians and prisoners of war interviewed in the **WRINGER** program, a modified **Royal Air Force** Canberra B-2 from 540 Squadron at **Wyton** photographed it on a flight from Giebelstadt in West Germany, which overflew Soviet territory in 1953 as Operation ROBIN and landed in Iran. The plane apparently sustained some damage from Soviet air defenses. Kapustin Yar, constructed in 1951 with German labor, remained the Soviet Union's principal IRBM development facility throughout the **Cold War**, and was a priority target for overflights. Telemetry from the range was monitored from a National Security Agency intercept station located across the Black Sea, at Sinop in Turkey. *See also* DIYARBAKUR; SOVIET UNION.

KATYN. In April 1943, German forces that had occupied the region around Smolensk since 1941 discovered the graves of 4,000 Polish officers in the forest of Katyn. Forensic examination proved that they had been murdered in 1940 when the area had been under Soviet control, but Moscow insisted the massacre had been a Nazi atrocity. An analysis undertaken in 1981 of the Luftwaffe's captured photoreconnaissance imagery by a **Central Intelligence Agency** photo interpreter, Robert G. Poirier, proved that the Soviets had been responsible for the crime, and had subsequently made considerable efforts to conceal it when the territory had been recaptured in September 1943.

KEYHOLE. U.S. Air Force codename for the imagery derived from the KH series of surveillance cameras taken aloft in aircraft and reconnaissance satellites. Commencing in 1959 with the **CORONA** series, the satellite systems included the **Argon** and **Lanyard**.

KH-11. U.S. Air Force designation of the **KEYHOLE** satellite system that went into operation in December 1976 employing new digital imaging equipment that allowed the data to be transmitted to ground stations, thereby ending a reliance on finite supplies of film canisters. Fifty feet long and 10 feet in diameter, the KH-11 weighed 22,500 pounds and had a duration of 770 days in space, but the system's capabilities were betrayed to the Soviets by a disaffected former **Central Intelligence Agency** officer, William Kampiles, who sold a KH-11 technical manual for $3,000 to a GRU officer, Major Mikhail Zavali, in Athens in February 1978.

On the day after his inauguration in January 1977, President Jimmy Carter was presented with KH-11 imagery of the ceremony as part of his indoctrination into the system's impressive capabilities, which included real-time downloads.

A ground station for receiving KH-11 imagery was established at Fort Belvoir, and later additional sites were added at Buckley Air National Guard Base in Colorado and Kapaun in West Germany. The next generation of KH-11 built for the **National Reconnaissance Office** was codenamed Advanced KENNAN and Improved CRYSTAL.

KHARTOUM. In August 1998, a chemical factory in Khartoum was destroyed by American-launched cruise missiles after faulty intelligence had linked it to al-Qaeda and the production of biological weapons.

KIM SOK HO. The pilot of a North Korean MiG-15, Kim Sok Ho defected to the **U.S.** Air Force at Kimpo on 31 September 1953. His aircraft was placed on display at the Wright-Patterson Air Force Base at Dayton, Ohio.

KJ-2000. The Chinese designation of the Ilyushin-76 early warning aircraft purchased from the Russians in 1999 and flown to Israel to be fitted with the Falcon early warning radar. After American protests, the equipment was removed and both KJ-2000 planes were flown to Nanjing, where Monopulse secondary radars supplied by the Telephonics Corporation were installed, despite congressional opposition. The planes went into service soon afterward, but in June 2006 one crashed in Guangde, 125 miles southwest of Shanghai, killing the entire crew of 35.

KNICKEBEIN. The German codeword (literally "crooked leg") for an aircraft navigational aid manufactured by Telefunken and based on beams of signals transmitted from 11 ground stations located on the continent, intended to guide **Luftwaffe** bombers on air raids over England during 1940. The transmitters' huge antennae were 100 feet high and 315 feet wide and moved on a circular track to focus on different targets. With a range of 270 miles, the accuracy at 180 miles was estimated to be one degree, enabling a bomber at 20,000 feet to be within a mile of its target. The **Royal Air Force** (RAF) codenamed the system HEADACHE.

Aircraft already equipped with Lorenz blind-landing receivers were able to follow the beam and reach their target, but when the system was compromised, by a combination of aircrew interrogation, examination of downed enemy planes and the monitoring of signals, 80 Wing RAF built transmitters, codenamed **ASPIRIN**, to jam the signals and send the aircraft off course. When the Luftwaffe pilots realized the British were interfering with KNICKEBEIN they were reluctant to use it, because they believed their destinations had become known and nightfighters would be waiting for them. Accordingly, KNICKEBEIN fell into disuse in 1941. *See also* WORLD WAR II.

KOBALT. Soviet designation of an I-band ground-mapping radar, copied from the American APS-15 that was fitted to the B-29 Superfortress.

KOMAKI. At the conclusion of the Korean War, the U.S. Far East Air Force established the 16th Tactical Reconnaissance Squadron at Komaki in Japan to fly RF-86Fs on missions over China and the **Soviet Union**. The variant were stripped of their weapons and equipped with panoramic stereo cameras, four drop tanks, and fake gun ports to make them indistinguishable from regular Sabres.

Between April 1954 and February 1955, nine overflights were completed successfully, and one was made by **Rudolf Anderson** Jr., who would later be killed in a U-2 over **Cuba**. His first flight, via an advance base at Kunsan, designated as K-8, in South Korea, was to photograph Dairen and Port Arthur from 54,000 feet with a wingman, Lieutenant Robert J. Depew.

KOREAN WAR. On 25 June 1950, North Korean forces unexpectedly crossed the 38th Parallel and invaded South Korea. At the time, the

North Korean Air Force consisted of 62 Il-10 ground-attack aircraft, 70 Yak-16 transports, and four Polikarkov Po-2 twin-seater trainers.

Until Chinese and Soviet pilots intervened in the conflict in October 1950, unarmed RB-29s of the 31st Strategic Reconnaissance Squadron were able to fly over North Korea without interference. However, on 9 November 1950, an RB-29 from Johnson Air Force Base in Japan was attacked by two MiG-15s over Sinuiju. Badly damaged, the plane limped home, but five of the crew were killed in the crash-landing. Thereafter, RB-29s were banned from flying near the Yalu River, and reconnaissance missions were flown by the less vulnerable RF-80s and by the versatile RB-45Cs. Altogether, 10 RB-29As were assigned to Korean reconnaissance operations by the 91st Strategic Reconnaissance Squadron flying from Yokota Air Force base in Japan, of which some had their rear gun turrets reinstalled to protect them from MiG-15s.

During the Korean War, air intelligence played a crucial role, with Allied aircraft easily outclassed by MiG-15 jet fighters flown by Soviet pilots, until the introduction of the F-86 Sabre late in December 1950. Altogether, 262 American aircrew were questioned by Soviet and Chinese interrogators and several F-86s were captured. The first was captured following a dogfight when the pilot was forced to land his damaged aircraft, but he himself was subsequently rescued. The F-86 was recovered to Andung airfield and then transported to Moscow for detailed examination. In May 1952, an F-86E model, flown by the commander of one of the two **U.S.** Air Force F-86 wings in Korea, Colonel Bud Mahurin, was recovered intact and also taken to Moscow.

During the conflict, the U.S. Far East Air Force lost 1,406 aircraft with 1,114 aircrew killed and 306 wounded. At the 1953 ceasefire, 235 PoWs were released in operation BIG SWITCH, but 35 were kept in North Korea until after June 1954. An estimated 59 PoWs underwent interrogation by KGB and GRU personnel.

Upon their release, the airmen, of whom two-thirds were officers, were interviewed by the Air Force Office of Special Investigations (AFOSI) in an attempt to identify personnel who had collaborated with the enemy. Captive aircrew were treated far worse than other prisoners and 59 had been singled out for harsh treatment by the Chinese to support a false claim made in February 1952 that the Americans had engaged in bacteriological warfare. Eventually, 38 airmen were forced to confess, and 23 of these bogus confessions were used for propaganda. The remainder endured up to 24 weeks of solitary confinement, limited rations, sensory deprivation, and continuous interrogation, but refused to cooperate.

KOSOVO. On 23 March 1999, an ultimatum given by the North Atlantic Treaty Organization (NATO) to President Slobodan Milosevic of Serbia expired, and as he had failed to withdraw his troops and engaged in genocide in the predominantly ethnic Albanian enclave of Kosovo, NATO aircraft embarked on a bombing campaign codenamed ALLIED FORCE. The operation, commanded by General Wesley Clark, lasted just six weeks, mainly because missions could not be flown every day due to poor weather, and on 9 June, as Yugoslav troops began their evacuation, NATO's air strikes were suspended. The capitulation of Milosevic, under pressure from the relentless and accurate air bombardment, saved the need for a ground invasion, which NATO planners had estimated would require more than 100,000 troops. ALLIED FORCE was also the first war to be won entirely by the application of air power, and the exploitation of air intelligence contributed by all 19 members of NATO.

Significantly, evidence of an earlier massacre of Muslim men and boys at Srebrenica in July 1995 was supplied by the **Central Intelligence Agency** in the form of overhead imagery that was declassified so it could be circulated to the United Nations Security Council as proof of President Milosevic's culpability for the ethnic cleansing.

Indicted on charges of war crimes and having initiated conflicts in Bosnia and Croatia, Milosevic would go on trial at the International War Crimes Tribunal in The Hague, but he died of natural causes before a verdict could be reached. *See also* CHINESE EMBASSY BOMBING.

KRASNOYARSK. The discovery in August 1983 by a KH-8 GAMBIT satellite that the Soviets were building a large phased array radar at Abalakova, north of Krasnoyarsk, 400 miles inside the Soviet Union's border with Mongolia, proved that the construction was a violation of the Anti-Ballistic Missile (ABM) Treaty that restricted the Pechora class radars to the country's periphery. Thus the stations at

Lyaki, Olenogrosk, Sary Shagan, and Micheleveka complied with the terms of the arms control treaty, but the Krasnoyarsk apparatus, 30 stories high, was oriented to the northeast, across 3,000 miles of Siberia and clearly intended to close a radar gap to provide early warning of Trident missiles launched from American submarines in the North Pacific. When challenged, the Soviets initially claimed that the site, on a spur line off the Trans-Siberian railway, was intended for tracking launches of spacecraft from Plesetsk and Tyuratam, but after foreign minister Eduard Sheverdnadze was shown the imagery privately at the United Nations headquarters, which proved the apparatus was a Pechora class radar, he ordered the entire facility to be dismantled, a task that began in September 1989. *See also* SOVIET UNION.

– L –

LACROSSE. A radar-imaging satellite codenamed INDIGO by the **Central Intelligence Agency**, LACROSSE required a space shuttle launch into orbit, and the first was carried aloft by the *Atlantis* in December 1987. Although well over budget, the LACROSSE fulfilled its objective of producing high-quality imagery through thick cloud cover.

LAND, EDWIN H. Always fascinated by polarized light, Edwin Land was born in Bridgeport, Connecticut, in May 1909 and registered his first patent while still a student at Harvard in June 1933. He established the Polaroid Corporation in 1937 and during **World War II** developed glare-free gun sights, periscopes, goggles, and rangefinders. In 1953, he was appointed to the **U.S.** Air Force's Scientific Advisory Board and later designed the cameras for the **U-2** and **CORONA**.

LANYARD. The **U.S.** Air Force designation for an unsuccessful high-resolution reconnaissance satellite program that was terminated after one flight in July 1963, when the camera malfunctioned after just 32 hours. The KH-6 camera was intended to capture imagery within a range of two feet of suspected missile launch sites around Leningrad, but the entire project was abandoned. *See also* ARGON; CORONA.

LAOS. A supposedly neutral country in southeast Asia during the Vietnam War, Laos reluctantly provided the North Vietnamese Army (NVA) with a safe haven and a route for the Ho Chi Minh trail to resupply the Vietcong. Initially reluctant to cross the border to confront the enemy concentrations hiding in Laos, President Richard Nixon authorized a clandestine campaign to deny the NVA respite facilities. The decision proved politically controversial for the Nixon administration although the intelligence evidence proving the NVA's exploitation of the frontier areas was compelling and consisted of impressive aerial reconnaissance imagery.

The **Vietnam War** transformed large provinces of Laos into a combat zone, managed from Vientiane by the **Central Intelligence Agency**, and from secret **Lima sites** that provided radar and signals intercept access across the frontier into North Vietnam. However, this secret war went largely unreported, either by the media or to Congress, although occasionally there were incidents, news of which proved hard to suppress. On 5 February 1973, a **U.S.** Air Force E-47Q Skytrain on an intelligence mission was hit by ground fire over Laos and crash-landed. Of the four crewmen aboard, two reportedly survived and were taken prisoner, although neither was ever released.

LEBANON. When Syrian air defenses unsuccessfully fired antiaircraft missiles at U.S. reconnaissance planes in December 1983, President Ronald Reagan ordered a retaliatory raid on the SAM sites, which resulted in the loss of two aircraft and one pilot. Its bombardier survived and was later released by the Syrians.

Lebanon was the subject of intensive aerial surveillance throughout the 1980s, following a suicide truck-bomb attack on the U.S. embassy in Beirut by Hezbollah in April 1983 that killed 63, among then 17 Americans. The same tactic was used in another attack in October 1983 on the embassy annex in West Beirut, which killed 23, including two Americans. However, subsequent scrutiny of satellite imagery of Hezbollah's headquarters at the Sheikh Abdullah barracks in the Bekaa Valley suggested that the compound included a driving course replicating the approach to the embassy annex. Although the pictures had been available prior to the attack, the photo interpreters had not realized their significance. The Sheikh Abdullah barracks, in Syrian-controlled territory, would later come under close examination when the local **Central Intelligence Agency** station chief, William Buckley, was abducted in March 1984.

LEGHORN, RICHARD S. The commander of the 30th Photo Reconnaissance Squadron at the end of **World War II**, Richard Leghorn participated in Task Force 1.52, observing and recording the atomic tests conducted over and under Bikini Atoll's lagoon in July 1946. Leghorn was a pilot, graduate of the Massachusetts Institute of Technology, and a physicist, and in 1947 rejoined Kodak, where he was working in April 1951 when he was recalled as a reservist to head the Reconnaissance Systems Branch of the Wright Air Development Center at Dayton, Ohio. There he advocated the development of a fast, high-altitude reconnaissance aircraft designed to enter Soviet airspace, and he chose to modify one of the new **Royal Air Force** Canberra, eliminating one of the pilots and the armor, and extending the wings to reduce weight and gain altitude. A sponsor of the first overflights of the Soviet Union, Leghorn played a key role in the development of the **U-2** and the cameras carried by the **CORONA** satellites. In 1957, he resigned from Kodak to buy Boston University's Optical Research Laboratory and form the Itek Corporation that, with funding from the **Central Intelligence Agency**, made the technological breakthroughs necessary to establish strategic aerial reconnaissance.

LEOPARD. The U.S. Air Force codename for photographic missions flown by the 72nd Strategic Reconnaissance Squadron in 1948 along the Chukotsky peninsula using oblique cameras to identify Soviet airfields.

LIAONING INCIDENT. On 12 January 1953, a **U.S.** Air Force B-29 of the 581st Squadron was illuminated by **radar**-guided searchlights and then shot down by Chinese MiG-15s from Antung airfield while on a night mission to drop an agent over Liaoning province. Three of the aircrew were killed and 11 were taken prisoner, including the pilot, Colonel John Arnold. They were tried on charges of espionage, their cover story of a leaflet drop having been disbelieved, and in November 1954, Radio Beijing announced their conviction. They were freed in August 1955 in Kowloon as the Geneva Conference on Indochina opened. *See also* CHINA, PEOPLE'S REPUBLIC OF; TROPIC.

LICHTENSTEIN. Luftwaffe codename for the SN-2 air interception radar that enabled tracker aircraft to identify Allied bomber streams and vector nightfighters onto them. Although the existence of the LICHTENSTEIN was known to air intelligence, because the apparatus included a very distinctive antenna, it was not until a Ju-88 was forced to land at Woodbridge in July 1944 that British experts were able to examine the SN-2 and develop a countermeasure.

LIMA SITES. During the **Vietnam War**, up to 3,000 clandestine airfields, designated as Lima sites, were constructed in (ostensibly neutral) **Laos** to enhance the logistical support of various covert facilities. Some were built to support local Hmong tribesmen recruited as mercenaries by the **Central Intelligence Agency**, while others were large **radar** stations and signals intelligence sites. As the number of American aircraft flying over the region increased, Tactical Air Navigation (TACAN) transmitters were installed at several Lima sites, including Phu Kate, near Saravane in the south of the country, designated as LS 44 and established in April 1966. There followed JANE at Long Tieng, LS 85 in northeastern Laos, LS 61 at Muang Phalane, and LS 85 at Phou Tha Thi. U.S. personnel assigned to these secret facilities were required to wear civilian clothes and were shown to have been working on MSQ-77, a classified U.S. Air Force radar program. As the North Vietnamese became aware of the strategic importance of the Lima sites, some were attacked. LS 44 was evacuated in the face of Pathet Lao pressure prior to the Tet offensive and LS 85 was captured after a surprise assault in March 1968. *See also* HEAVY GREEN.

LINNEY, BRIAN. On 28 July 1958, Brian F. Linney was sentenced to 14 years' imprisonment after he admitted having sold Rolls-Royce aero engine secrets to the Czech military attaché in London, Colonel Oldrich Prybl, with whom he had been in contact since May 1954. Linney had been caught holding a clandestine meeting with Prybl near his home in Worthing, Sussex, after the diplomat had been placed under surveillance on advice from the Federal Bureau of

Investigation (FBI). One of the FBI's sources in Washington, D.C., Frantisek Tisler, who was a cipher clerk at the Czech embassy, had reported to his handlers that his friend Prybl had recruited an important agent in England. A patient watch had been maintained on Prybl until he was spotted with Linney.

LONDONDERRY, LORD. The minister for air in **Stanley Baldwin**'s government, Lord Londonderry was sacked in June 1935 and replaced with Sir Philip Cunliffe-Lister when it emerged that the **Luftwaffe** had succeeded in overtaking the **Royal Air Force** (RAF) in aircraft strength. As a result of information from the French Deuxième Bureau in October 1934, the Air Staff revised the estimate of German front-line aircraft from 1,000 in 1939 to 1,296. However, in March 1935, Adolf Hitler claimed publicly that the Luftwaffe had achieved parity with the RAF, and this led to an increase in the estimates to 1,512 planes by April 1937, although in September 1935, signals analysis had identified 576 individual aircraft and 60 ground stations. In October 1938, the estimates reached 3,200 aircraft with 2,400 reserves, whereas the true figure was a total of 3,307 aircraft in the Luftwaffe. *See also* ESTIMATES OF NAZI AIR STRENGTH.

LOPATKOV, VIKTOR. On 27 June 1958, Senior Lieutenant Viktor Lopatkov led his wingman, Lieutenant Gavrilov, from their base at Yerevan to intercept a **U.S.** Air Force EC-130 that had strayed accidentally over the Soviet border with Turkey. The unarmed EC-130 from the 7406th Support Squadron, flying from Incirlik, had a flight crew of six, plus 11 men from Detachment 1 of the 6911th Radio Group Mobile based at Darmstadt, and was on a routine signals intelligence mission when Lopakov fired warning shots ahead of the aircraft. Lopakov's MiG-17 Fresco was joined by two others, from Leninakan, and when the EC-130 turned back toward Turkish airspace all four fighters attacked, causing the intruder to crash 25 miles inside Soviet territory, near the village of Sasnashen, causing the death of all 17 men aboard. This was the first occasion in which an American reconnaissance aircraft had been shot down over the Soviet Union and, initially unaware what had happened, the aircraft's parent unit, the 7499th Support Group in Wiesbaden, announced the cover story, that a C-130 engaged on radio wave propagation research was overdue and had come down somewhere in eastern Turkey beyond Trabzon. In fact, as the Air Force Security Service would soon learn from intercepts, Lieutenant Lopatkov had been ordered to destroy the plane by General Tsedrik over a VHF voice channel. As nine of the intercept positions on the plane had been manned by linguists, those aboard probably overheard the Russian radio exchanges.

To conceal the EC-130's true role, all personnel records of all the intercept operators were altered to show that they had been transferred to the 7406th Support Group. The Soviets waited until 12 September to announce that bodies and wreckage had been discovered in Armenia, following claims made in Washington, D.C., that Turkish border guards had witnessed the incident. In fact, the Air Force Security Service knew precisely what had happened, where, and when, but to reveal that knowledge would have compromised security, so the Air Force had mounted a prolonged, intensive, and very public airborne search of the Turkish side of the frontier. Finally, in December 1958, after the Soviets had surrendered just six bodies, the U.S. State Department challenged the Soviets, claiming that it had a recording of the conversations held between the MiG pilots and their ground controllers, and that the plane had been lured off course deliberately by Soviet transmissions emulating signals from the navigation beacons it had relied upon at Trabzon and Lake Van.

The loss of the EC-130 had a profound impact on the small unit that consisted of less than 100 airmen that had been formed in 1956, and a year after the incident it was renamed Detachment 1, 6900th Security Wing, and after a further six months was redesignated as the 6916th Radio Squadron Mobile.

LUFTWAFFE. Developed in secret in defiance of the terms of the Treaty of Versailles, the Luftwaffe trained its pilots under cover of glider clubs, but the aircrew were very uninhibited with their radio traffic, which allowed the signals to be intercepted and analyzed by operators in England, who logged the call-signs of every aircraft in training and every ground station. Until March 1935, when the Luftwaffe came into official existence, it took precautions to prevent foreigners from visiting their airbases and never published any official production figures so the true strength of the fighter and bomber wings could not be estimated accurately. In 1934, when the Luftwaffe had 550 aircraft, the British estimate was only 350, rising to 480 during the following year. In 1938, the estimate was 2,640, whereas the correct number was 3,000. In September 1939, the estimate was 4,320, while there were actually 3,647.

Although following the air raids on Madrid during the Spanish Civil War it was anticipated that the Nazis might attempt a knockout blow against London, the Battle of Britain during the summer of 1940 denied Reichmarschal Hermann Göring the air superiority needed to launch an invasion across the English Channel. Thereafter he concentrated on attacking civilian centers of population, but in May 1941 was obliged to transfer many of his bomber squadrons from France to the eastern front in anticipation of the assault on the **Soviet Union**.

The Luftwaffe's air intelligence branch, based at Oranienburg, near Potsdam, included a photo interpretation center on the Colombiastrasse in Berlin and provided comprehensive aerial photography for the Sudetan, Polish, and Norwegian campaigns. However, the unit suffered heavy losses during the Russian offensive, with 300 front-line aircraft destroyed, which led to a reorganization of air reconnaissance that hitherto had combined the interests of the Wehrmacht and the Luftwaffe. General Gunther Lomann replaced the Luftwaffe's General Paul Bogatsch. However, Lomann lasted only nine months, and a pilot, General Karl-Henning von Barswisch, took over until the end of the war, switching the emphasis to converted fighters.

Whereas for the first half of the war the Luftwaffe exercised virtual air superiority over most of Europe and was able to enhance German territorial gains across much of the continent and North Africa, the erosion of Nazi power in the second half of the conflict reduced the land bases from which the Luftwaffe could fly and sharply limited its reconnaissance operations. By December 1944, it was admitted than no flights had been made over British industrial centers in the past three years, and the inability to fly missions over southern England in the weeks before **D-Day** had made the High Command perilously dependent on the Abwehr's agents, most of whom turned out to have been operating under the enemy's control. *See also* GOERTZ, HERMAN; ROWEHL, THEODOR; WORLD WAR II.

LUNDAHL, ART. The founding director of the **National Photographic Interpretation Center** (NPIC), Art Lundahl made the **Central Intelligence Agency**'s (CIA) first presentation of the overhead imagery of SS-4 missile sites in **Cuba** on 16 October 1962 to President John F. Kennedy, thereby initiating the missile crisis, and played a key role in enabling the policy makers in the president's executive committee to understand the significance of the **U-2** photos, to identify the evidence of SA-2 emplacements, and to see the preparations under way for the deployment of Soviet MRBMs.

Born in Chicago in 1915, Lundahl served in the **U.S.** Navy during **World War II** at Adak, Alaska, studying photographs of Japanese targets in the Pacific. In 1945, he was transferred to the Naval Photographic Interpretation Center in Washington, D.C., first as chief of the photogrammetry division, and then as assistant chief engineer. In 1953, he joined the CIA's Photographic Intelligence Division, located in M Building, a temporary hut near the Reflecting Pool, and remained in charge for the next 20 years. He died in 1992.

– M –

MAGNUM. Codename for an American signals intelligence satellite first placed into geosynchronous orbit by the space shuttle *Discovery* in January 1985. By 1994, the dish of MAGNUM's latest version was 160 feet in diameter and weighed 2.7 tons.

MALAYA EMERGENCY. During the counterinsurgency operations mounted against Chinese Communist terrorists during the emergency, which lasted from 1948 to 1957, a single Lancaster was deployed on intercept patrols to monitor the guerrillas' wireless traffic and to home in on radio beacons ingeniously fitted to their weapons and other equipment.

MALTA. From September 1940, **Royal Air Force** photo reconnaissance flights in the western Mediterranean were flown by 431 Flight at Luqa. In January 1941, this unit was redesignated as 69 Squadron, and in February 1943 it became 683 (PR) Squadron until it was disbanded in September 1945.

MALTSBY, CHARLES. The pilot of a **U-2** on an air-sampling flight from Eielson Air Force Base on 27 October 1962, Major Charles Maltsby of the 4080th Strategic Reconnaissance Wing made a navigational error over the North Pole and strayed into Siberian airspace. A former member of the Thunderbirds formation flying team, Chuck Maltsby had been flying U-2s since January 1961, but the air-sampling missions had only begun from Eielson on 25 August 1962. Alerted by his C-54 chase rescue aircraft that he had strayed from his route, Maltsby immediately changed course, but by then Soviet MiGs had been scrambled to intercept an intruder detected by **radar** over the Chukotsky Peninsula. A pair of F-102 fighters took off in response, but Maltsby was able to reach American airspace safely. However, as he was running low on fuel he attempted to glide part of the way home, but was unable to reignite his engine and was obliged to crash-land on a small civil airfield, making his flight of 10 hours 25 minutes the longest unrefueled U-2 flight ever. Although unpublicized, the incident occurred on the same day that Major **Rudolf Anderson**'s U-2 had been shot down over **Cuba**, and an **RB-47** had crashed on takeoff at Bermuda at the start of what was intended to be a maritime patrol, killing all four crew.

MANDREL. British codename for an airborne jammer designed to confuse the German **FREYA** early-warning radar.

MEACON. British codename for transmitters located in England and designed to broadcast signals to interfere with enemy navigation beacons. By August 1940, 80 Wing had built nine MEACONS, part of the **ASPIRIN** antidote for **HEADACHE**.

MEDHURST, CHARLES. Britain's **Director of Air Intelligence** at the Air Ministry during **World War II** in succession to Archie Boyle, Charles Medhurst was originally commissioned into the Royal Inniskilling Fusiliers. He joined the Royal Flying Corps in 1915, aged 18, and then the **Royal Air Force** (RAF) in 1919. After serving in Iraq he was appointed deputy **director of Intelligence** in 1934, and three years later went to Rome as air attaché, covering Bern and Athens too. In 1941, he was promoted to assistant chief of the Air

Staff (Intelligence), but was replaced by Frank Inglis in 1942. He retired from the RAF in 1950 and died in October 1954.

MEDITERRANEAN ARMY INTERPRETATION CENTRE (MEIC). Photographic interpretation in the Mediterranean theater from 1943 processed imagery at two MEIC facilities, from 36 Spitfires flying in three **Royal Air Force** squadrons and eight Mosquitoes from a South African squadron.

MEDMENHAM. From October 1940, the **World War II** headquarters of the **Royal Air Force**'s Photographic Interpretation Centre (PIC), located at Danesfield House, in Medmenham, Buckinghamshire. When the **United States** joined the war it was renamed the Allied Central Interpretation Unit. The PIC was commanded by Wing-Commander Douglas Kendall, who from 1943 coordinated all air reconnaissance flights against the **V-weapons**.

MENWITH HILL. Located just outside Harrogate in Yorkshire, Menwith Hill is the largest U.S. National Security Agency facility outside North America and contains eight large radomes for receiving signals from **satellites**.

MERCATOR. The Martin P4M-IQ Mercator was the **U.S.** Air Force's principal electronic intelligence gatherer until it was replaced by the Douglas EA-3B Skywarrior. Two squadrons, the VQ-1 and VQ-2, were based at Arsugi, Japan, and Port Lyautey in Morocco, respectively, with the top gun turret removed to accommodate five intercept operators. On 22 August 1956, a VQ-1 Mercator operating from Iwakuni was shot down 32 miles off the Chinese coast with the loss of all 16 crew. In July 1959, two North Korean MiGs attacked a Mercator in international airspace, wounding the tail-gunner, and caused it to make an emergency landing at Miho, near Matsui.

MERKUR. The **Luftwaffe** codename for the invasion of the strategically important island of Crete in May 1941, organized as an airborne assault to capture the **Royal Air Force** airfields at Maleme, Retimo, and Heraklion, combined with a landing from the sea. The island was defended by 27,500 British and Empire troops, supported by 14,000 Greeks, and commanded by a New Zealander, General Bernard

Freyberg, who had the benefit of signals intelligence from Bletchley Park relayed to his headquarters from Cairo.

There was little doubt about the imminent offensive because the Allied signals intelligence, the source disguised as a well-informed spy in Athens, revealed the Luftwaffe's orders to conduct an extensive aerial reconnaissance of Cyprus, and to avoid bomb damage to the airfields or to the harbor in Suda Bay. Indeed, the Enigma traffic provided the entire German operational plan a clear three weeks before the attack, and even disclosed that Herman Göring had approved a 48-hour postponement until 19 May. An added advantage for the defenders was possession of a captured German paratroop manual, recovered in May 1940 in Holland, which detailed the tactics likely to be adopted by General Kurt Student's soldiers. Significantly, the document had revealed that German paratroops landed unarmed, and were required to find the containers bearing their weapons after they had reached the ground and discarded their parachutes. This, of course, left them terribly vulnerable if their landing-zone was well-defended, and their appearance had been anticipated, as indeed happened in Crete.

When the attack commenced, right on schedule, 15,750 airborne troops arrived by parachute and by glider, and a further 7,000 were intended to land from the sea, supported by 272 Ju-52 bombers, 180 fighters, 150 dive-bombers, and 40 reconnaissance planes. As the German paratroops were massacred, General Student concentrated his forces on Maleme and was able to land transports carrying reinforcements, under heavy fire, on the runway. This single achievement and the failure of the defending troops to mount a swift counterattack were to be decisive and ensure an eventual German victory.

Despite the quality of intelligence available to Freyberg, who was always handicapped by an almost total lack of air cover, the RAF's few planes having been withdrawn to Egypt, the Germans succeeded in occupying the entire island by the end of the month, although at a high cost. Royal Navy destroyers, acting on accurate signals intelligence, intercepted and sunk the poorly armed invasion *caiques*, and a convoy carrying the second wave returned to port. The Luftwaffe's crack Fliegerdivision 7 was decimated in the fighting, losing 6,000 men, and the Germans never rebuilt the unit nor resorted to parachute tactics again in the remainder of the war. About 15,000 of the defenders were evacuated to Alexandria from Sphakia and Heraklion, but 1,742 were killed, 1,737 wounded, and 11,835 taken prisoner.

The battle for Crete once again proved the value of overwhelming air superiority, even if the defenders were well-prepared and had the benefit of the very best intelligence about the enemy's intentions. *See also* WORLD WAR II.

MESSERSCHMITT-262. The world's first jet-propelled military aircraft, the Me-262 flew for the first time in July 1943. Designed in 1940 and reliant on the jet engine developed for the Heinkel-178, which had flown in August 1939, the Me-262's introduction was delayed because of Allied bombing of the factory at Dessau assembling the Jumo aero engine, so only 13 had been built by May 1944. The aircraft was first spotted by photographic reconnaissance on the ground at Augsberg and Lechfeld in January 1944, but details of its performance, with a speed of 527 miles per hour and armaments, with four 30-cm guns, would not be learned until signals intelligence revealed it required a 4,500 foot runway. According to the **Japanese Naval Mission** in Berlin, production was planned to supply 300 aircraft by September 1944 and reach 1,000 a month in January 1945.

Originally planned as a replacement for the Me-109 fighter, Adolf Hitler demanded that it be reconfigured as a bomber after the **D-Day** landings, which caused further delay. Hitler only agreed to the Me-262's use as a fighter in November 1944, by which time it had never flown over the beaches of Normandy. *See also* WORLD WAR II.

METEOR. In December 1950, No. 541 Squadron at **Royal Air Force** Benson in Oxfordshire was equipped with the first of 14 new Gloster Meteor PR-10 jets, and in June 1951 was transferred to Buckeburg, West Germany. The Squadron flew reconnaissance missions over eastern Europe for the 2nd Tactical Air Force until 1956, when they were restricted to peripheral flights because of the deployment of twin-engined, supersonic MiG-19s in East Germany. The squadron was disbanded in September 1957.

MICRO AIR VEHICLE (MAV). The search to develop an intelligence collection platform the size of an insect promises to provide an almost undetectable source of audio or video data. Components consisting of Mylar wings, silicon carbide jet engines, and tiny lithium batteries have been engineered to produce a MicroFly and other MAVs. *See also* DEFENSE ADVANCED RESEARCH PROJECTS AGENCY.

MIKADO. British codename for a planned raid on the Argentine airfield at Rio Grande by 22 Special Air Service in May 1982 in support of the task force sent to the south Atlantic to recover the Falkland Islands. The airbase had been selected for attack because its Super Etendard fighters were equipped with lethal Exocet missiles and had already sunk HMS *Sheffield*. The mission was aborted after a reconnaissance party was flown to the mainland on a stripped-down Sea King 4 helicopter, ZA 290, of 846 Naval Air Squadron from the carrier HMS *Invincible*, but it was compromised and flew on to Punta Arenas. Nine SAS troopers were evacuated through Santiago, but the helicopter's aircrew of three—Lieutenant Richard Hutchings, Alan Bennett, and winchman Peter Imrie—was arrested by Chilean Carabineiros after they had abandoned their aircraft at Agua Fresca, 22 kilometers south of the town. Chilean Air Force personnel quickly buried the Sea King and an investigation conducted by Major Jorge Rodriguez Marquez concluded that the Fleet Air Arm pilot had made a navigational error, enabling the trio to be repatriated through Santiago.

MIL-GEO. The German mapping service responsible for drawing up accurate maps of the Soviet Union for the Wehrmacht based on **Luftwaffe** aerial photography. The Mil-Geo archive was recovered from Bad Reichenhall in 1946, in an Anglo-American operation codenamed DICK TRACY, and later distributed with the designation GX. These maps remained the basis of Western knowledge of the Soviet Union until the **U-2** overflights. *See also* KATYN.

MIMOYECQUES MARQUISE. Photographic reconnaissance conducted in 1943 over northern France, within a range of 130 miles from London (estimated to be the limit of new German weapons), revealed some large construction work in seven locations. Two sites, at Watten and Wizernes, appeared to photo interpreters to be similar to, and perhaps associated with, the rocket experiments known to be under way at Peenemünde, but the third, at Mimoyecques Marquise in the Pas-de-Calais, proved a mystery, despite frequent overflights and reports from agents. The concrete structures were bombed extensively on the assumption that they were likely to be missile launch pads, but when Allied experts arrived following the liberation, they learned that the facility had been intended to accommodate the Hochdruckpumpe, a multi-barreled rocket-firing gun.

MINSK. In 1982, the Japanese minister of defense was shown rare satellite imagery to prove that a floating dry-dock, sold by the Japanese to the Soviet Union on condition it would not be used for military purposes, had repaired the aircraft carrier *Minsk*. The demonstration had been intended to warn Tokyo about future exports of dual-use technology.

MISAWA. Located on the northern tip of Japan's Honshu Island, the Misawa Air Base is the National Security Agency's principal intercept base staffed largely by the **United States** Air Force's 501st Intelligence Squadron and the 6920th Electronic Security Group that perform "satellite communications processing and reporting."

MISSILE GAP. Based on Nikita Khrushchev's public declaration in December 1958 that the Soviets possessed an **inter-continental ballistic missile** (ICBM) that could carry a five-megaton warhead 8,000 miles and in November 1959 that Soviet warhead production had reached 300 a year from a single factory, assessments made by American intelligence analysts proved to be extremely inaccurate. In December 1957, a Special National Intelligence Estimate predicted the development of a Soviet ICBM with a range of 5,500 miles and suggested that up to 10 prototypes could be ready between mid-1958 and mid-1959. A year later, a National Intelligence Estimate predicted 1,000 Soviet ICBMs would be in place by 1961, whereas Senator Stuart Symington insisted a figure of 3,000 by the end of 1961 would be more accurate. The gap was reflected by American plans to deploy only 130 Atlas and Titan ICBMs by 1962, and the Polaris and Minuteman missiles were not scheduled to become operational until 1963. Evidence given to Congress in January 1960 ranged from testimony from the director of central intelligence Allen Dulles that the

Soviets then had about 10 ICBMs, to the statement of Air Force General Nathan Twining averring the correct figure to be around 100.

U-2 imagery persuaded the **Central Intelligence Agency** (CIA) to reduce the 1960 estimate of ICBMs in the Soviet arsenal in 1963 to 400 although the **U.S.** Air Force preferred 700. According to the CIA's spy Oleg Penkovsky, the actual figure of Soviet ICBMs in 1962 was three, with some doubt about one of them. He revealed that the Soviets regarded all missiles with a range of more than 600 miles as strategic, and they were on the test ranges where they took a long time to fuel. The SS-6, powered by a volatile mixture of kerosene and liquid oxygen, while useful as a rocket for space launches, was entirely unsuitable as an ICBM and Khrushchev had lied to buy time until the smaller, solid-fueled, silo-launched SS-7, SS-8, and SS-9 could go into production. Although President Dwight D. Eisenhower knew there had been only four SS-6 launches in 1957 (including two *Sputniks*) and only one in 1958, he was unwilling to compromise the U-2 by stating publicly that no Soviet tests had taken place in 1955 or 1956. The next successful test launch would not take place until 1959, although some failures were observed.

The Soviets regarded the missile gap controversy as a triumph of deception, and between his recruitment in 1955 and his arrest in 1966 received confirmation from a KGB mole in the Pentagon, Colonel William Whalen, that the Americans had grossly overestimated the Soviet threat. The disadvantage for the Kremlin was that the fear of numerical inferiority led the Americans to accelerate the development of the Minuteman ICBM and the submarine-launched Polaris. In reality, the **United States** had always maintained a significant numerical advantage in nuclear weapons, and by 1962 the ratio was 17 to 1, with the respective arsenals being 5,000 to 300. *See also* ESTIMATES OF SOVIET AIR STRENGTH; SOVIET UNION.

MISSILE AND SPACE INTELLIGENCE CENTER (MSIC). A branch of the U.S. Defense Intelligence Agency, the MSIC is located on the Redstone Arsenal at Huntsville, Alabama, near the Marshall Space Flight Center and collects intelligence relating to missile technology.

MISSION 4019. The first **Central Intelligence Agency** signals intelligence flight with a **U-2** took place over the Black Sea on 22 December 1956.

MOBY DICK. Central Intelligence Agency codename for a 1954 project to launch reconnaissance **balloons** equipped with cameras into the jet stream in Scotland and retrieve them after they had overflown the **Soviet Union**. The plan was abandoned when the balloons ended up over Yugoslavia and north Africa.

MOGUL. Codename for a high-altitude air-sampling project designed to monitor Soviet atomic tests at long range by the clandestine collection and analysis of radioactive dust. Flights over the plutonium producing reactor at Hanford, Washington, in 1944 had proved that emissions of telltale xenon could be detected by aircraft equipped with air filters but no such low-level missions could be flown over the two suspected reactor sites in the Soviet Union. Therefore, MOGUL was initiated at the Air Force Watson Laboratories at Fort Monmouth, New Jersey, in 1946 to perfect a system of remote particle analysis. Experiments following the TRINITY test detonation at Alamogordo, New Mexico, in July 1945 proved that a significant increase in the level of atmospheric radioactivity had been measured 1,400 miles away at Annapolis, Maryland, within 13 hours, suggesting that dust in the jet stream traveled at 110 miles per hour. Air sampling proved more effective than seismic monitoring because the Soviets occasionally used large quantities of TNT on major civil engineering schemes, such as dam construction, and it was impossible to distinguish seismically between the results of a huge conventional detonation and a low-yield nuclear weapon test. Similarly, air pressure monitoring, which had registered the seven atmospheric pulses created by the catastrophic eruption of Krakatoa in August 1883, was another potential indicator, but the CROSSROADS/ABLE air-burst test at Bikini Atoll in May 1946 demonstrated that air-sampling, even 4,700 miles away in San Francisco, was more efficient and accurate. Sensitive seismographs located much closer failed to register CROSSROADS/ABLE but did detect a second test, CROSSROADS/BAKER, which was detonated just under the surface of the sea. Work on an acoustic monitor, based on the principle that a sound channel existed at high altitude (similar to one found deep underwater), also proved impractical although experiments were conducted at the White Sands Proving Ground in New Mexico with captured V-2 rockets. The MOGUL remote measurement results were kept secret and published reports suggested that atmospheric testing was unreliable beyond 2,000 miles. *See also* ALSOS; FITZWILLIAM.

MONTES, ANA. One of the most successful spies in the history of the **United States**, 44-year-old Ana Belen Montes was arrested in her sixth-floor office at the Defense Intelligence Analysis Center at the Defense Intelligence Agency (DIA) headquarters at Bolling Air Force Base in September 2001 and pleaded guilty to having passed classified information to her Cuban Direcion General de Inteligencia handlers for 16 years. During that period, she compromised every U.S. intelligence source and technique she gained access to and effectively neutralized air and signals intelligence operations she had been cleared for.

Of Puerto Rican parentage, and with a brother and sister employed by the Federal Bureau of Investigation in Miami, Montes was a graduate of the University of Virginia, with a postgraduate degree from Johns Hopkins University, and at the time of her arrest was a GS-15 **Cuba** specialist and the acting chief of her branch. She was about to be posted for a year to the National Intelligence Council at Langley and have access to the planning for the invasion of Afghanistan, when she was taken into custody. The DIA's investigation into suspicions that she had been a spy had begun in 1996 but had stalled for lack of evidence until November 2000, when, codenamed BLUE WREN, she was finally identified by the **Central Intelligence Agency** in an operation codenamed SCAR TISSUE and a Foreign Intelligence Surveillance Act warrant was issued in February 2000.

During her career as an analyst, she collected many awards and was selected to participate in the Director of Central Intelligence's Exceptional Analyst Program, completing a study on the Cuban military. Her participation in the research for assessments and her access to highly classified sources covering all the armed forces enabled her to compromise U.S. plans across Latin America and to influence policy.

In a plea bargain dependent on her cooperation with a damage assessment, Montes received 25 years' imprisonment, a sentence she is serving in Fort Worth, Texas. She did not receive any financial reward for her espionage and apparently acted from ideological motives, convinced that American policy toward Fidel Castro's regime was mistaken. *See also* BROTHERS TO THE RESCUE; CUBA.

MONTGOLFIER, ÉTIENNE-JACQUES. Soon after the brothers Étienne-Jacques and Joseph-Michel Montgolfier were taken aloft on

21 November 1783 by a hot-air **balloon** in Paris, Benjamin Franklin wrote that such craft could be used to "convey Intelligence." This achievement is generally acknowledged to gave been the first manned free flight.

MOONSHINE. British codename for a **World War II** electronic countermeasure that detected enemy **radar** pulses and then returned them greatly amplified, thus giving the false impression of the existence of a significant force. MOONSHINE proved especially effective during Operations **GLIMMER** and **TAXABLE**, both **D-Day** deception ploys intended to suggest ships concentrating off Cap d'Antifer and Boulogne, respectively.

MOON SQUADRONS. So called because these clandestine units usually only flew missions into Nazi-occupied territory at night during the period of the full moon, the **Royal Air Force** Special Duties squadrons were equipped with Westland Lysander and Lockheed Hudson aircraft. The original Moon Squadron consisted of the four Lysanders of the Special Duties unit, 419 Flight (based initially at North Weald, Essex, and then at Stapleford, Abbots, and Stradishall), which was amalgamated with three Whitley and two Halifax bombers to form 161 Squadron at Tempsford in February 1942 before being disbanded in June 1945.

Meanwhile, 138 (Special Duties) Squadron had been formed at Newmarket in February 1941 and combined with the King's Flight (419 Flight). In August 1941, 419 Flight became 138 Squadron, with eight Whitleys and two Lysanders, which were replaced with the Halifax in October 1942. Based at Tempsford, the Halifax was replaced with Stirlings in September 1944, and in March 1945 was transferred to Bomber Command and reequipped with Lancasters. All these units acted on behalf of the Secret Intelligence Service (SIS) and Special Operations Executive, and the first such mission of **World War II** was the dropping into France in October 1940 by the 419 Flight Whitley of a SIS agent, Philip Schneidau, who was collected from Montigny 10 days later by a Lysander from Stradishall, via Tangmere, flown by Wally Farley.

In the Mediterranean theater, 267 Squadron, equipped with Dakotas, was transferred from Heliopolis in Egypt to Bari in Italy to perform Special Duties in the Balkans. In February 1945, the squadron was posted to Burma, but flew regular transport missions. In September 1943, 1575 Special Duties Flight at Blida, Algeria, was redesignated as 624 Squadron and flew clandestine missions to France, Italy, Czechoslovakia, and the Balkans until it was disbanded in September 1944. Also flying into Poland from the Mediterranean was 1586 Flight, staffed with Polish personnel. It was redesignated as 301 Squadron in November 1944, to fly missions over the Balkans, and was disbanded in December 1946.

In the Far East 240 Squadron (based at Redhills Lake, Madras, and equipped with Catalinas) flew Special Duties flights from April 1943, landing agents on the Burmese coast. Missions to Malaya and the Dutch East Indies followed, and the squadron was disbanded in July 1945. Also at Redhills Lake were three Catalinas of 357 Squadron, previously formed at Digri in February 1944 from 1576 (Special Duties) Squadron with seven Hudsons and three Liberators. The 357 Squadron was disbanded in November 1945. The 628 Squadron, at Redhills Lake from March 1944, infiltrated Force 136 personnel into Burma and Malaya with Catalinas until it was disbanded in October the same year. The 1576 Flight (formed at Chaklala, India, in June 1943) flew flights over Burma, using a forward base at Dum Dum, Calcutta, and was disbanded in February 1944.

In January 1945, 358 Squadron had a brief existence at Digri with 16 Liberators, dropping supplies across southeast Asia until it too was disbanded in November 1945.

The Moon Squadrons relied on four main aircraft, with the slow but sturdy Lysander, with a range of 800 miles, proving the most reliable for pickup operations, capable of carrying up to four passengers. Also popular were the long-range B-24 Liberator and the PBY-1 Catalina flying boat for amphibious operations. The Whitley, which was obsolete at the outbreak of war, with a range of 1,500 miles, was used to drop agents into Nazi-occupied Europe until late in 1942, when it was replaced by the Halifax with a range of 1,860 miles.

MORISON, SAMUEL LORING. An analyst at the Naval Intelligence Support Center in Suitland, Maryland, and grandson of the famous naval historian Samuel E. Morison, Samuel L. Morison was also a part-time correspondent for *Jane's Fighting Ships*, and in July 1984 he supplied the publishers with some **KH-11** computer-enhanced imagery of the *Leonid Brezhnev*, a 75,000-ton Soviet nuclear-powered aircraft carrier, designated as Black Sea Combatant II (Black Com II) under construction at the Nikolayev 444 shipyard. The photograph also showed the stern section of the *Kharkov*, the fourth Kiev-class carrier, and an Ivan Rogov–class amphibious assault ship. This was published in *Jane's Defence Weekly*, and when the photographs were recovered in London they were found to have Morison's fingerprints on them. In a search of his apartment at Crofton, Maryland, several hundred other classified documents were recovered, and Morison was prosecuted under the 1917 Espionage Act. He was sentenced to two years' imprisonment.

MOSAIC THEORY. Allied air intelligence during **World War II** developed into the model used throughout the **Cold War**, and subsequently became known as mosaic theory, a synthesis of information from numerous sources, ranging from signals intelligence, overhead imagery, open sources, diplomatic reports, agent reports, the interrogation of prisoners of war, and the interviewing of refugees. When analyzed together, the emerging mosaic provided a credible picture of the true situation, with overlapping sources serving to provide a measure of verification.

– N –

NANOOK. Codename of an air intelligence operation conducted over the Arctic for three years from June 1946 by the U.S. Strategic Air Command's 46th Squadron based at Ladd Air Force Base in Alaska. The objective was to survey the polar wastes of the Arctic Ocean to identify land that could be claimed as American territory for a possible forward air base to provide early warning against Soviet attack. Equipped with B-29 Superfortresses carrying ground-mapping **radar**, no islands were found, although several large ice islands were discovered.

NATIONAL AIR AND SPACE INTELLIGENCE CENTER (NASIC). In June 2007, the National Air and Space Intelligence Center at

Wright-Patterson Air Force Base, at Dayton, Ohio, was reorganized and absorbed into a new **U.S.** Air Force Intelligence, Surveillance and Reconnaissance Agency.

NATIONAL GEOSPATIAL INTELLIGENCE AGENCY (NGIA). Created in November 2003 under the control of the **U.S.** director of national intelligence and the secretary for defense, the NGIA is responsible for the coordination, collection, analysis, and distribution of imagery to the intelligence community and to military consumers.

NATIONAL IMAGERY AND MAPPING AGENCY (NIMA). Created in October 1996, NIMA was an amalgamation of the United States **Central Imagery Office**, the **National Photographic Interpretation Center**, the Defense Mapping Agency, the Defense Dissemination Program Office and branches of the Defense Intelligence Agency, the **Defense Airborne Reconnaissance Office**, and the **National Reconnaissance Office**. In November 2003, NIMA was renamed the **National Geospatial Intelligence Agency**.

NATIONAL PHOTOGRAPHIC INTERPRETATION CENTER (NPIC). Created initially within the **Central Intelligence Agency** in 1953 as the Photographic Intelligence Division, NPIC was established in 1961 in a windowless block in a **U.S.** Navy compound on M Street in southeast Washington, D.C., but was subsumed into the **National Imagery and Mapping Agency** in 1996. NPIC was headed until June 1973 by the legendary photo interpreter **Art Lundahl**. *See also* BRUGIONI, DINO.

NATIONAL RECONNAISSANCE OFFICE (NRO). Created in August 1960 as part of the U.S. Department of Defense, the National Reconnaissance Office designs, develops, and procures the construction of American reconnaissance **satellites** and operates some 30 ground stations across the globe. In addition, the NRO was responsible for **U-2** and **SR-71** flights, although its existence was not disclosed officially until 1992. The NRO's first directors were Joseph Cheryk (1961–1963) and Brockway McMillan, a Massachusetts Institute of Technology mathematician appointed in 1963, who feuded with the **Central Intelligence Agency** over control of the U.S.'s reconnaissance satellite programs. He was dismissed in 1965. Other directors have been Alexander Flax (1965–1969), John McLucas (1969–1973), James W. Plummer (1973–1976), Thomas Reed (1976–1977), Hans Mark (1977–1979), Robert Hermann (1979–1981), Edward Aldridge (1981–1988), Jimmie Hill (1988–1989, 1993–1994), Martin Faga (1989–1993), Jeffrey Harris (1994–1996), Keith Hall (1996–2001), Peter Teets (2002–2005), and Donald Kerr (2005–present). The NRO had intended to keep the exact location of its headquarters secret, but was forced to disclose its existence in Westfield, Virginia, to the Fairfax County authorities to claim a federal exemption from local property tax.

Initially the United States Air Force and the **Central Intelligence Agency** (CIA) shared responsibility for developing and managing the country's satellite program, accepting tasking from the **United States Intelligence Board**. Broadly, the CIA supervised the satellite systems and the U.S. Air Force provided the launcher vehicles and ground stations. In 1965, the NRO appointed an executive committee consisting of the director of central intelligence, an assistant secretary of defense, and the president's principal scientific adviser. In 1998, the NRO was absorbed into the **National Imagery and Mapping Agency**.

NAXBURG. German codename for a receiver, mounted on the **WURZBURG** dish antenna, introduced in September 1943 that could take precise bearings on the emissions of the H2S centimetric ground-scanning **radar** equipment carried by Bomber Command. The Luftwaffe had examined an H2S set in March 1943 retrieved from a crashed British bomber.

NEPTUNE. The Lockheed P2-V Neptune was widely deployed by the **U.S.** Navy as a long-range maritime reconnaissance aircraft, with ASW squadrons based from Bangor in Maine to Key West in Florida, and others in Iceland and the Azores. On 18 January 1953, an aircraft crash-landed in the sea off the Chinese port of Swatow after being hit by gunfire. A Martin PBM Mariner seaplane attempted to rescue the crew but crashed on takeoff, killing 10 of the 21 men aboard. During the **Cold War**, a total of three Neptunes were shot down, two by the Chinese and one by the Soviets in the Bering Sea. The latter incident occurred on 22 June 1955, when a U.S. Navy Neptune was attacked by MiGs and crash-landed on St. Lawrence Island, Alaska. All 12 of the crew survived, and when the State Department submitted a bill to the Soviets for $1.5 million (the aircraft's value), the Soviets unexpectedly paid half in January 1956, the first and last time compensation was paid.

NICARAGUA. In March 1980, American satellite imagery revealed the existence of large-scale construction work on Nicaraguan airfields, apparently intended to extend the runways to accommodate MiG-21 Fishbed fighters and provide them with reinforced revetments. An **SR-71** sortie from Beale Air Force Base provided further imagery that was presented to the media by John Hughes of the Defense Intelligence Agency as proof of Cuban and East German military support for the Sandinista regime that had seized power in 1979. Also photographed were Mi-8 helicopters, lines of T-54 and T-55 tanks, 36 new garrison barracks, and vehicle sheds at Diriamba. In November 1981, photographs taken by a **U-2** over Montelimar showed expanded aprons and a runway 6,721 feet long. Combined with intelligence that up to 70 Nicaraguan pilots were undergoing flight training on MiGs in Bulgaria and **Cuba**, which had received two squadrons of MiG-23 Floggers, analysts concluded that the Sandinistas were planning to export revolution across the region. The airfield at Puerto Cabezas, for example, photographed in January 1982, was 6,000 feet long, whereas a fully loaded MiG-21 required 6,000 feet to take off with 3,500 pounds of ordnance. Covered the same day was the commercial airport at Sandino, which was defended by several batteries of Soviet antiaircraft guns. In addition, the Sandinista minister of defense, Humberto Ortega, boasted that the main runway at Punta Huete, 13 miles from Managua, was to be extended to 14,000 feet and a second runway 12,000 feet long was planned.

No MiGs were ever photographed in Nicaragua, although a KH-11 satellite took pictures of a Bulgarian freighter, the *Bakuriani*, at Nikolayev in September 1984 that the **crateologists** suggested might be a consignment of disassembled fighters. Curiously, the ship avoided transiting the Panama Canal and rounded Cape Horn, presumably to avoid declaring the nature of the cargo, but when she arrived at Corinto in November, only four Soviet patrol boats and two helicopters were unloaded.

According to the Sandinistas, there were 124 violations of Nicaraguan airspace by American reconnaissance aircraft in 1982, with 62 in the first four months of 1983. Most of these were RC-135 missions flown by the newly formed 38th Strategic Reconnaissance Squadron from Patrick Air Force Base in Florida and from Howard Air Force Base in the Panama Canal Zone. Overflights of Nicaragua and Costa Rica were also made by Lockheed AC-130 Spectre aircraft on missions codenamed BIELD KIRK, and by Royal Duke Beechcraft Queenairs of the 114th Army Security Agency's Aviation Company on signals interception flights from Honduras.

NIHON KOKU JIEITAI. The Air Wing of the Japanese Self-Defense Force, equipped with American jet interceptors controlled from Fuchu, near Tokyo, has been responsible for monitoring local airspace since 1958. During the **Cold War**, Soviet Tu-16 Badgers, Tu-95 Bear-Ds, An-12 Cub-Bs, and H-20 Coot-As made almost weekly incursions from bases at Sokolovka, Sovetsky Gavan, and Vladivostok to test reaction times of fighters based at **Misawa**, Hyakuri, and Chitise. Another objective was to monitor activity at the National Security Agency listening posts at Kamiseya and Torrii Station on Okinawa.

NIMROD. The **Royal Air Force**'s (RAF) reconnaissance version of the Comet airliner, the Nimrod entered service in 1974 at **Wyton**. Although the aircraft was deployed in a maritime surveillance role, a conversion to airborne early warning proved costly and ineffective. On 2 September 2006, an MR-2 variant, usually based at RAF Kinloss, crashed near Kandahar in Afghanistan, killing all 14 crewmen and technicians aboard. The coroner's verdict was that the accident, which had occurred immediately after a mid-refueling operation, was due to an avoidable design fault.

9/11. The coordinated seizure of four civilian airlines in the **United States** on 11 September 2001 by a group of 19 al-Qaeda suicide terrorists led by an Egyptian, Mohammed Atta, resulted in two of the aircraft being flown into the twin towers of the World Trade Center in lower Manhattan and a third crashing into the Pentagon, killing 189. Passengers on the fourth plane attempted to wrest control of their United Airlines flight 93, from Newark bound for San Francisco, over Pennsylvania, causing it to crash into an open field. An estimated 3,500 people died in the atrocity, which had been planned by al-Qaeda in Afghanistan. As a consequence of the perceived failures of U.S. intelligence, a 9/11 Commission was impaneled by President George W. Bush, which recommended a restructuring of the entire community and the establishment of a Department of Homeland Security, headed by Governor Tom Ridge, and the appointment of a director of National Intelligence, John Negroponte.

The hijackers responsible for taking control of American Airlines Boeing 767 flight 11 from Boston were Mohammed Atta, Abdul Aziz Alomari, Salam al-Suqami, Waleed al-Shehri, and Wail al-Shehri. Meanwhile, Hamza al-Ghamdi, Fayez Ahmed, Mohand al-Shehri, Ahmed al-Ghamdi, and Marwan al-Shehhi seized another Boeing 767, United Airlines flight 175, also from Boston. A Boeing 757, American Airlines flight 77, from Virginia bound for Los Angeles, was taken over by Khaled al-Mihdhar, Majed Moqed, Nawaf al-Hazmi, and Salem al-Hazmi and flown into the Pentagon by Hani Hanjour. Saeed al-Ghamdi, Ahmed al-Nami, Ahmed al-Haznawi, and Ziad Jarrah failed in their attempt to fly United 93 to their target.

Sixteen of the hijackers were Saudi and four were qualified pilots, although Hanjour, who had overstayed on his F-1 student visa, was considered hardly competent by his instructors at Bowie, Maryland, despite 600 hours flying. Fifteen of the 19 had been granted tourist visas, including Atta and al-Shehhi, who both had overstayed previously.

Another of the conspirators, French-born Zacarias Moussaoui, had been arrested by the Immigration and Naturalization Service (INS) in Minneapolis in August while attending a flight school, charged with overstaying on his visa by three months. Of Moroccan origin, he had been living in London, where he had gained a master's degree at the Southbank University in international business, and he was being held for deportation to France when the Direction de la Surveillance du Territoire linked him to Islamic rebels in Chechnya, and he was still in custody when the attacks took place. Accordingly, he was to be the only one of the terrorists to be charged with conspiracy and convicted. Significantly, the Federal Bureau of Investigation (FBI) field office in Minneapolis days previously had been refused permission to examine Moussaoui's laptop computer, which was later found to contain flight simulation programs and details about crop-dusters.

The FBI's investigation of Moussaoui revealed that he had received money from Ramzi bin al-Shibh, another radical who had lived with Mohammed Atta, Marwan al-Shehhi from the United Arab Emirates, and a Lebanese, Ziad Jarrah, in Hamburg where Atta and bin al-Shibh had been employed in the same computer warehouse. Bin al-Shibh had been refused American visas when he had applied for them while still in Hamburg in May and June 2000. A third attempt, made by him from Yemen in September 2000 had also been rejected, as had his fourth, submitted in Germany a month later. Nevertheless, al-Shibh had transferred money from Germany to al-Shehhi's account in Florida in September 2000, and then in December he had moved from Hamburg to London. In August 2001, while back in Germany, he had wired $14,000 from Western Union offices in the railway stations in Hamburg and Dusseldorf to Moussaoui, then attending the Airman Flight School at Norman, Oklahoma, the same facility previously visited by Atta and al-Shehhi in early July 2000. Both had gained their pilot's licenses in December 2000. Evidently al-Shibh had intended to learn to fly in the United States, for Ziad Jarrah had tried to enroll him in a flying course at Venice, Florida, in August 2000, and even arranged to make a money transfer from Germany to the flight school.

The FBI also found a letter from a Malaysian, Yazid Sufaat, confirming Moussaoui's work as a salaried marketing consultant for a company, Infocus Tech. In fact, Sufaat, who held a degree from California State University in Sacramento, was an al-Qaeda biologist who had experimented with anthrax spores at a secret laboratory in Kandahar. He was also known to the **Central Intelligence Agency** (CIA) as a terrorist whose apartment at a golf resort in Kuala Lumpur had been placed under surveillance by the Malaysian Special Branch, and had been used by the men who had planned the attack on the USS *Cole* in Aden on 12 October 2000 for a conference that had taken place on 5 January 2000. Although Infocus Tech was a genuine company, the letter itself was a forgery. Moussaoui was also traced by the FBI in Afghanistan, where in April 1998 he had attended a notorious al-Qaeda training camp at Khaldan.

Apart from Moussaoui, others among the 9/11 terrorists had appeared on the CIA's radar screen. Nafal al-Hazmi, a 25-year-old Saudi from Mecca, who had fought in Bosnia and Chechnya, had been logged by the National Security Agency (NSA) as a terrorist suspect, his full name having come up in a telephone conversation monitored in Sanaa, capital of Yemen. The telephone had belonged to Ahmad al-Hada, a veteran of the Afghan jihad, whose daughter Hoda had married 26-year-old Khaled el-Mihdhar, a Saudi originally from Yemen and a Flight 77 hijacker. Flagged as an al-Qaeda terrorist by the Saudi security service, Mihdhar's passport had been copied in Dubai during a clandestine break-in conducted by the local CIA station, and details of the multiple-reentry American business visa it contained passed to ALEC, the CIA's dedicated al-Qaeda unit. Al-Hada's phone, routinely intercepted by the NSA, had also implicated al-Hazmi, el-Mihdhar's boyhood friend, also from a wealthy background in Mecca, with whom he had attended the January 2000 meeting in Kuala Lumpur. A few days later, on 15 January 2000, they had both flown together from Bangkok to Los Angeles. Later, they would live together in San Diego at an apartment owned by an FBI informant and worship at the same mosque, headed by a radical imam. Thus, other 9/11 hijackers were known to the CIA; their significance as al-Qaeda plotters was not fully appreciated until the forensic investigation was initiated, but the links between the members of the Hamburg cell were clear. Atta and al-Shehhi had visited a flight school at Decatur, Georgia, together in February 2001, and had attended a local health club. Then in June, al-Shehhi had joined a gym in Florida with Safam al-Suqami, who had overstayed on an expired business visa, and Waleed al-Shehri.

While Moussaoui may not have been the ringleader or 9/11's central planner, he was demonstrably linked to al-Shibh who, though not one of the hijackers himself, was closely connected to three of the pilots, Atta, Jarrah, and al-Shehhi. In turn, al-Shehhi had associated with al-Shehri and Safam al-Suqami. Furthermore, through Yazid Sufaat it had been possible to tie in Moussaoui with Nawaf al-Hazmi, who had overstayed on a tourist visa, and el-Mihdhar, traveling on a legitimate business visa, establishing a relationship between him and no less than seven of the dead 19 terrorists. The fact that he had been in federal custody at the time of the attack, which doubtless he had advance knowledge of, served to support criticism that the entire episode had been a lapse of intelligence, or at least a failure of coordination between the various agencies responsible for U.S. counterterrorism. By the time the ALEC station had circulated details of al-Hazmi and el-Mihdhar for the State Department, Customs, INS, and FBI, the pair had been in the United States for eight months. As for Atta, there had been a missed opportunity when he had been summoned for reckless driving and driving without a license, but he had failed to turn up at the court hearing. His driver's license had been obtained legitimately in Florida, having been exchanged for his Egyptian permit.

From an intelligence perspective, 9/11 was an unprecedented, unanticipated debacle, even if the perpetrators exercised minimal tradecraft to protect themselves. They used their own identities and authentic travel documents, relied on the same banks, including the Florida SunTrust bank, used ATMs and Visa cards to transfer cash from Sharjah to Florida, and communicated with pay-as-you-go cell phones purchased in Canada. They even cited the same motel as their home addresses when applying for driving licenses, or the same false addresses when obtaining the state photo identification cards issued in Virginia. Their travel patterns were similar and their links to al-Qaeda fairly overt, even if their own families had failed to recognize they had been radicalized. They came from relatively well-educated middle-class environments and appeared not to have made much of an effort to prevent cross-contamination by operating independently in isolated cells. Chatter picked up by the NSA indicated an imminent, momentous event, and there were references to "the big wedding," enough for the CIA to issue a general alert on 2 July warning of an al-Qaeda "spectacular," but the dots were not joined until after the attack had taken place.

In the aftermath, a memo to headquarters from Kenneth Williams of the FBI's field office in Arizona, dated 10 July 2001, identified one of Hanjour's associates as a likely terrorist, one of eight listed, and recommended that the FBI pursue concerns about Middle Eastern men attending the Embry-Riddle Aeronautical University at Prescott, Arizona. No action had been taken, and another FBI special agent, Colleen Rowley, protested the obstruction she had experienced in Minneapolis when she had tried to investigate Moussaoui. He had attracted attention because when he had attended the Pan Am Flight Academy at Eagan, he had paid $8,000 cash for a course intended to convert him to Boeing 747s when his previous experience had been limited to single-engined Cessnas. A timely, intensive investigation of the surly Moroccan might have led the FBI to the other four pilots, or maybe to pursue the Williams memorandum that, after the tragedy, looked all too prescient.

NORDEN BOMBSIGHT. The astonishingly accurate Norden bombsight was invented by an eccentric Swiss-educated Dutch genius, Carl Norden, who worked for the **U.S.** Navy's Bureau of Ordinance. The instrument itself was a technological marvel, with the inner mechanism consisting of gears, mirrors, electronic motors, gyros, and a telescope covered by 35 patents, allowing aerial bombardiers to drop their ordnance on a target with unprecedented precision, thereby transforming the potency of heavy bombers. Norden's device, which he invented in 1922 but perfected with the Mark XV a decade later, made him extremely vulnerable to espionage and abduction by hostile powers anxious to learn his secrets. Before **World War II** he was placed under the protection of the Federal Bureau of Investigation (FBI).

Blueprints of his device were to be stolen by Herman Lang, who commuted daily from his home in Glendale, Queens, to work in Manhattan at the Lafayette Street offices of the manufacturer, the C.L. Norden Company. Lang, aged 27, had been brought to the United States from Germany in 1927 but had remained passionately patriotic, although he had taken care not to confide in his wife or daughter about his thefts. His accomplice, who worked as an engineering inspector at the Sperry Gyroscope plant in Brooklyn, was 44-year-old Everett Roeder, also German-born and an enthusiastic spy.

Lang's Abwehr controller was Fritz Duquesne, an extraordinarily colorful character who claimed that he had once been young Winston Churchill's jailer and had witnessed British troops maltreat his mother and sister during the Boer War. Originally from the Cape Colony in South Africa, where allegedly he had spied against the British, Duquesne claimed in a sensational book published in New York in February 1932, *The Man Who Killed Kitchener: The Life of Fritz Joubert Duquesne 1891* (written by a journalist, Clement Wood), that he had been responsible for the loss of the cruiser HMS

Hampshire in the North Sea in June 1916, while carrying the field-marshal to Petrograd. Although the British Admiralty had always believed that the cruiser had hit a mine, Wood reported that Duquesne had slipped aboard, disguised as a Russian officer, to signal a U-boat waiting to torpedo her, and then had made his escape before she sank.

Duquesne was a writer, and lived with his mistress, Evelyn Lewis, who was a sculptress from a wealthy southern family, at West 76th Street, calling themselves "Mr. and Mrs. James Dunn," but he had also volunteered his services to the Abwehr as a professional spy. After his offer had been accepted and he had established himself in a small, one-room office at 120 Wall Street operating under the name Air Terminal Associates, the building had been placed under surveillance by the FBI following a tip from an informer, William Sebold.

Sebold also rented a three-room office, suite 629, in the Knickerbocker Building at 152 West 42nd Street, under the name of the Diesel Research Company, and the FBI wired the room for sound and installed a two-way mirror on a wall-mounted medicine cabinet, behind which a 16mm movie camera filmed every visitor. Every word was recorded and a team of FBI special agents fluent in German transcribed the conversations. One, held between Duquesne and Sebold, in which they discussed active sabotage, and identified the General Electric plant at Schenectady, New York, as a target, led to their arrest. In addition, Duquesne asserted that he was working on a plan to assassinate President Franklin D. Roosevelt at his Hyde Park estate.

Despite his fury at being arrested, Duquesne retained his sense of humor and appeared amused to watch the surveillance footage of his incriminating visits to Sebold's office. A clock on the wall and a flip-over calendar placed on Sebold's desk made an accurate, verifiable record of every conversation. He said he always wanted to be in the movies, but had been disappointed by his performance. The film was showed in court and proved to be damning evidence.

The leads from the Duquesne case resulted in 19 pleas of guilty and a total of 32 convictions. It also spawned a Hollywood movie, *The House on 92nd Street*, which won several awards. The case ended with prison sentences totaling 300 years, and fines of $18,000. Duquesne received the longest sentence, of 18 years, while his mistress, Evelyn Lewis, received a year and a day.

During World War II, elaborate precautions were taken to protect the Norden Bombsight, and many models included a thermite bomb intended to destroy the analog computer at the heart of the machine if there was any danger of it falling into enemy hands. Altogether, 45,000 American bombardiers were sworn to secrecy and trained to operate the device, which performed less accurately above 20,000 feet where the jet stream affected the trajectory of falling bombs.

NORTH KOREA. As a totalitarian society, the People's Democratic Republic of North Korea has always posed a significant intelligence collection challenge to the West because of the limited numbers of knowledgeable refugees and defectors available for interrogation, the restrictions on diplomatic representation, and the paucity of opportunities to penetrate the regime. In such circumstances and in the absence of other sources, there is inevitably a heavy reliance on technical methods, with air intelligence playing a significant role, especially after the delivery of a small Soviet five-megawatt nuclear research reactor to Yongbyon, 70 miles north of Pyongyang, which became operational in 1965 and became subject to International Atomic Energy Authority (IAEA) controls in 1977. However, two years earlier, Yongbyon technicians had succeeded in separating small quantities of plutonium from the spent uranium fuel. In May 1992, the IAEA conducted an inspection of the site to verify previous North Korean declarations and investigate a suspected newly constructed plutonium separation plant that had been identified on satellite imagery that had been collected since at least March 1967, the date of the first declassified **CORONA** pictures. The IAEA delegation saw a second, 200-megawatt reactor under construction, and flew to Taechon to inspect the site of a third reactor intended to produce 800 megawatts. Significantly, there was no external evidence to suggest that these facilities were connected to the national electricity grid. Final proof that the North Koreans had been working on a nuclear device came in October 2006 when a small underground detonation was announced, registered on seismographs in Australia, and detected by U.S. air-sampling flights from Japan.

Armed with Scud-B missiles with a range of 185 miles, the Scud-C missile with a range of 320 miles, and the Neodong-1 missile with a range of 620 miles, the North Koreans later developed the much more sophisticated three-stage Taepo Dong-1 and Taepo Dong-2 missiles and test-fired them over Japan in August 1992 and July 2006. The North Koreans claimed in September 1998 that they had successfully placed a **satellite**, the Kwangmyonggsong-1, into orbit with a multistage rocket, but the launch went undetected. According to defector reports, 40 percent of the Taepo Dong-1's semiconductors and gas burners had been imported from Japan, which promptly placed an embargo on further exports of strategic matèriel.

Satellite imagery of a Taepo Dong-2 was taken over the Sannum Dong Research and Development Facility in 1994 that showed it to be 105 feet long, with a 59-foot first stage, an 8-foot diameter, and an estimated range of 2,170 to 3,720 miles. The Taepo Dong-2 was exported to Iran, and Iranian delegates had been present in May 1993 during the only known test firing of the Nodong-1.

In April 1994, following satellite imagery showing the probable development of nuclear weapons at the research reactor at Yongbyon, the **United States** delivered four batteries of Patriot missiles to Pusan for deployment to vulnerable ports and airbases. The Patriot is a possible defense against a surprise missile attack, but is impotent against any free-fall bomb delivered by one of the 20 Soviet-made Il-28 bombers in the North Korean Air Force. *See also* SEOUL OLYMPICS.

NORTHWEST AFRICAN PHOTOGRAPHIC RECONNAISSANCE WING (NWAPRW). Created in September 1942 from the U.S. Army Air Force's 3rd Photo Group, South African Air Force, and the **Royal Air Force**, the NWAPRW was commanded by Colonel Elliott Roosevelt and undertook missions in anticipation of Operation TORCH, the Allied invasion of North Africa. *See also* WORLD WAR II.

NORWAY. As a North Atlantic Treaty Organization frontline country during the **Cold War**, Norway monitored Soviet military activity in the Kola peninsula, and in August 1952, a Royal Norwegian Air Force C-47 participated in Operation PEDAR, a mission to identify the location of **Voiska Protivovozdushnoi Oborony** (VPVO) control centers in Salmijari and Belomorsk.

PEDAR was followed in 1954 by MINERAL, which used a Beaver single-engined reconnaissance aircraft to take oblique imagery of Soviet military installations within 10 kilometers of the border. Poor weather hampered the mission, which was replaced by MINERAL 2 and conducted by a C-47 until 1959, which was often monitored by MiG-13s from Luostari. In addition, RETINA, FOKUS, and VEGA flights were flown by RF-84F Thunderjets to collect imagery of target sites, and KORNELIUS missions were mounted to provoke VPVO **radar** and signals activity. These exercises were held jointly with British and American aircraft, although the Norwegian government placed a permanent ban on incursions into Soviet airspace by allied planes operating from Norwegian bases, and limited those flights to an area east of 24 degrees, being a safe 300 kilometers from the Soviet coast. When in May 1954 a U.S. RB-47E made a long-range overflight of the Kola peninsula through Norwegian airspace, exiting through Finland, the Norwegian Intelligence Service's Vilhelm Evang complained to the **Central Intelligence Agency** and received a personal apology from Allen Dulles.

In October 1957, MiG-17 and MiG-19 fighters were scrambled to intercept a high-flying, unidentified American aircraft, and in January 1959, the Soviets issued a formal protest regarding reconnaissance flights from Bodo although none had penetrated Soviet airspace. Undeterred, in that same month the British sought and obtained permission to fly Canberra missions from Bodo, and the Americans initiated DREAMBOAT, a series of signals intelligence collection flights up and down the Barents Sea, completed by C-130s operating from Germany.

In February 1960, Evang was invited to London to be indoctrinated into the **U-2** program, which was to be coordinated with flights made by C-130s. However, the proposal for 19 missions, averaging two a month, was rejected by the Norwegian government, and when the plane flown by **F. Gary Powers** failed to appear on 1 May 1960, the project was canceled, with the Norwegians complaining that they had not been informed that his U-2 had been engaged in precisely the kind of overflight that had been banned. The final straw was the loss, exactly two months later, of an RB-47H from **Royal Air Force** Brize Norton, Oxfordshire, over the Barents Sea, a flight that was monitored on Norwegian **radar** at Vardo, which confirmed the aircraft was in international airspace when it was attacked by a single MiG-19, flown by Captain Vasili Polyakov of the 17th Guards Fighter Aviation Regiment. The RB-47H returned fire with 20mm cannons, but plunged into the sea, killing four of the crew of six. The incident sparked protests from the U.S. State Department and from Prime Minister Harold Macmillan, who wrote an open letter to Nikita Khrushchev.

The copilot and navigator, who ejected successfully, were picked up by a Soviet trawler and underwent six months of interrogation by the KGB in the Lubyanka without declaring their capture to the U.S. State Department, which listed them as missing, presumed dead. In January 1961, the Kremlin announced their captivity, and they were released later the same month, on the day of President John F. Kennedy's inauguration. *See also* BABYFACE.

NUREMBERG RAID. The mass Bomber Command attack on Nuremberg on 20 March 1944 was one of the most controversial of **World War II**, with the **Royal Air Force** (RAF) suffering heavy losses. Of the 795 bombers on the raid, 94 failed to return and 71 were damaged, leading to accusations that the disaster was a major failure of Allied air intelligence, and maybe the result of a breach in security concerning the objective.

A detailed postmortem analysis conducted by air intelligence revealed that a combination of factors had been responsible for the debacle. Unpredicted, freak weather conditions created highly visible condensation contrails behind the bombers, which had been spotted by the Germans as they had assembled over East Anglia and switched on their distinctive H2S centimetric ground-scanning **radar**. Documents captured in Normandy in June 1944 indicated that the Luftwaffe routinely monitored up to eight transmissions from RAF aircraft, including Identification Friend or Foe transponders, the OBOE bomb-aiming device, and MONICA radar.

Accordingly, the **Luftwaffe** had early warning of a mass attack and gathered 200 twin-engined nightfighters from across the country, which were vectored onto beacons at Aachen and Frankfurt. Coincidentally, these beacons were on the route chosen by the **Royal Air Force** to the target, and most of the casualties were inflicted before the bombers reached Nuremberg. The Luftwaffe also detected the three decoy raids, mounted by Mosquitoes that dropped **WINDOW** over Aachen, Cologne, and Kassel, because the fighters were not equipped with the H2S radar.

Finally, the toll on the attackers was especially heavy because air intelligence was then still ignorant of the SCHRÄGE MUSIK upward-firing cannon, an innovation that exploited a blind spot under British bombers. Allied air intelligence improved dramatically after **D-Day**, when several Luftwaffe airfields were captured, and in July 1944, following the forced landing in Wales of a German nightfighter.

NURRANGAR. Located deep in the Australian outback, 11 miles from Woomera and far from electronic interference from Soviet spy ships, a joint Australian and American satellite control station was opened at Nurrangar in 1970.

– O –

OFEQ. The Hebrew word for "horizon," OFEQ was the codename of **Israel**'s first reconnaissance **satellite**, launched from the Negev Desert in September 1988. Following the intelligence failure of the Yom Kippur War of October 1973, when the Israeli Defense Force was taken by surprise, the need was identified for an independent Israeli satellite system to provide early warning of hostile troops movements in Egypt, Jordan, and **Syria**. OFEQ-2 was launched in 1990 and was followed by OFEQ-3, weighing 415 pounds and placed into orbit in April 1995 by an Israeli-made Sahvit-1 rocket. Reportedly, the OFEQ-3 satellite boasted a resolution of 3.3 feet. The launch of OFEQ-4 in January 1998 failed, but OFEQ-5 successfully replaced OFEQ-3 in May 2002. The launch of OFEQ-6 failed in September 2004 when a booster malfunctioned, sending the rocket plunging into the Mediterranean off Ashdod. OFEQ-5 reportedly has a life of five years and the development of a replacement system, Techstar, was speeded up when **Iran** commenced its satellite launch program in January 2005 with **Sinah-1**. *See also* EROS.

OPEN SKIES. The proposal made by President Dwight D. Eisenhower at the summit in Geneva in July 1955 to allow American and Soviet aircraft the freedom to overfly each other's territory was rejected by Nikita Khrushchev, who suspected that the suggestion was merely an attempt to identify suitable targets inside the **Soviet Union**. Accordingly, Eisenhower authorized the **Central Intelligence Agency**'s unilateral program of overflights.

ORION P-3. In July 1962, the **U.S.** Navy was equipped with the Orion P-3 to replace the P-2V Neptune as a maritime patrol aircraft, powered by four turboprop engines. Over the next 38 years, a total of 628 of the aircraft were built. On 26 October 1978, an antisubmarine warfare plane from Patrol Squadron 9, based at Adak on the Aleutians, ditched in the northern Pacific after experiencing an engine fire, and 10 survivors of the crew of 15 were rescued after 12 hours in the water by the *Mys Sinyavin*, a Soviet trawler that took them to Petropavlovsk in Kamchatka. Thereafter the crew were moved to Khabarovsk and then repatriated to Nigita, Japan, on 2 November, where they underwent two days of debriefing. *See also* SOVIET UNION.

OSIRAK. On 7 June 1981, eight unmarked Israeli Air Force F-16s, escorted by six F-15 Eagles, flew from a desert airbase near Eilat and attacked the Iraqi nuclear reactor nearing completion at Osirak. Built by the French, the site was heavily guarded, but the Israeli aircraft flew undetected through Jordanian and Saudi airspace to their target and delivered 16 2,000-pound bombs into the plant, destroying it entirely. All the aircraft returned safely, having taken the local air defenses entirely by surprise.

OSIRIS. French codename for a **radar** detection **satellite**.

OSLO REPORT. In November 1939, British air intelligence received an unexpected windfall, an anonymous package containing technical details of the latest German scientific breakthroughs, and a sample of a proximity fuse. Because the 10 pages had been delivered to the British embassy in Norway's capital, the material became known as the Oslo Report. Studied by **R. V. Jones**, it was eventually realized that the information, which included references to a pilotless glider-bomb under development at **Peenemünde** (the Ju-88 long-range bomber, a pilotless aircraft designated as FZ-10), was authentic. Also mentioned was a German radar effective at a range of 120 kilometers, due to be installed across Germany by April 1940.

After the war, Jones learned that the donor was a disaffected Siemens electrical engineer, Professor Hans Mayer. The fact that Jones originally was in a minority of experts who disbelieved the content of the documents illustrates the relative lack of knowledge in England of advances made in Nazi Germany. *See also* WORLD WAR II.

OUTWARD. British codename for a **World War II** balloon operation conducted against Nazi Germany intended to disrupt the local electricity distribution grid by destroying pylons and aerial cables. OUTWARD's greatest success was the destruction of a power station at Leipzig.

OVERCALL. U.S. Air Force codename for photographic missions flown from October 1948 by the 72nd Reconnaissance Squadron to identify 28 potential targets in the Soviet Far East, including airfields at Anadyr, Velkel, and Lavrentiya. Similar flights were codenamed STONEWORK and RICKRACK. OVERCALL was terminated in July 1949.

OVERCAST. Anglo-American codename for an operation, headed by Colonel Gervaise Trichel of the U.S. Army's Ordnance Department's Rocket Development Branch, and conducted from July 1945 to identify and capture 350 key Nazi scientists who had worked on the V-2 rockets. Most were offered work at the White Sands Proving Ground in New Mexico, while a parallel British research project, codenamed BACKFIRE and headed by Sir Alwyn Crow at the Ministry of Supply, test-fired weapons at a range outside Cuxhaven. In March 1946, following a breach of security, the codename was changed to **PAPERCLIP**.

OXCART. Central Intelligence Agency codename for the A-12 supersonic high-altitude, single-seated reconnaissance aircraft that flew for the first time in December 1966 but was quickly replaced in 1968 by the twin-seated **Blackbird**. Capable of flying at more than three times the speed of sound and at the edge of space, only 15 were built by Lockheed Martin at the Skunk Works in Burbank.

– P –

PAN AM 103. The destruction of Pan Am's Flight 103 over Lockerbie in Scotland on 21 December 1988 prompted the largest antiterrorist investigation ever conducted by the British Security Service, MI5. All 259 people aboard were killed and forensic reconstruction of the bomb, concealed inside a radio-cassette recorder, revealed components that were traced to Switzerland. Clothes found in the same suitcase, luggage that had been checked in at Malta, was linked to a pair of Air Libya employees, Ali al-Magrahi and Khalifa Fahima, and United Nations (UN) sanctions were imposed on Libya when Colonel Mu'ammar Gadhafi refused to surrender the two suspects. Eventually, in April 1999, Gadhafi relented and, following an agreement brokered by the UN and South Africa's President Nelson Mandela, a trial was held in The Hague under Scottish jurisdiction. In January 2001, Fahima was acquitted by a panel of three Scottish judges, but al-Maghrabi was convicted and sentenced to 20 years' imprisonment.

PAPERCLIP. The Anglo-American codename selected in March 1946 for an extension of **OVERCAST**, a secret project that identified German technicians with valuable skills. The scientists were offered one-year contracts in the **United States** and during their absence, their families were accommodated at a former German cavalry barracks at Landshut, Bavaria. By May 1948, 1,136 PAPERCLIP Germans were in the United States, with 127 rocket specialists working at Fort Bliss, El Paso, and 146 experts at Wright Field, Ohio. German scientists taken to England were accommodated at a branch of the Royal Aircraft Establishment, Farnborough, located at Westcott, where research on rocket motors was concentrated until the cancellation of the BLUE STREAK missile project in 1962.

PARR, IAN. A 45-year-old former soldier, Ian Parr was arrested in March 2002 for selling classified information from British Aerospace Systems in Essex, where he had worked as an electrical engineer since October 1986. During Operation DRAGONFLY, MI5 personnel masqueraded as Russian intelligence officers and paid Parr £130,000 for computer diskettes containing data relating to STORM

SHADOW, a stealth system designed to protect cruise missiles, and HALO, an artillery location device. In January 2003, Parr was sentenced to 10 years' imprisonment at the Old Bailey.

PEACE PEEK. Codename for the Breguet Atlantic electronic surveillance aircraft flown by the 2nd Staffel of the Federal German No. 3 Naval Air Squadron (*Marinefliegergeschwader*) at Nordholtz, which was modernized in 1980.

PEARL HARBOR. The surprise Japanese air raid on Oahu on the morning of Sunday, 7 December 1941, intended to eliminate the U.S. Navy's Pacific Fleet, was the culmination of a lengthy espionage operation conducted from Oahu by the local Japanese consul-general, Nagao Kita, from his two-story consulate on Nuuana Avenue. There he was assisted by 29-year-old Takeo Yoshikawa, an intelligence professional who had been sent from Tokyo in March 1941.

As well as employing his subordinates to collect information on the locations of Hawaii's air defenses and details of the torpedo nets in Pearl Harbor, Kita was in contact with a German academic, Dr. Bernard Kühn, who had taken up residence in Honolulu in August 1935, accompanied by his wife Friedel and her daughter Ruth.

While the German scholar, who had connections with the Brazilian coffee industry, busied himself with a study of Polynesian culture, financed by payments made from the Rotterdamsche Bank in Holland, his wife and his beautiful stepdaughter opened a hairdressing salon that developed a clientele among the wives of U.S. Navy personnel based at Pearl Harbor.

In October 1940, the Federal Bureau of Investigation (FBI) began an investigation of the Kühn family after a tip that suggested that Ruth was making regular visits to Japan and returning with large amounts of cash, which she laundered through a doctor on the *Lurline*, a Matson Line ship sailing between Honolulu and the West Coast. No evidence of espionage was discovered then, although the Kühns' bank transactions were monitored, but shortly after the surprise attack, Bernard Kühn was arrested and charged with espionage, a wireless transmitter having been discovered during a search of his substantial villa.

In an agreement reached with his FBI interrogators to save him from the death penalty, Kühn admitted that he had been recruited by the Sicherheitsdienst, had been sent on a mission to spy for the Japanese, and had reported to the local Japanese vice consul Otojira Kuda. To facilitate their observations and communications, Ruth bought a beach house at Kalama on Lanakai Bay and used a pre-arranged system of lights in certain rooms at particular times to signal to Japanese submarines offshore the number of Pacific Fleet ships in the anchorage. The FBI special agent in charge, Robert L. Shivers, was able to obtain Kühn's cooperation because of incriminating documents and messages found in the incinerator at the Japanese Consulate-General that Kita had failed to destroy entirely. They clearly implicated the Kühn family, and when questioned, Bernard confirmed that he had taken his instructions from Ruth. His death sentence was commuted to 50 years' hard labor, but Ruth and Friedel were interned. At the end of the war, the women were deported to Germany, but upon his release from Fort Leavenworth Penitentiary, Bernard was accommodated on Ellis Island, New York, until December 1948, when he was given permission to emigrate to Argentina.

In the aftermath of the attack, the FBI arrested 770 suspected Japanese agents, although only one, named Mori, appeared to have been in direct contact with Tokyo. Reliant on wiretaps, the FBI concluded that Mori had been reporting the movements of warships in Pearl Harbor over the telephone in a rather primitive code in which he had referred to particular vessels as flowers supposedly blooming on Oahu.

The scale of the Japanese success at Pearl Harbor was enhanced by the American decision, endorsed by General Walter C. Short, to protect military aircraft from sabotage by enemy agents and assemble the planes in closely guarded compounds at Hickam, Wheeler, Bellows, Kaneohe, and Ewa. The tactic of gathering the USAAF's fighters and bombers in dense concentrations made the task of the Japanese pilots much easier than if their targets had been widely dispersed. Short, who had only arrived in Hawaii in February 1941, protested that he had not been warned of the possibility of a surprise air raid, although more senior officers in Washington had learned of ominous intercepted and decrypted wireless messages exchanged between

Tokyo and the Japanese ambassador, but he was made to shoulder the blame, as was Admiral Husband E. Kimmel. While Short's strategy would have offered maximum protection against infiltrators, its actual effect was increase the destruction achieved by the enemy. *See also* WORLD WAR II.

PEENEMÜNDE. Located on the island of Usedom on Germany's Baltic coast, 50 miles from Stettin, Peenemünde was the site of the **Luftwaffe**'s principal **World War II** research establishment and the focus of attention from British air intelligence after it had been identified as an important target by the anonymous author of the **Oslo Report** in 1939. In March 1943, a prisoner of war interrogation mentioned that two captured Afrika Korps officers, Generals Ritter von Thoma and Crüwell, had been recorded discussing a new long-range rocket. This information coincided with Secret Intelligence Service agent reports from Peenemünde, so a series of photographic reconnaissance missions were flown over the area in May and June 1943. A Cabinet minister, Duncan Sandys, was appointed to chair a committee, codenamed **CROSSBOW**, to assess the intelligence. By the end of June, photo interpreters at Medmenham, as documented by Constance Babington-Smith in her memoir *Evidence in Camera*, had identified a rocket estimated to be 35 feet long. On 17–18 August, 600 Bomber Command aircraft attacked the site, killing 600 foreign workers and 130 German scientists including Dr. Thiel (the principal jet engine designer), at the loss of 60 aircraft. The raid effectively ceased further experiments at Peenemünde and forced the Germans to abandon their plans to mass-produce rockets at the Zeppelin works at Friedrichshafen. Instead, an assembly plant was built underground at Nordhausen, causing a further delay in bringing the weapons into service. *See also* A-4; BODYLINE; V-WEAPONS.

PERSIAN GULF WAR. On the first night of the war, 16–17 January 1991, F-15E Strike Eagles attacked the fixed Scud-B sites designated as H-2 and H-3 in western Iraq and destroyed 36 launchers and 10 mobile erectors. By the end of the Gulf War, designated as Operation **DESERT STORM**, 2,493 sorties had been flown to eliminate the Scud threat. The air war lasted seven weeks and resulted in the establishment of total air superiority for the coalition forces.

Eighty-eight of the Al-Hussein variant of the Scud-B missile were fired from Iraq between 17 January and 25 February 1991, consisting of 41 against Israel, 43 against Saudi Arabia, and two against Bahrain. Each launch was monitored by three satellites that transmitted the data to ground stations at Kapaun in Germany, Buckley Air National Guard Base in Colorado, and on Ascension Island. Perfecting the satellite early-warning system had been assisted by three Scud tests conducted in December 1990, fired from Basraq in southeast Iraq, west to an impact site near the H-3 airfield.

The only military casualties inflicted during a Scud attack occurred at Dhahran on 26 February, when a missile disintegrated and killed 28 soldiers and injured more than 100 others accommodated in a warehouse directly below. Notoriously inaccurate, the performance of the Scuds was not improved by the need for the Iraqis to avoid using the same launch site twice. On the first day of the war, eight launches against Israel from four sites near Rutbah, Wadi Rutgah, and Wadi Al Jabariyah resulted in immediate retaliatory air strikes, forcing the surviving estimated 15 to 20 transporters to avoid using **radar** or deploying weather balloons, and to adopt sites that probably had not been surveyed previously. Without calculating the exact coordinates of each launch site and entering the data into the missile's navigation system, such accuracy as the weapon possessed deteriorated. In consequence, the daily launch rate dropped from 4.7 per day during the first week of the conflict to 1.5 per day at the conclusion five weeks later.

Partially dependent on ground reconnaissance conducted by American, British, and French Special Forces, the first missions, undertaken by the French 13 Regiment de Dragons Parachutistes (13 RDP) were compromised and withdrawn. Not a single Scud was destroyed by a Patriot missile. Few, if any, were destroyed by the 22nd Special Air Service (SAS) patrols dispatched into Iraq to distinguish ingenious East German-built decoys from authentic targets and guide A-10 aircraft onto the missile transporters, which invariably were camouflaged and concealed under bridges during daylight and emerged at night to prepare for a launch. SAS road-watching patrols were inserted into the "Scud box," 350 square miles along the Baghdad to Amman highway, where an estimated 10 to 14 mobile launchers were believed to be operational, and into two other search areas farther south. U.S. Delta Force troops were active in "Scud boulevard," along the Syrian frontier west of Al Qaim, where a total of 16 reserve launchers were claimed destroyed. The claims and counterclaims for the destruction of Iraqi Scud missiles by British and American Special Forces remain controversial. The SAS's D Squadron later claimed a total of six Scuds destroyed, with A Squadron having attacked a facility described as a transporter repair and maintenance complex.

Overall, air intelligence made an unprecedented contribution to the successful prosecution of the war, first by providing the target information that eliminated the enemy on the ground and in the air, and second by providing almost instantaneous, accurate battle-damage assessments that allowed the coalition commanders to monitor the conflict's progress and leave them better informed than in any previous major military engagement.

PHOTOGRAPHIC RECONNAISSANCE UNIT (PRU). Established by the **Royal Air Force** (RAF) in 1940, the PRU flew converted Spitfires from **Wyton** and other airfields in East Anglia to provide imagery for the photographic interpreters at RAF **Medmenham**. By the end of the war, there were four PRU squadrons deployed in Europe.

In October 1942, No. 4 PRU was transferred from Benson, Oxfordshire, to Maison Blanche in Algeria. This was redesignated as 682 (PR) Squadron in February 1943 and was disbanded in September 1945. In the Middle East, the Intelligence Photo Flight at Heliopolis began operations in June 1940 and in March 1943 was redesignated as No. 2 PRU. In February 1943, 2 PRU was retitled 680 (PR) Squadron and was disbanded in September 1946. *See also* WORLD WAR II.

PHOTOINT. The acronym for photographic intelligence, covering the collection and analysis of imagery collected by cameras.

PIED PIPER. The **U.S.** Air Force codename for the first satellite project involving a recoverable capsule containing photo imagery. Proposed by the RAND Corporation in 1955, the Advanced Reconnaissance System contract was awarded to Lockheed in October 1956 as Weapons System 117L and later renamed **Discoverer**.

PINE GAP. Located in the MacDonnell Ranges, 19 kilometers southwest of Alice Springs in Central Australia, Pine Gap is the site of the **United States**–Australian Joint Defence Space Research Facility. Codenamed MERINO and opened in 1968 after three years of negotiations conducted by the **Central Intelligence Agency** station chief in Canberra, William B. Caldwell, Pine Gap controlled American geosynchronous signals intelligence **satellites**, including the **RHYOLITE**. The compound contains eight large antenna radomes and is one of the largest satellite ground stations in the world, employing more than 580 personnel, comparable only to **Menwith Hill**, Yorkshire, Buckley in Colorado, and Rosman, North Carolina.

PIONEER. An American-manufactured **unmanned aerial vehicle** (UAV), the distinctive twin-tailed Pioneer was deployed by the **U.S.** Navy during Operation URGENT FURY in Grenada in October 1983, and later over **Libya** and by U.S. troops during DESERT STORM in 1991, to provide a tactical reconnaissance capability. The Pioneer was later replaced by more sophisticated UAVs.

POLLARD, JONATHAN. Responsible for probably the greatest loss of highly classified **satellite** imagery ever, Jonathan Pollard had been an analyst at the Naval Intelligence Support Center (NISC) at Suitland, Maryland, since September 1979. A graduate of Stanford University, Pollard had later dropped out after two years readying for another degree at Tufts University, Boston, and was subsequently turned down for a job at the **Central Intelligence Agency** (CIA) when he failed a polygraph test and admitted drug use. At NISC, which was unaware of his attempt to join the CIA or a rejection from the American Israel Public Affairs Committee, Pollard had been assigned to the Anti-Terrorist Alert Center, where he had enjoyed access to top-secret compartmented intelligence, including imagery from the **National Photographic Interpretation Center**. He was arrested in November 1985 and charged with supplying unauthorized information to **Israel**. In his confession, he admitted to having sold thousands of documents to his Israeli contacts for $2,500 a month since 1981. He also admitted having passed information to South Africa and Pakistan, although he was not charged with those offences. Nor was his coconspirator, his wife, Anne Henderson Pollard, charged with having possession of classified material concerning the People's Republic of **China** and with having approached PRC diplomats in Washington, D.C. According to the damage assessment completed by the Department of Defense, over 18 months he passed 360 cubic feet of documents he removed from classified archives, libraries, and message centers to other countries, amounting to more than a million items altogether. Included were satellite photographs of the Palestine Liberation Organization's Headquarters in Tunisia, which had assisted the Israeli air raid in October 1985, and imagery of a nuclear facility outside Islamabad in Pakistan.

So much of the information was not directly relevant to Israel, but would have been of great assistance to the Soviets, that there was a suspicion that either the Israelis had traded some it with Moscow, perhaps in exchange for the release of refugees, or that it had been passed on to the KGB by one, or all, of the three Soviet spies caught in Israel: Shabtai Kalmanovitch, Marcus Klingberg, and Colonel Marcus Shinberg.

In March 1987, Pollard pleaded guilty to espionage and was sentenced to life imprisonment. His wife was given five years.

POLYARNY. The principal Soviet Red Banner Northern Fleet submarine base, north of the headquarters in Sevoromorsk, Polyarny, was a target for American air reconnaissance, especially when the Kremlin ordered a five-year plan to modernize the submarine fleet and introduce Hotel-class nuclear-powered boats armed with surface-launched theater missiles. Also studied constantly were the shipyards at Severodvinsk, Nilolayev, in the Black Sea, and Komsomolsk-on-Amur in the Far East.

In the absence of human signals intelligence sources, Western analysts were dependent on air reconnaissance to monitor Soviet developments and assess their impact on the strategic balance. In January 1961, a Whiskey-class diesel was lost with all hands in the Barents Sea following a schnorkel failure, and the first Hotel, the K-19, suffered a reactor failure while attempting a test launch in July 1961. Nevertheless, the Hotel, armed with three R-13 Sark missiles with a range of 350 nautical miles, was misrepresented to the world's media as having achieved a successful submerged missile launch. As it attempted to return to its base, the K-19 suffered a further coolant pump fracture and had to be evacuated. To launch an R-13 required preparations on the surface that took an hour and a half, and in fact, the Soviets were unable to achieve an underwater launch until February 1962.

In January 1962, Polyarny suffered widespread damage when a Tango submarine was destroyed in a torpedo-leading accident that also sank a Whiskey diesel moored on the same pier. Plagued by accidents, the Soviet submarine program was monitored continuously, first by **U-2** aircraft and then by satellites. The imagery collected proved the numbers of Soviet nuclear-powered missile submarines represented a low threat to the **United States** unless they could get into launch range undetected. *See also* SOVIET UNION.

POWERS, FRANCIS GARY. Trained as a fighter pilot, Captain F. Gary Powers became a **U-2** pilot for the **Central Intelligence Agency** in 1956. After he had undergone training at Groom Lake, he was given a cover transfer to the National Aeronautical and Space Administration but instead was posted to Incirlik in Turkey, where he flew missions along the Soviet border. Altogether, he had flown 27 U-2 missions, including one overflight of the Soviet Union, one over China, six signals intelligence flights along the Soviet border, and 19 other flights in the Middle East.

Following the discovery of a hitherto unknown missile launch center at **Tyuratam** on 5 April, a further overflight, codenamed GRAND SLAM, was scheduled from Peshawar in Pakistan, across the Soviet Union to Bodo in Norway, to be flown by Powers. The 3,800-mile route, exploiting a gap in the southern Soviet radar defenses, would take him over Chelyabinsk, the plutonium production unit at Kyshtym, the inter-continental ballistic missile sites at Yurya and Plesetsk, the nuclear submarine construction yards at Sverodvinsk, and the Northern Fleet naval bases at Murmansk and **Polyarny**. However, over Sverdlovsk he lost control of his U-2, possibly after the close detonation of a SA-2 Guideline missile, but managed to parachute safely to the ground, where he was taken into the KGB's custody. The Soviets later disclosed that a volley of 18 SA-2s had been fired at the U-2, and one had accidentally brought down a MiG-19 interceptor from Kaitsova, killing the pilot, Lieutenant Yuri Safronov.

Sentenced to 10 years' imprisonment, Powers was released in February 1962 in exchange for a Soviet spy, Willie Fisher, alias Colonel Rudolf Abel, convicted of espionage in the **United States** in 1957 and then serving a 30-year prison sentence. Upon his return to America, Powers wrote a book describing his experiences and was employed as a test pilot by Lockheed. He was killed in August 1977 while working as a traffic reporter when his helicopter experienced fuel starvation over Los Angeles.

Following the loss of Powers's U-2, all the other aircraft were fitted with burst transmitters, codenamed BIRDWATCHER, which provided regular information concerning the status of each flight. *See also* SOVIET UNION.

PREDATOR. An **unmanned aerial vehicle** developed for the U.S. **Central Intelligence Agency** by General Atomics Aeronautical Systems to fly reconnaissance missions and transmit tactical intelligence in real-time to a pair of controllers operating the aircraft remotely. The RQ-1A Predator, manufactured in San Diego, was flown operationally for the first time over Kosovo in 1999. It is 27 feet long and has a wingspan of 49 feet. Since 2001, the aircraft has been armed with two air-to-ground Hellfire missiles, deployed to attack terrorist targets. In November 2001, al-Qaeda's military commander in Afghanistan, Mohammed Atef, was hit by a missile fired from a Predator.

Another Predator in Yemen destroyed a vehicle in November 2002 in which seven al-Qaeda high-value targets were traveling 100 miles east of the capital, Sana'a. Among them was Qued Salim Sinan al-Haethi, known as "Abu Ali," who had planned the attack on the USS *Cole* and the French oil supertanker *Limburg* in October 2000. The Hellfire missile, developed at the U.S. Army's Aviation Center at Fort Ruckner, weighs 101 pounds and is a laser-guided precision weapon. In this case, the Predator had been launched from Djibouti, and to be quite certain of accurate identification Abu Ali was on his cell phone in conversation with a fellow al-Qaeda terrorist, albeit one in American custody, at the moment of impact.

Pushed by a propeller, the Predator is low and slow, flying at 10,000 feet at a speed of 90 miles per hour, which makes it vulnerable to antiaircraft fire, and it is unable to fly in poor weather conditions. However, it has a long flight duration and can supply a live video link to its controllers, who have undergone specialist training at Elgin Air Force Base. Each Predator costs $3.7 million, and a complete system, including four aircraft, costs $25 million.

In May 2005, Haitham Yemeni was killed by a Predator in Pakistan, and in December Abu Hamza Ramia was targeted. Both were senior al-Qaeda terrorists. On 13 January 2006, a Predator fired Hellfire missiles at a house owned by Bakhtpu Khan in Damadola, northeastern Pakistan, killing 18 people. Although the intended target had been the al-Qaeda leader Ayman al-Zawahiri, he was not among the casualties, although five senior terrorists were killed, including al-Zawahiri's son-in-law Abd al-Rahman al-Maghrebi, Midhat Mursi al-Sayid Umar, Abu Abayda al-Misri, and Abu Khabab, who formerly had commanded the notorious Darrunta training camp.

PRISONERS OF WAR (PoW). Captured prisoners of war have been a valuable source of information concerning an adversary's aircraft and German PoWs proved exceptionally important during **World War II** for Allied air intelligence, especially after mid-1943. A shortage of manpower in the Luftwaffe had led to a policy decision to draft repair and maintenance workers and technicians as aircrew, and this meant that the knowledge of PoWs increased considerably, as did their willingness to cooperate with their captors, apparently motivated by resentment that they had been transferred from the jobs they had been originally trained to undertake. Accordingly, prisoner of war intelligence became a very significant source of technical intelligence for Allied air intelligence.

PRIVATEER. The PB4Y-2 Privateer was a **U.S.** Navy reconnaissance variant of the B-24 Liberator. In April 1950, the *Turbulent Turtle* of Patrol Squadron 26, on a mission from Wiesbaden to Copenhagen, was shot down by Soviet La-11 fighters off Latvia with the loss of all 10 crew.

PR/SUCCESS. The **Central Intelligence Agency** (CIA) codename for the operation to remove the pro-Soviet Jacobo Guzman Arbenz from power in Guatemala in June 1954, a scheme that was dependent on persuading the dictator that he was in imminent danger of an invasion by a force led by Colonel Castillo Armas, who had also assembled a sizeable air force. In fact, Armas never attracted more than 150 supporting rebels to his camp in Honduras and relied upon a wing of CIA pilots managed by a former barnstormer, Jerry DeLarm, who dropped grenades and dynamite over selected, highly visible targets in Guatemala City from P-47s to give the impression of a major conflict. The spurious campaign was supported by broadcasts from a covert CIA-run radio station, the Voice of Liberation, which dominated the airwaves with reports of costly defeats for the government forces in skirmishes with the rebels. When a single Guatemalan Air Force pilot defected, he was tricked into recording a drunken appeal to his former colleagues, which resulted in Arbenz grounding all his country's aircraft in fear of a mass defection. DeLarm then strafed the capital and blew up the oil reserves, an event that persuaded Arbenz to resign and pass the presidency to his chief of the armed forces, Colonel Carlos Diaz. DeLarm then flew another mission to destroy the government's powder reserves. Diaz promptly resigned, after only a single day in power, and turned over the government to a junta headed by Castillo Armas.

– Q –

QUICKMOVE. The **Central Intelligence Agency** codename for the procedure of flying **U-2** reconnaissance aircraft accompanied by support personnel and equipment to advance airfields immediately prior to an overflight of the Soviet Union and China. QUICKMOVE required the deployment of a 20-man ground crew and fuel to be moved by C-124 transports from the permanent base at Adana in Turkey to the forward runway at Peshawar in Pakistan. QUICKMOVE was necessary because the Turkish government had declined to authorize incursions into airspace from its territory, even by Detachment B's British pilots.

– R –

R-1. The official designation of the first Soviet ballistic missile that was test-fired in October 1947 and designated as the SS-1a Scanner. Built largely by a team of 5,000 German prisoners led by Helmut Groettrupp, who had worked at **Peenemünde**, and Sergei Korolev, the R-1 was a modified V-2 rocket designed at the secret Scientific Research Institute at Kaliningrad known only as NII-88, and at a center on Gorodomyla Island in Lake Seliger. Work was also begun on the R-2, with an intended range of 365 miles, designated in 1950 by North Atlantic Treaty Organization as the SS-2 Sibling, and on a massive R-3, weighing 75 tons. The latter project was canceled after Stalin's death in 1953 and replaced with the giant R-7 inter-continental ballistic missile, which later went into service as the SS-6 Sapwood. Hugely expensive, the R-7's disadvantage was a relatively primitive guidance system that required signals from two ground stations 300 miles downrange, to maintain accuracy. The mainstay of the Soviet rocket force, the R-16, proved to be an ineffective weapon because, unlike the American Minuteman, it could only be fueled a few hours before launch because of corrosion.

RADAR. Throughout the 1930s, American, British, French, Dutch, Japanese, and Soviet scientists sought to perfect aircraft detection and ranging equipment, and by the outbreak of **World War II**, the Gema Company had developed the **FREYA** air early-warning apparatus, with a range of 75 miles, and the Seetakt naval device for sea search and gunnery support. Meanwhile, as eight FREYA stations had been built on Germany's northwest coast, Telefunken worked on a mobile system, the **WURZBURG**, with a 25-mile range.

Although the WURZBURG proved a highly effective support for radar-directed flak that could identify targets concealed behind heavy cloud cover, the Allies developed a jammer, codenamed CARPET after the device had been captured on the French coast in October 1942 during Operation BITING.

In contrast to the relatively small, mobile German radars, the British Home Chain air defense radar consisted of 19 towers, each 300 feet tall, carrying the antenna that transmitted a signal that could detect the height of an approaching aircraft at 120 miles.

Although air intelligence quickly established that some characteristics of a radar system, such as its operating frequency, could be determined by airborne interception, there was no substitute for physical possession, and the capture of a rather primitive Japanese Mark 1 by U.S. Marines in Guadalcanal in August 1942 revealed that its valves were copies of those manufactured by General Electric.

Once radar had become established, it became an essential instrument of war. The need to develop improvements and find countermeasures became compelling for all protagonists, and the competition, to refine the devices and protect them from countermeasures became a continuing feature of the **Cold War**, when all sides indulged in **ferret** tactics to test their adversaries' air detection systems.

RADIOSONDE. The **U.S.** Army Air Force designation of high-altitude balloons carrying monitoring equipment that were released in 1946 to detect radioactivity in the upper atmosphere for the purpose of monitoring an anticipated Soviet nuclear test. The experiments were discontinued when airborne air-sampling by Operation **FITZWILLIAM** proved more effective. *See also* SOVIET UNION.

RAM-M. The North Atlantic Treaty Organization designation of a Soviet high-altitude reconnaissance aircraft spotted by a satellite at Ramenskoye, a flight test center north of Moscow.

RAVEN. An unmanned aerial vehicle first deployed in Iraq in 2006, the Raven is a lightweight Styrofoam plane coated with Kevlar and equipped with two cameras, one for use in daylight and the other using infrared technology at night. Dismantled, the Raven fits into a handheld duffle bag and can be assembled in minutes. It is controlled by a team of two soldiers, one acting as the remote pilot, the other as navigator using GPS technology. The cameras provide live imagery to a tactical operations center, but being noisy it also fulfills the function of territory denial as adversaries can hear its approach from some distance and in Iraq prevented insurgents from leaving improvised explosive devices in the path of coalition patrols.

RAVENS. The name applied to the pilots contracted to fly unarmed spotter O-1 planes from secret bases in **Laos** during the **Vietnam War** and act as forward air controllers and guide strike aircraft to their ground targets along the Ho Chi Minh trail. Once the enemy had been spotted Operation HUNT would be initiated, with heavily armed AC-130 Spectre gunships deployed to fire their large-caliber weapons.

RB-29. U.S. Air Force designation of the reconnaissance variant of the B-29 Boeing Superfortress, equipped with cameras that could reach 100 miles into Soviet territory. On 22 October 1949, two La-7 fighters intercepted an unarmed RB-29 over the Sea of Japan and fired cannon across the nose, but then broke off the engagement. During the course of the **Cold War**, five RB-29s would be shot down by Soviet aircraft. On 13 June 1952, an RB-29 disappeared over the Sea of Japan; on 7 October, another was shot down in the same area by MiG-15s; on 15 March 1953, Colonel Robert Rich's plane, from the 38th Strategic Reconnaissance Squadron was engaged by Soviet fighters off Kamchatka, but returned to Alaska.

RB-45C. U.S. Air Force designation of the reconnaissance variant of the Tornado, a fast, medium bomber with a crew of three that could be refueled in the air. Three RB-45Cs were deployed in Korea and on 4 December 1950, Captain Charles E. McDonough was shot down by a MiG-15 of the Soviet 164th Fighter Aviation Corps near Sinuiju with the loss of three of his crew. McDonough bailed out but was later interrogated by Colonel Viktor A. Bushuyev, the Red Air Force's deputy chief of staff for intelligence.

Three other RB-45s were lent to the British in 1952 and painted in **Royal Air Force** (RAF) ivory to undertake **radar** mapping of targets deep inside the Soviet Union from RAF Sculthorpe, and in April flew missions over Estonia, Latvia, and Lithuania. All three returned safely, although one plane landed at Copenhagen to clear some frozen oil filters, and then had to divert to Prestwick because of poor weather. In April 1954, the exercise was repeated, although one aircraft, having encountered heavy flak over Kiev, was obliged to refuel at Furstenfeldbruck, having failed to refuel from an airborne KB-29 tanker.

Powered by four turbo jets, the Tornado carried a crew of two and three cameras, and could fly at 570 miles per hour with a ceiling of 37,550 feet. *See also* KOREAN WAR.

RB-47E. U.S. Air Force designation of the Boeing B-47 Stratojet bomber, with a ceiling of 47,000 feet, converted for aerial reconnaissance duties. Introduced at the end of 1953, it could photograph

100,000 square miles in three hours flying at 39,000 feet. The RB-47H variant was a signals intelligence variant that carried three "**Ravens**," the nickname of the electronic warfare officers who were accommodated in a separate compartment in the bomb bay only four feet high, away from the flight-deck crew of pilot, copilot, and navigator. To reach the classified intercept space, the three Ravens were obliged to crawl down an access tunnel after takeoff and return for landing.

During the **Cold War**, three RB-47s were attacked by Soviet fighters and two were shot down. On 8 May 1954, three RB-47Es of the 91st Strategic Reconnaissance Wing from the **Royal Air Force** (RAF Fairford, Gloucestershire) flew toward Murmansk, and two turned back from Soviet airspace as a diversion, leaving one to fly across the Kola peninsula and exit over Finland. Having refueled, the mission continued over Sweden and **Norway**, but was attacked by newly operational MiG-17s. The fighters, designated as Fresco by the North Atlantic Treaty Organization and introduced into service the previous year, failed to press home their attack because of 20mm cannon fire from the RB-47's M-24 rear turret. The pilot, 29-year-old Harold R. Austin, completed his assignment and photographed nine Soviet airfields. Although damaged, the aircraft refueled again and returned to Fairford safely.

The first RB-47 was lost, with a crew of three, on 18 April 1955, east of Kamchatka while on a photoreconnaissance mission from the 4th Strategic Reconnaissance Squadron at Eielson Air Force Base, Alaska, but no statement acknowledging the incident was released by Moscow until 1992, when Soviet documents were declassified that revealed that the plane had been attacked by two MiG-15s. Because the Americans had no proof that their aircraft had been shot down, no protest was registered with the Soviets.

The second loss occurred on 1 July 1960, when an RB-47H from RAF Brize Norton was shot down over the Barents Sea with the loss of four members of the crew. The copilot and navigator ejected to safety and were imprisoned at the Lubyanka until they were released in January 1961.

RB-50. On 29 July 1953, MiG-15 Fagot fighters shot down an RB-50 of the 343rd Strategic Reconnaissance Squadron based at Yokota, over the Sea of Japan, 90 miles southeast of Vladivostock. Of the crew of 17, only the copilot survived.

On 10 September the following year, another RB-50 from Yokota was lost over the Sea of Japan, only on this occasion the most likely explanation was not a Soviet attack, but adverse weather conditions created by Typhoon Emma. The flight crew of nine, from the 6091st Reconnaissance Squadron, and seven **Air Force Security Service** personnel, including four Russian linguists, all members of the 6924th Security Squadron, simply disappeared without trace.

RB-57A. In August 1955, the 7406th and 7407th Support Squadrons based at Rhein-Main were equipped with two variants of the RB-57A, the HEART THROB photoreconnaissance aircraft, and the SHARP CUT combined electronic and photographic-capable version. On 11 December 1956, three RB-57Ds flew from Yakota, Japan, on separate missions over Vladivostock. MiG-17s were scrambled to intercept them, but none could climb to 64,000 feet. A formal Soviet protest was delivered on 15 December, and President Dwight D. Eisenhower terminated the program.

In June 1959, they were replaced by the RB-57D with longer wings, but the unit was eventually disbanded, having been made redundant by the **U-2** and following the loss of an RB-57F from Incirlik with a crew of two over the Black Sea in December 1965. The pilot seems to have lost control of his aircraft at its cruising altitude of 80,000 feet and plunged into the sea. Part of a wing was recovered by a Turkish destroyer in international waters and other wreckage was winched aboard Soviet trawlers.

RB-69. The **U.S.** Air Force designation of the signals intelligence variant of the Lockheed Neptune, deployed from 1957 to Eglin Air Force Base, Florida, and to Japan, **Taiwan**, and Wiesbaden. Equipped with sideways-looking airborne radar, seven of the aircraft undertook peripheral reconnaissance flights for the **Central Intelligence Agency** before they were converted to the SP-2H antisubmarine role.

RC-135. The intelligence collection variant of the Boeing 707, the RC-135 was flown by the 55th Strategic Reconnaissance Wing of the U.S. Strategic Air Command based at Offut Air Force base in

Nebraska. Permanent detachments were posted to **Royal Air Force** Mildenhall in England, Kadena on Okinawa, and Eielson in Alaska.

On 16 September 1980, an RC-135 of the 922nd Support Squadron flying from Hellenikon, outside Athens, was attacked in international airspace over the Mediterranean by two Libyan MiG-23s. The Boeing took evasive action and escaped, but five days later a second mission was intercepted by four Libyan Mirages, two MiG-23s, and a pair of MiG-25s. On this occasion, three F-14 Tomcats were scrambled from the USS *John F. Kennedy*, and Libyan ground control was heard to order the Syrian pilots to break off the confrontation.

On 24 February 2004, an RC-135S flying from Kadena on a **COBRA BALL** signals intelligence collection mission in international airspace over the Sea of Japan was intercepted by two North Korean MiG-23 Floggers and a pair of MiG-29 Fulcrums and shadowed for 20 minutes. *See also* RIVET JOINT.

REDFA, MUNIR. A top Iraqi fighter pilot, Munir Redfa flew his MiG-21 Fishbed to Israel in August 1966. A Maronite Christian, Redfa had been motivated to defect because of the regime's indiscriminate bombing of Iraqi Kurds. Reportedly persuaded to defect by his American lover, whom he had met in Paris, Redfa's plane was refueled in Turkey before completing its flight to Israel. The information gleaned from the Fishbed proved important and showed that although the plane had limited range and short wings that reduced its dog-fighting performance, it was essentially a rocket, reaching Mach 2.3. Despite some poor workmanship, the aircraft was very durable and, unlike its American rivals that were invariably stored in hangars, was usually kept in the open, in extreme temperatures of heat and cold. During the **Cold War**, more than 10,000 MiG-21s would be flown in more than 40 countries.

REGAN, BRIAN. A year after taking up his post as a contractor for the **National Reconnaissance Office,** former **U.S.** Air Force sergeant Brian Regan was arrested at Dulles Airport as he attempted to board a Swissair flight for Zurich. The 40-year-old Regan had left the Air Force in August 2000 but the father of four had accumulated debts of $116,000 when he approached the Iraqis, the Chinese, and the Libyans with an offer to sell them classified information for $13 million. He was arrested in August 2001 and was sentenced to life imprisonment without parole in February 2003 after some 10,000 documents and a collection of CDs had been recovered from caches buried in Virginia and Maryland.

RENDITION. The process of detaining terrorist suspects and transporting them to covert interrogation centers was known as "extraordinary rendition" and was dependent upon a global air transport system using civil aircraft chartered by the **Central Intelligence Agency** (CIA) to collect and deliver the prisoners. The planes included a Boeing 737, registered N313P, and a Gulfstream initially registered N379P and later as N8068V. The operation began in 1998 and was extended following the occupation of Afghanistan in October 2001, but the disclosure that such an extralegal strategy had been adopted caused embarrassment to the administration of President George W. Bush and to the governments of Poland and Romania, which had provided secure accommodation for the detainees removed from third countries. The air charter companies providing transport to the CIA included Apache Aviation, Aviation Specialties, Bayard Foreign Leasing, Braxton Manufacturing, Centurion Aviation Services, Devon Holdings, Gemini Leasing, Keeler & Tate Management, Phoenix Aviation, Premier Executive Transport Services, Rapid Air Transport, Tepper Aviation, Richmor, and Stevens Express Leasing. These companies were often the successive registered owners of the same fleet of 24 executive jets that flew regularly, sometimes with military pilots, between Guantanamo Bay, Jordan, Egypt, Afghanistan, Germany, and the United Kingdom, with permission to land at U.S. military airfields.

The detention centers operated by the CIA were located at an abandoned brick factory near Kabul known as the "Salt Pit," a military base close to Szcytno-Szymany airport in northeast Poland, at Tamara outside Rabat in Morocco, and at the Mikhail Kogalniceanu military airfield in Romania.

RENO, FRANKLIN VINCENT. A brilliant young mathematician working on the development of aerial bombsights at the U.S. Army's Aberdeen Proving Grounds in Maryland, Frank Reno was identified in 1939 by the defector Whittaker Chambers as a Soviet spy. Chambers claimed that Reno, who had been a Communist Party of the

United States of America (CPUSA) activist under the alias Lance Clark, had worked for a Colonel Zornig to calculate bombing tables for the **Norden Bombsight**, and had supplied information about them to the GRU illegal *rezident* in the United States, Colonel Boris Bykov. When interviewed in 1948, Reno, who was still working in the same place, confirmed Chambers's allegations, and in July 1952 at Denver, Colorado, was sentenced to three years' imprisonment at Leavenworth Federal Penitentiary for having concealed his prewar membership in CPUSA.

RESSAN, AHMED. A petty criminal of Algerian background living in Montreal, Ahmed Ressan was arrested by a U.S. Customs inspector at Port Angeles, Washington, on 14 December 1999 as he attempted to drive a car over the border. His behavior was considered suspicious, and when challenged, he attempted to flee on foot. When searched, his vehicle was found to contain four timers and large quantities of urea and sulfate, both components for a homemade explosive, and under interrogation he confessed that he had intended to attack Los Angeles International Airport.

Ressan was also carrying the telephone number of a contact in Brooklyn, New York. Abdul Ghani Meskini, also an Algerian, an illegal immigrant who was placed under surveillance and then, on 30 December, arrested on immigration charges as he had stowed away and slipped ashore in Boston. Both men eventually agreed to cooperate with the authorities, as did a third suspect, Abdel Hakim Tizegha, another illegal immigrant from Algeria.

RHYNE, JAMES. In 1980, Jim Rhyne flew a Twin Otter fitted with extra fuel tanks into Iran to establish DESERT ONE, the airstrip from which Delta Force intended to rescue the U.S. Embassy hostages held in Tehran. When the Operation **EAGLE CLAW** failed, a second attempt was planned, and Rhyne was selected to go to Nevada to train H-53 pilots in the use of image-intensifying goggles and to fly at night. However, the project was canceled when the Iranians released their hostages.

The son of a pharmacist in La Fayette, Georgia, Rhyne was a teenager when he bought his first plane, a Piper J-3 cub, with a school friend, Paul Robinson. He joined the Air Force in 1954 but left after aircrew flight time was cut as a budgetary measure. In 1960, while running a small airport, he joined Air America to fly in India and then Laos. As a senior pilot, one of his tasks was to drop sensors on the Ho Chi Minh trail and then monitor them remotely. He also started a small factory in northern Thailand with 50 sewing machines to make the parachutes used for Air America's thousands of supply drops each month.

On 15 January 1972, while dropping leaflets offering a reward for a missing air crew member, Rhyne was badly wounded by ground fire. The pilot immediately flew to Thailand as another member of the crew drove his knee into Rhyne's groin to stem the bleeding from Rhyne's shredded leg, saving his life. Six months later Rhyne was flying again with a prosthetic leg, having been awarded the **Central Intelligence Agency** (CIA) Star.

In 1975, Rhyne moved to Saigon, where Air America flew until the city fell in April. In 1978, Rhyne delivered the eulogy for his friend Berl King, an experienced pilot with 70,000 hours and the only other Air America pilot to be hired permanently by the CIA, after his plane crashed near Fort Bragg, killing two CIA paramilitary officers and a Special Forces soldier aboard.

Rhyne, the holder of the CIA's top two medals for valor, retired in 1979. He moved to Clayton, North Carolina, and opened Aero Contractors Ltd. at the Johnston County Airport, not far from Fort Bragg. With 20,000 hours of experience, Rhyne had moved to a home with a small airstrip in Moore County with his wife Jearanai. Rhyne was killed in an air crash in April 2002, aged 66, flying a homemade Steen Skybolt belonging to a friend, a local doctor. The aircraft dived into a swampy forest immediately after takeoff and Rhyne was conscious when rescuers cut him out of the plane, but died an hour later at Johnston Memorial Hospital.

RHYOLITE. An American signals intelligence satellite system, manufactured by TRW at Redondo Beach, California, the first RHYOLITE was launched in 1970 from Cape Canaveral and transmitted signals to ground stations at **Pine Gap** and **Menwith Hill**. Three RHYOLITES were successfully placed in orbit 24,000 miles above the earth, and in 1975 the system was replaced by an enhanced version, the Argus. In May 1977, a second generation, codenamed **AQUACADE**, was brought into service and there were three further launches. Both systems were compromised in 1976 by a TRW employee, **Christopher Boyce**. *See also* BYEMAN.

RIVET AMBER. U.S. Air Force codename for a series of signals intelligence collection missions flown outside Soviet airspace during the **Cold War** to monitor air defense emissions. On 5 June 1969, the sole RC-135E, specially converted with a massive radome on the front of the fuselage, disappeared without trace in the Bering Sea with all nine aircrew. *See also* SOVIET UNION.

RIVET BALL. U.S. Air Force codename for signals intelligence collection flights flown over the Bering Sea during the **Cold War** by RC-135 ELINT aircraft of the 24th Strategic Reconnaissance Wing of the 6th Strategic Wing stationed at Eielson in Alaska. Other similar codenames in the series included RIVET BRASS, RIVER QUICK, COMBAT SCENT, and COMBAT PINK. *See also* SOVIET UNION.

RIVET JOINT. U.S. Air Force codename for signals intelligence collection flights flown outside Soviet airspace during the **Cold War** by RC-135 ELINT aircraft to monitor air defense emissions. The aircraft were based at Offut Air Force Base, near Omaha, Nebraska; Eielson Air Force Base in Alaska; Hellenikon Air Force Base near Athens in Greece; Kadena in Okinawa, Japan; Howard Air Force Base in Panama; and **Royal Air Force** Mildenhall in England.

ROBIN. Royal Air Force codename for air reconnaissance flights undertaken between 1953 and 1955 by Canberra aircraft of No. 540 Squadron over Soviet and Eastern Bloc airspace, including missions to photograph the missile launch site at **Kapustin Yar**.

ROOSTER-53. Israeli codename for a raid undertaken in December 1969 on an Egyptian air defense **radar** site at Ras-al-Ghaleb on Green Island in the Red Sea. After *Sayeret Maktal* paratroops from the elite Unit 269 had captured the station in a night attack, two Sikorsky CH-53 helicopters removed the entire communications caravan and radar antenna to Israel, while another lifted the four tons of Soviet radar equipment. The heavy load caused one of the helicopters to crash land, and a third almost had the same experience. Subsequently, the hardware was studied by Israeli technicians before being passed to the **United States**. The coup enabled the Israeli Air Force to introduce countermeasures that neutralized Egyptian radar coverage over the Suez Canal. *See also* WAR OF ATTRITION.

ROWEHL, THEODOR. Prior to the outbreak of **World War II**, the **Luftwaffe** conducted a series of aerial photographic flights across Europe in an He-111 twin-engined bomber painted in Lufthansa livery and flown by Theodor Rowehl. A reconnaissance pilot in World War I, Rowehl was renowned for having penetrated British airspace in his Rhomberg C-7. After the war, he had continued to fly a chartered aircraft until he began to supply the newly formed Abwehr with photos he had taken over Poland and East Prussia. Having begun with a single Junkers W-34 based in Kiel, Rowehl soon gathered a group of pilots around him to form an experimental high-altitude flight of five aircraft based at Staaken, but training at Lipetsk, the Luftwaffe's secret airfield in Russia. His work impressed Herman Göring and he was transferred to the command of Otto ("Beppo") Schmid, head of the Luftwaffe's intelligence branch at Oranienburg, to fly specially adapted Heinkel 111s equipped with cameras designed by Carl Zeiss.

Under Rowehl's leadership, the Luftwaffe's air reconnaissance wing grew from three squadrons to 53 on the outbreak of war in September 1939, amounting to 602 aircraft, by which time much of Germany's neighboring territories had been mapped. The organization was divided into 342 short-range aircraft, dedicated to tactical support, and 260 longer-range planes, mainly Junker 88Ds and Dornier 17Fs, undertaking strategic missions.

In December 1943, following the death of his wife in an Allied air raid, Rowehl resigned his command and his unit was renamed **Kamfsgruppe 200**.

ROYAL AIR FORCE (RAF). From June 1943, all British photographic reconnaissance missions from England were undertaken by No. 106 PR Wing at Benson, under the operational control of the assistant chief of the Air Staff (Intelligence). The unit, consisting of 80 aircraft in four squadrons, worked in parallel with the 7th Photo

Group of the U.S. Eighth Air Force and in May 1944 was fully integrated as the 106th Reconnaissance Group, operating with four squadrons of Spitfires and Mosquitoes under the supervision of the Joint Photographic Reconnaissance Committee.

ROYAL AUSTRALIAN AIR FORCE (RAAF). In July 1941, the Royal Australian Air Force established a signals intelligence organization, the Central Bureau, at Victoria Barracks in Melbourne, which was supplied with intercepted Japanese traffic collected from a station at Darwin. The following year, another intercept site was established in two houses in the Pimlico suburb of Townsville, in northern Queensland, and the two stations were renamed RAAF 1 and 2 Wireless Units.

RYAN 147. Known to the **U.S.** Air Force as Lightning Bugs, the Ryan 147 was an unmanned **drone** deployed during the Vietnam War from DC-130 aircraft. Operated by the 408th Reconnaissance Wing from Bien Hoa under the codename BLUE SPRINGS, the Ryan 147 was designated as the AQM-34 and replaced **U-2**s in missions when North Vietnam acquired improved SA-2 missiles. These high-risk flights were codenamed COMPASS COOKIE and UNITED EFFORT, and some 200 aircraft were shot down over enemy territory.

The drones were also flown over **China** and **North Korea** from Osan, and at the conclusion of their flights dropped to the ground on a parachute for recovery by helicopter. Later versions of the jet-powered aircraft, known as the Buffalo Hunter, flew at altitudes of 70,000 feet with a cruising speed of 435 miles per hour.

The Ryan Aeronautical Company had pioneered the development of pilotless Firebee target drones, and the Firefly was an intelligence-collection version that became operational in May 1962, in the 4080th Strategic Reconnaissance Wing. During the early stages of the **Cuban missile crisis**, General Robert Breitweiser, the Air Force's chief of intelligence, recommended the use of a Firefly over the island, but his suggestion was rejected.

– S –

SAMOS. U.S. Air Force codename for a video satellite system developed in 1960 and subsequently abandoned because of the poor picture resolution and the success of **CORONA**.

SATELLITES. Since October 1957, when the first *Sputnik* went into orbit, satellites have been launched in primarily reconnaissance and communications roles, and in 2006 there were some 2,700 nonmilitary satellites circling the earth. Satellites range in size from very big systems, supported by large solar panels, down to the latest miniaturized nanosatellites designed to destroy other target satellites in the event of a terrestrial conflict.

Satellites have played the major post–**World War II** role in air intelligence because they have fulfilled three vital functions. First, they have provided accurate information from denied areas, and have collected data on military installations, weapons, industrial production, and even agricultural land use. Second, in military terms, satellites effectively eliminated the possibility in the **Cold War** of a surprise attack. Third, they offer an opportunity to verify obligations made under arms control agreements.

During the Cold War, the **United States** intelligence satellites collected imagery and signals, and from August 1960, their activities were controlled by the **National Reconnaissance Office** (NRO). Initially, the first imagery satellites returned their exposed films in jettisoned canisters that were retrieved as they descended by parachute, but from December 1976 the data were transmitted in digital form via a communications satellite in a higher orbit to a ground station, thereby allowing (with a 20-second delay for transmission) almost instantaneous access to the imagery on electronic screens, from which prints could be taken. This breakthrough was achieved by the **KEY-HOLE** series, first launched in 1959, with the KH-11 being the first to download the imagery in digital form. The sixth generation of KEYHOLE platforms was the KH-12, a 32,000-pound satellite designed to be delivered into orbit by the space shuttle and carrying 6,500 pounds of hydrazine fuel to maneuver it into the correct position.

The NRO's signals intelligence platforms began with the **RHYO-LITE**, which was replaced in June 1979 with the **CHALET** system, later renamed **VORTEX**, and the ARGOS, the AR designation meaning "Advanced RHYOLITE." Their precise purpose and capabilities remain classified, and the true roles of platforms such as JUMPSEAT can only be guessed at, based on their orbits and performance. Nevertheless, these signals intelligence systems undertake orthodox collection functions, ranging from monitoring radar station emissions to verifying treaty compliance, to the interception of telemetry, radio, and other communications traffic. *See also* BYEMAN; SOVIET UNION.

SCHULZE-BOYSEN, HARRO. A senior intelligence analyst at the Reich air ministry in Berlin, Arvid Harnack regularly briefed Reichminister Hermann Göring and routinely read reports submitted to Berlin from German air attachés posted across the world. However, he was also a Soviet spy, having been recruited by the NKVD *rezident* Alexander Korotkov, who had been based at the Soviet embassy under diplomatic cover.

Born into a noble family, Schulze-Boysen married Libertas Eulenburg, a beautiful blonde from an even more aristocratic background, in 1936, two years after he had joined the **Luftwaffe**'s intelligence branch. Codenamed SENIOR, Schulze-Boysen was stationed at Wildpark Werder, near Potsdam, where he collected information for a Communist espionage network headed by a close friend, Arvid Harnack, codenamed CORSICAN. The Soviet spy ring, dubbed the Rote Kapelle by its Gestapo investigators, was eventually broken up when the GRU sent an agent from Brussels to reestablish contact with the organization that, after the closure of the Soviet embassy in June 1941, had lost its conduit to Moscow. In August 1941, Anatoli Guryevich received a wireless message instructing him on how to find CORSICAN and SENIOR, and he traveled to Berlin in October to deliver new ciphers, radio schedules, and mailing addresses in Stockholm, Paris, and Brussels. This crucial message was intercepted by the Funkabwehr but not decrypted until July 1942, just two weeks after Johann Wenzel, a GRU radio operator, was caught as he communicated with Moscow. From that moment, the entire network in Germany was doomed, for the German cryptographers were able to read Guryevich's signal and quickly identified CORSICAN as Arvid Harnack and SENIOR as Schulze-Boysen, and they were promptly arrested. A week later, Libertas was also arrested by the Gestapo as she attempted to leave Berlin by train.

By March 1943, 129 suspects had been taken into custody, of whom 19 were women, who were sentenced to death for a variety of crimes, ranging from war treason to the distribution of subversive leaflets, and the Schulze-Boysens were executed in Plotzensee prison. *See also* WORLD WAR II.

SCUD. The principal Soviet-supplied ballistic missile system, with Scud-B and Scud-C variants, the Scud was launched operationally during the Yom Kippur War in 1973, the eight-year Iran-Iraq War, the Soviet occupation of **Afghanistan**, and Operation **DESERT STORM**. In 1986, as the **United States** confronted Libya, Iraq fired a single Scud-B at the North Atlantic Treaty Organization air base at Lampedusa, Italy. All these launches were monitored by satellite early-warning systems linked to Cheyenne Mountain, Colorado. *See also* SOVIET UNION.

SEELÖWE. The German codename for the planned invasion of England in 1940, Royal Air Force **Photographic Reconnaissance Unit** flights discovered an armada of 1,700 enemy barges and 200 ships massing in Antwerp and Amsterdam in July 1940 and monitored their movement to Ostend and the Channel ports, before they dispersed as the project was abandoned. *See also* WORLD WAR II.

SEETAKT. German codename for a precision naval search **radar** built by the Gema company and used on warships and coastal batteries during **World War II**.

SEMIPALATINSK. The Soviet nuclear test site in the remote desert 100 miles south of Semipalatinsk in Kazakhstan was the location of the first Soviet atomic explosion on 29 August 1949. Codenamed POLIGON, the site included a 165-foot tower on which the weapon was detonated in a test codenamed PERVAYA MOLNIYA (MORNING LIGHT). Dust particles were carried 3,000 miles eastward where they were detected by **U.S.** high-altitude air-sampling aircraft, components of Operation **FITZWILLIAM**. The bomb had been constructed from plutonium developed in a reactor near Sverdlovsk, an exact replica of the Hanford 305 reactor. *See also* SOVIET UNION.

SENIOR BOOK. U.S. Air Force codename for **U-2** signals intelligence collection missions flown along the Chinese border by the 349th Strategic Reconnaissance Squadron from Takhli, a base near U-Tapao in Thailand between 1970 and 1978.

SENIOR BOWL. U.S. Air Force codename for a long-range, air-launched high-altitude reconnaissance **drone** developed by Lockheed as the D-21 that was the result of a 1963 classified contract code-named TAGBOARD. SENIOR BOWL, intended to fly at 90,000 feet after being dropped from an adapted B-52, was operational for two years from 1969, but experienced technical problems that could not be overcome.

SENIOR RUBY. U.S. Air Force codename for ELINT operations conducted from Turkey by **U-2R** aircraft in the 1970s.

SEOUL OLYMPICS. In an effort to disrupt the South Korean presidential elections and the Olympic Games scheduled to be opened in Seoul in September 1988, North Korean agents flew on KAL 858 from Baghdad to Abu Dhabi in November 1987, leaving explosives in a bottle of liqueur and a detonator linked to a timer in an overhead compartment. As the plane flew on to Seoul, the bomb destroyed the aircraft and killed all 115 aboard. The two North Korean agents responsible for planting the device were arrested but one, Kim Sung Il, age 70, swallowed cyanide and died while his companion, Kim Hyon Hui, age 26, confessed and in December 1987 was extradited to Seoul. In a statement made in January 1988, she revealed that they had been trained to act as Japanese tourists by an abducted person, Megumi Yakota, who had been seized from her home by North Korean agents in Japan in 1977 when she had been age 13. Kim Hyon Hui claimed that she had been briefed on her mission by Kim Jong Il, son of the North Korean president.

SEVEROMORSK. The site of the Soviet Red Banner Northern Fleet's main munitions storage depot, Severomorsk is north of Murmansk in the Kola Peninsula and experienced a huge explosion in May 1984 that was monitored by a **KH-11** satellite. Comparison with earlier imagery, taken in July 1979, showed the extent of the blast that was estimated to have killed up to 400 technicians, some of whom had attempted to disarm weapons before they detonated in a chain reaction. Fires raged for many hours and analysts later reported that among the weapons destroyed were 580 SA-N-1 and SA-N-3 missiles; 320 SS-N-3 and SS-N-12 missiles; 80 SS-N-22 nuclear-capable missiles; an unknown quantity of SS-N-19 antiship missiles; and some SA-N-6 and SA-N-7 antiaircraft missiles. The scale of the loss had a significant impact on the operational effectiveness of the Red Banner Fleet. *See also* SOVIET UNION.

SHADOW. An **unmanned aerial vehicle** deployed by the U.S. Army, the Shadow 200 has a payload of 330 pounds and has a surveillance and artillery-spotting role, operating at an altitude of 10,000 feet for up to five hours. It has been deployed in Iraq and over the demilitarized zone in Korea.

SHELL HOUSE RAID. On 18 February 1945, a low-level raid was mounted on the Gestapo headquarters in Copenhagen, which were located in Shell House, by 18 Mosquito Mk VIs of 140 Wing flying from **Royal Air Force** Fersfield. Escorted by 31 Mustangs of 64, 126, and 234 Squadrons from Bentwaters, the raiders reached Copenhagen shortly before midday, a time when the planners from the Danish Section of Special Operations Executive believed most of the Germans would be at their desks. Accordingly to Svend Truelsen, who briefed the aircrews, the raid was essential because so much of the local resistance leadership had been caught by the Gestapo and the entire movement was in danger of collapse. He explained that following other raids the Germans had imprisoned their detainees in cells under the roof, but as they all expected to be executed anyway, they preferred to die in an Allied raid rather than by Nazi bullets.

As the raid began, the lead aircraft, flying at rooftop level and armed with two 500-pound bombs, collided with a mast and crashed close to a school that caught fire when the Mosquito's bombs exploded, killing 86 Danish children and 10 of their teachers. A further 67 children were injured, and the Mosquito's pilot and navigator were killed. Confused by the fire, two of the aircraft in the second wave dropped their bombs on the school, adding to the casualties.

Altogether, nine of the aircrew failed to return to base and six of the Gestapo's prisoners died in the attack. Several others escaped, and between 100 to 200 Germans and Danish collaborators were killed. The toll on the Gestapo was not as great as expected because most of the senior personnel were attending the funeral of a colleague who had shot himself. *See also* WORLD WAR II.

SIGNAL CORPS. In November 1942, the U.S. Army's Signal Corps established the 1st Radio Squadron Mobile (RSM) and recruited second-generation Japanese, known as Nisei, to intercept enemy wireless and voice traffic in the Pacific. The 1st RSM was posted to Australia and then landed at Tacloban Bay on Leyte in the Philippines before moving up to Luzon, where two C-54s were made available for airborne interception operations over Formosa and Kyushu.

Having also trained at Camp Pinedale, near Fresno, the 8th RSM was posted in November 1944 to Guam and flew signals intelligence flights in modified Army Air Corps RB-24 Liberators, with their nose gun turrets removed, before moving to Palau, Saipan, and Iwo Jima in March 1945. Both units were disbanded at the end of 1945 when the Army Security Agency was created out of the Army Signal Security Agency, but were reestablished in 1948 when the **Air Force Security Service** was formed.

SINAH-1. This Russian-built satellite, weighing 275 pounds, was launched into space by a Kosmos-3M rocket from Plesetsk for the Iranians in October 2005. Placed into orbit 600 miles above the earth, circling the globe 14 times a day, it boasts a resolution of 150 feet. As Iran's first reconnaissance satellite, its launch had a strategic significance in the region, especially for Israel. The Sinah-1 was the first of a series of Russian satellites contracted by Iran, the next being the Zohreh ("Venus") and Mesbah ("Lantern") telecommunications systems.

SIX DAY WAR. In June 1967, the Israelis launched a preemptive attack on Egypt after the Straits of Tiran at the entrance to the Gulf of Aqaba were closed by President Abdel Nasser. The blockade prevented Israeli access to the Red Sea, so the Israeli Air Force struck simultaneously against the Egyptian, Jordanian, and Syrian airfields. All together, 304 of 419 Egyptian aircraft were destroyed on the ground, 53 of 112 Syrian planes, and the entire Jordanian force of 28 aircraft. The day after the raids, a telephone conversation between the Egyptian president and King Hussein of Jordan was intercepted in which the former asserted that the attack had been made by British and American planes in collusion with the Israelis. The conflict lasted six days and remains a model of the effective collection and exploitation of air intelligence.

SKUNK WORKS. The nickname of Lockheed's Special Projects Division, located at a secure compound at Sunnyvale, next to Burbank Airport, California, the Skunk Works was where many of the most secret American aircraft were designed and built, including the **U-2** and the **SR-71**. The legendary director of the site was Clarence "Kelly" Johnson.

SLICK CHICK. U.S. Air Force codename for the RF-100 supersonic photoreconnaissance fighter introduced in May 1955 at Bitburg, West Germany. Three of the aircraft flew operations until July 1958 when Detachment 1, 7407th Support Squadron, was disbanded.

SLOW WALKER. Codename of a **satellite** infrared sensor that was designed in the mid-1980s in the **United States** to detect the telltale flares associated with ballistic missile launches, which was found to be effective at tracking the Soviet Tu-22 Backfire bomber in flight.

SNIFDEN. High-altitude air sampling missions flown to detect the radioactive residue from Soviet atomic tests conducted on Novaya Zembya were known by the crews that flew the Boeing WB-29s of the 72nd Reconnaissance Squadron as "snifden." A "weather flight" from this squadron returned to Alaska with traces of the first Soviet atomic test conducted in August 1949. *See also* SOVIET UNION.

SOFT TOUCH. The **Central Intelligence Agency** codename for a series of **U-2** overflights of nuclear production centers and test sites in Soviet Central Asia and Siberia that began in August 1957. They included the test site at **Semipalatinsk**, a huge gaseous diffusion plant at Tomsk, and the launch area of **Tyuratam**.

SONNIE. The codename for a U.S. Office of Strategic Services (OSS) operation to evacuate 2,000 Norwegian refugees from neutral Sweden, commencing in March 1944, and fly them via Scotland to training camps in Canada. Altogether, 80,000 Scandinavians and a further 150,000 refugees from neighboring Baltic countries had found asylum in Sweden, and the OSS plan was to enable some of them to join the Allied forces. The airlift was led by a famous arctic aviator, Bernt

Balchen, who had acquired American citizenship following his participation in several of Richard Byrd's pioneering flights across the poles. The flights, completed by unarmed B-17s and B-24 Liberators, took place daily between **Royal Air Force** Leuchars and Stockholm's Bromma airport. Balchen's principal contact in Sweden was Dr. Harry Soederman, the director of the Criminal Institute, who in 1944 arranged for the wreckage of a V-2 to be loaded aboard a C-47 for examination at Farnborough. *See also* PEENEMÜNDE; WORLD WAR II.

SON-2. Soviet designation of an early gun-laying radar, copied from the British Mark 2 design, that had entered service in England in 1940. In 1951, ELINT operators of the 91st Strategic Reconnaissance Squadron detected the telltale signals of the SON-2 defending Pyongyang in Korea.

SOUTH AFRICA. The Republic of South Africa's impressive aerial reconnaissance capability, dependent on 20 Albatross maritime reconnaissance aircraft, undertook the task of monitoring shipping around the Cape throughout the **Cold War**. The planes were deployed from the Winfield South African Air Force Base north of Cape Town at Fort Ikapa and relayed intercepted wireless traffic to the South African Navy's underground facility at Silver Mine, where analysts accommodated in a bunker three levels below the surface identified all shipping in the region and passed encrypted communications to a separate office, designated as Room 100, where they came under cryptographic attack.

SOUTHERN AIR TRANSPORT (SAT). A proprietary air charter company owned since 1960 by the **Central Intelligence Agency** (CIA) with offices in **Taiwan** and Miami, SAT operated until 1973 and was financed by loans made from other CIA fronts, including Cactus Technology and **Air America**. SAT was intended to operate in Latin America, but lack of demand by the CIA enabled it to undertake regular commercial business. In October 1986, an SAT C-123 was shot down over Nicaragua, killing the pilot, William Cooper, and his copilot, Wallace "Buzz" Sawyer. One of five CIA air crews based in Hopango, El Salvador, flying C-123s and a pair of Caribous, they had been making air-drops to the Nicaraguan contras when they had been brought down by a shoulder-fired Sandinista missile. Like the dropmaster, Eugene Hasenfus, who survived the crash by using his parachute, they were CIA contractors and ex–Air America.

SOVIET UNION. During **World War II**, the Soviet Union was the subject of intensive aerial reconnaissance by the Luftwaffe, which produced imagery-based maps for the other fighting services that were used following BARBAROSSA in June 1941. This imagery subsequently fell into American hands and provided the basis of **Cold War** targeting data. Of particular interest were atomic facilities at Beloyarsk, Cholyabinsk, Semipalatinsk, and Troitsk; Red Fleet bases at Lokanga, Petropavlovsk, and Vladivostock; shipyards at Nikolayev, Novolitovsk, and Severodvinsk; and missile production and test centers at Plesetsk, Tyuratam, Sary Shagan, and Vladimirovska.

During the Cold War, Tupolev Bear air reconnaissance flights would enter the U.S. Aerospace Defense Identification Zone, which extends 200 miles into the Atlantic, up to 70 times a year in "fence-testing" exercises, intended to monitor American response times. In the 30 years following 1961, Soviet intruders were intercepted in American airspace on 306 occasions, although no shots were ever fired. Toward the end of the Cold War the statistics escalated, with 33 incidents recorded in 1987 and 15 in 1991. Soviet reconnaissance aircraft also operated in the Mediterranean from an airbase at Mersa Matruh, flying Tu-16 Badgers, Il-38 Mays, and Beriev Be-12s on missions over the U.S. 6th Fleet, until the Soviet expulsion from Egypt in July 1972. After 1975, Soviet long-range reconnaissance aircraft were based at former American military airfields at Cam Ramh Bay and Da Nang in Vietnam.

SPECIAL DUTIES SQUADRONS. Royal Air Force personnel selected for clandestine operations during **World War II** were assigned initially to 419 Flight at North Weald to fly Lysanders into Nazi-occupied France. In September 1940, 419 Flight moved to Stapleford Abbots and in October 1940, to Royal Air Force Stradishall in Suffolk, where it was equipped with three Whitley bombers. This unit later became 138 (Special Duties) Squadron and in August 1941, 161 (Special Duties) Squadron was formed at Rowley Miles, Newmarket.

In April 1942, 138 and 161 Squadrons were transferred to Royal Air Force Tempsford in Bedfordshire and became known as the "**Moon Squadrons**" because of the flights to Europe undertaken by the light of the full moon.

SPUTNIK. The first Soviet **satellite** placed into orbit was the *Sputnik-1*, on 4 October 1957, which weighed 184 pounds. Although the technical achievement was considerable, *Sputnik-2*, launched three weeks later, was of far more strategic significance because the payload was 1,119 pounds, more than enough for a nuclear warhead. In May 1957, *Spunik-3* weighed two and a half tons. In contrast, the closest American competitor was the relatively puny Atlas, which was only half as powerful.

The unexpected launch of *Sputnik* had a profound impact on the **U.S.** government, which reacted by altering the country's education policy to encourage more engineers. *See also* SOVIET UNION.

SQUARE DEAL. **Central Intelligence Agency** codename for a **U-2** overflight of **Tyuratam** from Peshawar in April 1960. Mission 4155's route took the aircraft over Sary Shagan, the nuclear test site at **Semipalatinsk**, and the nuclear storage area at Dolon. Although a pair of Su-9 fighters were scrambled to intercept the U-2C over Mary, they never came close to its improved altitude of 74,000 feet and the pilot, Bob Ericson, landed safely at Zahedan in Iran after a flight lasting six hours.

SR-71. Official designation of the **Blackbird**, the prefix "SR" being the abbreviation of strategic reconnaissance.

SS-6. Designated as the Sapwood by the North Atlantic Treaty Organization, the SS-6 was the first Soviet inter-continental ballistic missile and was launched at Tyuratam successfully at the third attempt on 15 May 1957. Known to the Soviets as the R-7, one of its five booster rockets failed 98 seconds into the flight, and the **inter-continental ballistic missile** (ICBM) crashed to the ground 400 kilometers downrange. A second SS-6 failed to launch three times on 10 and 11 June and was removed from the pad. A third was launched on 12 July, but self-destructed after 38 seconds. A fourth was launched on 21 August, but the dummy warhead separated from the second stage as the rocket reentered the atmosphere.

In November 1959, the **Central Intelligence Agency** issued a National Security Estimate that suggested that there had been about 18 SS-6 test launches, of which a high proportion had reached the Klyuchi impact area on the Kamchatka Peninsula, and on that basis it was believed that 10 ICBMs would be operational by January 1960. The deployment of the SS-6 was relatively easy to monitor because it was so large it could only be delivered to its launch sites by rail.

STARFISH. British codename for decoy fires that were ignited during German air raids in December 1940 to attract enemy bombers from their real targets in England. In the first attempt, made on 2 December 1940 as the **Luftwaffe** attacked Bristol, 66 high explosive bombs were dropped on the STARFISH site, which established the countermeasure. The **Royal Air Force**'s 80 Wing supervised 27 sites and employed 2,000 personnel on STARFISH operations.

STEALTH. The combination of low **radar** signature design and infrared suppression in the construction of aircraft is colloquially known as stealth technology, most dramatically demonstrated by the futuristic Lockheed F-117A Nighthawk that was test flown in June 1981 after three years of development. The objective of stealth is to make an aircraft virtually undetectable to hostile radar systems, and although this aim was achieved by the single-seater Nighthawk, one aircraft was lost through random ground fire while participating in a raid on Belgrade during the North Atlantic Treaty Organization's Operation ALLIED FORCE in March 1999. The aircraft, flying from the 49th Fighter Wing at Holloman Air Force Base, New Mexico, also made significant contributions to DESERT STORM in 1991 and IRAQI FREEDOM in 2003.

Stealth technology is a result of detailed knowledge of hostile air defense systems, and therefore itself becomes a significant target for intelligence agencies. In June 1981, a Polish intelligence officer, **Marian W. Zacharsky**, was arrested in California while suborning an avionics engineer to sell him stealth secrets.

STINGER. The shoulder-held, infrared heat-seeking missile manufactured at Poloma, California, by General Dynamics, turned the tide in Afghanistan during the Soviet occupation. The decision to arm the Mujahideen resistance with the weapon was authorized by NSDD-66, President Ronald Reagan's National Security Decision Directive, which offered the hard-pressed guerrillas support by "all means available," which came to mean selling an initial 400 missiles to the Saudis (who had asked for three times that number) and arranging (with President Zia's consent, obtained by DCI William Casey personally in January 1986) for their onward transmission to the Mujahideen (after 100 had been retained for use by the Pakistanis, together with some air-to-air Sidewinders, to protect against the threat of Soviet retaliatory incursions). The deployment of the Stinger meant a significant change from the established policy of only supplying non-U.S. government hardware, but the main objection had come from the U.S. Army, which argued, long but finally unsuccessfully, that foreign sales would compromise the technology and deplete their own stock of 3,000 weapons.

The arguments against deployment diminished when a GRU defector, Sergei Bokhan, revealed that the Stinger's technology had already been acquired by the Soviets. The GRU's deputy *rezident* in Athens until May 1985, Bokhan confirmed that the Stinger's design and components had been compromised and were to be copied to manufacture a clone, later designated as the SAM-14.

The Stingers would drive the Hind gunships from the skies, destroying an estimated 350 Soviet aircraft, with the losses running at one point in the conflict to one a day. The official **Central Intelligence Agency** (CIA) statistics, based on verified intelligence from satellite imagery, show 269 helicopter kills in 340 engagements, which amounts to an astonishing attrition ratio of 79 percent.

The first consignment of 200 Stinger grip stocks was delivered via Dhahran in July 1996, and they were deployed to engage a flight of eight Hind gunships coming in to land at Jalalabad's airfield on 25 September. Although the missiles had a ceiling of around 10,000 feet, these targets were low and slow, at an altitude of 4,500 feet and a range of 7,500 feet, entirely unable to outrun the warheads closing at 1,200 miles per hour, and wholly unprepared to drop decoy flares or other countermeasures. Three of the helicopters were destroyed and the others abandoned their approach and fled the scene, which was recorded on videotape by an excited Mujahideen. The CIA acquired excellent imagery of the still-smoking wreckage, taken by a **KH-11 KEYHOLE** reconnaissance satellite that passed overhead soon after the incident.

According to the after-combat reports received in Pakistan, and subsequently confirmed by comparison of the satellite imagery of the individual hits and the video footage taken by the guerrillas, the first 187 missiles downed an astonishing 150 aircraft. Hitherto, the ancient SAM-7, the Milan, and the Chinese wire-guided Red Arrow antitank missiles had accounted for less than 10 percent of Soviet air losses, most of which had been hit on the ground in surprise rocket attacks on vulnerable airbases. The SAM-7 was especially unpopular as it was heavy to handle, tended to cause casualties by backfiring, and trailed a very distinctive telltale white plume that threatened to precisely identify the firing position and also allowed a quick-witted pilot to spot the threat and take evading action. As for the unwieldy British Blowpipe, manufactured by Short Brothers in Belfast, which had performed so badly in the Falklands, it confirmed its reputation as a highly dangerous weapon. It posed the biggest threat to the gunner who carried it and was expected to keep an approaching target in his optical sights, remotely guiding the missile to impact by transmitting course adjustments by radio.

The Soviets, so widely perceived as aggressors in Afghanistan, were powerless to retaliate, and their initial response was to limit their sorties to night operations. This gave them a brief respite, but the carnage continued when the CIA distributed night vision image-intensifying equipment to the Mujahideen. From that moment, the pilots were on the defensive, making their bombing runs from high altitude, well above 10,000 to 12,000 feet, and thereby abandoning accuracy. The alternative was low-level, high-speed approaches, but the terrain made such tactics highly dangerous and very unpopular with aircrews, who suffered more accidents and even found themselves under attack from machine guns and RPG-7s sited above them. The Stinger's effectiveness was quickly reflected in the casualty statistics. In 1985, 2,013 Soviet military operations resulted in 13 Afghan deaths per 1,000 of the population. Two years later, the operations had increased to 4,450, but the deaths had fallen to just nine per 1,000.

By the time the Soviets started to withdraw in mid-May 1988, the CIA's Afghan budget had reached $700 million and a total of 900 Stinger missiles had been shipped to the docks in Karachi on non-U.S. cargo vessels or flown into the Pakistani airbase at Chaklala from Dhahran.

STRATOCRUISER. The EC-97G was the electronic reconnaissance version of the Boeing Stratocruiser bomber and was based until 1976 with the **U.S.** Air Force's 7405th Combat Support Squadron at Wiesbaden. It was then replaced by C-130A-Hs of the 7406th, operating from Rhein-Main.

STRELA. Soviet codename for a clandestine **satellite** communications system used to relay messages to and from KGB illegals, agents who had been infiltrated into the **United States** to remain dormant as sleepers until deployed on missions to sabotage American military facilities in the event of hostilities.

SUEZ CRISIS. The political crisis created when **Egypt**'s President Abdel Gamal Nasser nationalized the Suez Canal in August 1956 concluded in the Anglo-French invasion in October, but in the meantime three distinct air intelligence operations were undertaken. The first, by the French, was to supply the Israelis with 60 Mystere fighters, although only a sale of 12 was publicly declared. Both the French and the Israelis recognized that recent Egyptian purchases of Soviet equipment from Czechoslovakia were the precursor to an inevitable war in the Middle East, so Marcel Dassault restored the balance of air power in breach of a United Nations ban on the sale of weapons in the region. The **Central Intelligence Agency** (CIA) discovered the size of the new Israeli Air Force when the country was overflown by a **U-2** on 29 August 1956. Shortly before the offensive, further French jets were flown to Israel via Cyprus to participate in the conflict, but only after the pilots had been issued with bogus Israeli identity papers and their planes had been repainted.

Shortly before hostilities commenced between Israel and Egypt in October 1956, the Israelis learned that much of the Egyptian general staff was visiting **Syria**, and when one of the Il-28s carrying the senior officers from Damascus to Cairo was over the Mediterranean it was attacked and destroyed at night by an Israeli Gloster Meteor. The Egyptians assumed that their aircraft had been lost in an accident as no public statement was made about the incident in Israel for 50 years.

SYRIA. As a front-line Arab state equipped almost exclusively with Soviet weaponry, Syria has provided Israel and Western air intelligence agencies with the opportunity to match air defense systems and thereby acquire vital information with a wider relevance. During a dogfight over Damascus in April 1967, six Syrian MiGs were shot down by Israeli fighters. During the Yom Kippur War in October 1973, the Israelis lost six Phantoms in one day in a futile effort to eliminate Syria's deadly SA-6 batteries. A plan, codenamed DOUG-MAN V, had been prepared for the elimination of Syria's SA-6 launchers in a preemptive strike, but by the time the planes were airborne, delayed a vital day by low cloud cover, the highly mobile SA-6 launchers had moved, and only two out of 30 launchers were destroyed, for the loss or capture of 12 aircrew. However, the Syrians soon expended their stock of missiles and were forced to rely on SA-2s and SA-3s, for which the Israelis had developed effective countermeasures. When the Soviets declined to resupply the Syrians, the northern offensive faltered and Israeli troops captured the strategic Golan Heights.

In June 1982, during the Israeli invasion of **Lebanon**, 17 out of Syria's 19 SA-6 sites were destroyed in a single strike, and so were 29 Mig-21 and Mig-23s sent to defend them. On the second day of attacks, Syria's last two SA-6 sites were demolished and another four replacements were eliminated a week later, along with three batteries of advanced SA-8s, with their LAND ROLL radars, that were hastily deployed into the Bekaa Valley. By the time the cease-fire was declared on 12 June, 80 Syrian jets had been shot down, for the loss of a single Israeli A-4 Skyhawk and two helicopters, brought down by ground fire.

Since the cessation of hostilities, a proxy conflict has been fought, with the Syrians depending on Hezbollah forces mounting attacks on Israel from southern **Lebanon**.

– T –

TAIWAN. Since the air battle of July 1958 over Quemoy, when Chinese MiG-17 Shenyangs were mauled by F-86F Sabres, American reconnaissance aircraft have been based continuously at Taoyuan, near Taipei, to patrol the Straits of Formosa. Initially, three Martin RB-57D were deployed in Nationalist livery, until October 1959, when one was shot down by a MiG-19. In 1962, the RB-57s were withdrawn and replaced by **U-2s**. Although no exact statistics are available, up to nine U-2s, three RB-57s, and two RF-101s flown from Hsinchu were lost over the mainland. The first U-2 lost was an aircraft that failed to return from a mission over Nanchang in September 1962. Another crashed near Shanghai in September 1962, and others were lost in November 1963, July 1964, January 1965, and September 1967, probably to SA-2 missiles. Two **Central Intelligence Agency**–trained pilots, Major Ye Changi and Major Zhang Liyi, were captured and "rehabilitated." The wreckage of four aircraft, equipped with long-range oblique cameras, were put on public display in Beijing in April 1965. The CIA's Taiwanese pilots, known as "black bats," flew an estimated 800 clandestine missions between 1953 and 1967.

The U-2Rs were flown by Taiwanese pilots until October 1974, when the remaining aircraft were returned to the **United States** at Davis-Monthan Air Force Base. *See also* CHINA, PEOPLE'S REPUBLIC OF.

TALENT-KEYHOLE (TK). The **U.S.** intelligence community codename for special compartmented intelligence originating from aircraft and **satellites**. Personnel with the need to access this source require a TK clearance that authorizes them to study the relevant imagery or signals intelligence intercepts. *See also* BYEMAN.

TAXABLE. British codename for a **D-Day** deception scheme perpetrated by 617 Squadron, which distributed **WINDOW** above the English Channel off Cap d'Antifer to simulate the appearance of a large air armada.

TAYLOR, CHARLES E. The U.S. air attaché attending the annual May Day parade in Red Square in 1955, Colonel Charles Taylor counted 28 of the new Myasishchev M-4 Molot Bison bombers in the fly-past. His report heightened fears of a "**bomber gap**," although subsequently it was alleged that he had simply seen the same bombers circle twice and participate in the show as part of a deliberate deception campaign to exaggerate the true numbers of Soviet strategic bombers. Whether Taylor was duped or made an accurate observation remains controversial and unresolved. In the mistaken belief that the Soviets had embarked on a crash program to manufacture the four-jet intercontinental bomber, the **Central Intelligence Agency** estimated that 50 would have been built by the end of 1957 and 250 would be in service by mid-1959.

TEAL AMBER. U.S. Air Force codename for a powerful space telescope located at Malabar in Florida, which monitors satellites in orbit. A similar system at Mount Haleakala on Maui is codenamed TEAL BLUE.

TECHSTAR. An advanced Israeli satellite equipped with synthetic aperture **radar** that is planned to give Tel Aviv a photoreconnaissance capability at night and through cloud cover.

TELECOMMUNICATIONS RESEARCH ESTABLISHMENT (TRE). The wartime center of British **radar** research, the Telecommunications Research Establishment was transferred from its vulnerable site at Swanage to Malvern College in 1942 in anticipation of a retaliatory raid following Operation **BITING** to Bruneval. The TRE was the center of much innovation, including the Brock's rocket designed by Sam Devons, which was deployed on merchantmen in the Channel to force enemy aircraft to fly at over 1,000 feet, an altitude where they could be spotted by radar. This invention, though of limited effectiveness as a means of defense for shipping, proved to be a noisy and highly visible weapon that achieved its objective of persuading low-flying raiders to gain height and become visible on radar.

TELINT. The abbreviation for telemetry intelligence, TELINT consists of the downrange performance information transmitted from rockets during test firings. The data include engine thrust, burn time, fuel consumption, heading, and altitude, all vital statistics for technicians and analysts alike. Before going into production, an **intercontinental ballistic missile** (ICBM) probably requites 20 or 30 test firings.

When the first SS-6 was on the launch pad preparing for the test conducted on 3 August 1957 at Tyuratam, the rocket was photographed by the **U-2**, and when the firing occurred the TELINT was intercepted by a **U.S. Air Force Security Service** station at Karamursel in Turkey. Later tests were monitored by new intercept facilities built at Trabzon and Samsun. There were two Soviet ICBM tests in 1957 and two *Sputnik* launches, but after the launch of *Sputnik-3* in May 1958, there were no further test launches until 1959. *See also* SOVIET UNION.

THOMAS, DENNIS. A **Central Intelligence Agency** contractor, Dennis Thomas was shot dead by FARC guerrillas in February 2003 when his Cessna Hk-1116 experienced mechanical problems during a flight from Bogota to the U.S. Special Forces base at Larandia. The aircraft, on a routine antinarcotics surveillance flight, landed at a jungle airstrip controlled by members of the FARC's notorious Teofilo Forero, who shot Dennis and a Colombian, Sergeant Jose Luis Cruz, and seized three other American passengers as hostages. By the time troops reached the clearing to find the aircraft, the FARC guerrillas had disappeared with their three prisoners.

THUNDERBOLT. German **Luftwaffe** codename for an operation conducted in February 1942 to provide an air screen of 280 fighters for the covert daylight movement of three cruisers, the *Scharnhorst*, *Gneisenau*, and *Prinz Eugen*, from Brest up the English Channel to **Wilhelmshaven**. British **radar** stations along the south coast were swamped with jamming signals, and the huge convoy of the three warships and their escorts were not spotted until 1030, when a pair of Spitfires on routine patrol accidentally encountered enemy fighters. The information, which was not reported by the pilots until they had landed because of the need to maintain radio silence, was confirmed at 1233 by Royal Navy motor torpedo boats (MTB) from Dover that were engaged by Kriegsmarine E-boats. The first air attack occurred soon afterward, when six ancient Swordfish biplanes, escorted by 10

Spitfires, attempted to launch their torpedoes but were shot out of the sky. Of 18 aircrew, only five survived to be picked up by MTBs. At 1530, the *Scharnhorst* struck a mine, one of more than 100 laid in its path by the **Royal Air Force** (RAF) and was delayed temporarily, but was soon under way, and her escorts beat off a raid by three RAF bombers and also an attack from HMS *Worcester* and four other destroyers from Harwich. A running air battle continued until poor weather closed in, by which time both the *Gneisenau* and the *Scharnhorst* sustained damage from mines but had reached the Kiel Canal. By nightfall, the British had lost 49 aircraft and a destroyer was badly damaged, while the German losses amounted to a single E-boat and 17 fighters.

The episode was an embarrassing failure of air intelligence for the British and a considerable success for the Germans, even if all three ships would later endure further damage at the hands of the RAF. *See also* WORLD WAR II.

TIROS-1. A weather satellite developed by the U.S. National Aeronautical and Space Administration and placed into orbit on 1 April 1960, the Tiros-1 had no obvious intelligence purpose because its cameras produced only low-grade pictures of cloud cover, but the fact that the Kremlin lodged no protest as it passed over the Soviet Union encouraged the Eisenhower administration to accelerate the **CORONA** program.

TIRPITZ. Until the *Tirpitz* was sunk in a Norwegian fjord in November 1944, the German pocket battleship was the fastest, most heavily armed warship afloat and represented a grave danger to Allied shipping on the Atlantic and Arctic convoys. During the first 12 months of the war, the **Royal Air Force** flew 20 photographic reconnaissance (PR) missions to **Wilhelmshaven** to confirm the presence of the *Tirpitz*, which was bombed unsuccessfully on several occasions. The warship then moved to Kiel for sea trials in the Baltic, where there were further ineffective air raids, and in January 1942, a combination of signals analysis and air intelligence showed it sailing to Trondheim. While the *Tirpitz* sheltered in Norway, 14 air raids involving 412 aircraft were mounted, with the loss of 23 aircraft, and in addition, in September 1944, an attack by midget submarines left the bows damaged. In September 1944, the ship was disabled in the Kaa

Fjord by a force of 27 Lancasters flying from Yagodnik, near Archangel in Russia, and was attacked again in October by 39 Lancasters. Finally, on 12 November in Tromso, the ship capsized after being hit by three specially designed Tallboy bombs. Although the precise number of PR flights flown against the *Tirpitz* is impossible to calculate, more were flown against this single enemy warship than any other during the course of the war. *See also* WORLD WAR II.

TOKATY, GRIGORI. A Soviet military intelligence officer and aeronautical engineer, Colonel Grigori Tokaty defected to the British in Germany in 1947 and revealed that the Politburo had decided to develop a long-range bomber capability. Tokaty was resettled in England as Grigori Tokaev and was appointed professor of aeronautical engineering at London University.

TOKEN. The North Atlantic Treaty Organization designation of the Soviet P-20 early-warning and ground-controlled intercept radar, copied from the CPS-6 and introduced into service in 1947. *See also* SOVIET UNION.

TOLKACHEV, ADOLF. A Soviet aviation engineer, Adolf Tolkachev was arrested in June 1985 and convicted of spying for the **Central Intelligence Agency** (CIA). A volunteer spy, Tolkachev was a political dissident who worked for the Research Institute for Radiobuilding, Phastron, and had approached the CIA in Moscow in 1976. He had been run by a legendary case officer, John Guilsher, and his information included details of the MiG-25's improved avionics and the Soviet Identification Friend or Foe. Tolkachev's execution was announced in October 1986. *See also* SOVIET UNION.

TOM-TOM. The **U.S.** Air Force codename for a plan in 1952 to launch an F-84F Thunderflash fighter from under a B-36F bomber. The objective was to enable the smaller aircraft to be carried to its operating area and then be recovered by connecting with a dock. The project, intended to provide a stop-gap reconnaissance capability before the RB-47 came into service, proved too dangerous and was abandoned at the end of 1953.

TOPPER. The **Central Intelligence Agency** codename for a series of four **U-2** overflights into China to collect imagery of Tibet in 1960. The first two were flown successfully on 30 March, but the third mission, on 4 April, resulted in the U-2 crash-landing in Thailand due to fuel starvation.

TOUCHDOWN. **Central Intelligence Agency** codename for a **U-2** overflight, Mission 4125 flown by Martin Knutson from Peshawar in July 1959, to photograph Soviet nuclear facilities in the Urals that had been built in the late 1940s, including the plutonium production site at Kyshtym, a gaseous diffusion plant at Verkh Neyvinsk, and a weapons assembly and storage area at Nizhnaya Tura. His mission ended successfully when he landed at Zahedan in Iran with only 20 gallons of fuel left in his tanks. *See also* SOVIET UNION.

TRIMETROGON. The system of fitting three K-17 cameras in an aircraft, providing two oblique pictures and one vertical, gave photo interpreters unprecedented quality and was pioneered during **World War II**.

TROPIC. The **Central Intelligence Agency** (CIA) codename for an operation conducted in 1952 to drop Formosan agents into eastern Manchuria from a C-47 and a B-17. When the CIA's unmarked C-47, based in Atsugi but flying missions from Seoul, was shot down near Antu in Jilin province on 29 November, two crewmen, Robert C. Snoddy and Norman A. Schwartz, were killed, and 24-year-old Richard G. Fecteau and 27-year-old John T. Downey were captured. They had been attempting to "air-snatch" documents from an agent with a Fulton Sky-Hook but had been lured to the area by messages sent by agents who had been operating under Chinese control.

Two years later, the Chinese announced the conviction of the pair and 11 other Americans, aircrew from a B-29 downed over **Liaoning**, on espionage charges and they remained in Chinese captivity until 9 December 1971 and March 1973 respectively, when they were released over the Lo Wu bridge into Hong Kong. Both were newly recruited CIA officers and under interrogation revealed what information they had, Fecteau having had less than five months' experience in the agency. Downey had joined the CIA from Yale in June 1951 and after three months' training at Fort Benning, Georgia, had been posted to Atsugi.

Between 1951 and 1953, a total of 212 agents were parachuted into mainland China, of whom 101 were killed and 111 captured. The initially unexplained loss of the C-47, which effectively terminated CIA paramilitary operations in **China**, was a result of the capture of the team of agents, led by Chang Tsai-Wen, which had been inserted in July after training on Saipan. The plane had been lured into a trap while attempting to exfiltrate Li Chub-ying, who had been delivered the previous month on an inspection mission. *See also* CHINA, PEOPLE'S REPUBLIC OF; TAIWAN.

TUNISIAN RAID. On 1 October 1985, the Israeli Air Force pulled off an astonishing coup when 10 F-15s flew 1,280 miles across the Mediterranean to attack the Palestine Liberation Organization's (PLO) headquarters at Hammam el-Shat, having been refueled by 707 tankers. The bold raid killed 47 PLO personnel and injured 56, but Yasser Arafat narrowly escaped death as he had left the Force 17 building only a few minutes before it was destroyed by a bomb. The beach resort, 13 miles east of Tunis, had accommodated the PLO following its evacuation from Beirut in 1982, and clearly had been thoroughly surveyed by the Israelis in preparation for the raid.

TUPOLOV TU-4. Copied from one of the three **U.S.** Army Air Force B-29 Superfortress bombers that were stranded near Vladivostock after making emergency landings during an air raid on Manchuria in July 1944, the Tu-4 was reverse-engineered by Andrei Tupolov's design bureau. The three aircraft were not returned to their base in China, but were dismantled and their components measured and photographed so exact replicas could be reproduced accurately. The only item the Soviets had difficulty in replicating were the aircraft's rubber tires, which subsequently were purchased in the United States.

TUPOLOV-16. Designated as Badger by the North Atlantic Treaty Organization, the Tu-16 variants D, F, and K conducted electronic surveillance, mainly in the Baltic, while the Badger-E was a photoreconnaissance variant. With a crew of seven, the Tu-16 could be refueled in the air, thus extending its range to 4,350 miles. In May 1968, a Badger-F crashed into the Norwegian Sea, having flown at low altitude past the aircraft carrier USS *Essex*. A wingtip hit the sea as the plane's pilot attempted to avoid a helicopter taking off from the USS *Wasp* and cartwheeled out of control. Four of the Soviet crew were killed instantly and a further two were rescued from the sea alive, but later died aboard the carrier.

Another Tu-16 crashed in June 1980 near Sado in the Sea of Japan while attempting to bank at low altitude near the Japanese patrol boat *Nemuro*, which rescued three of the crew of seven.

Badger incursions along the coast of Alaska, mainly from bases at Providenia and Kytrtkyn, became so frequent during the **Cold War** that F-15 fighters were deployed to King Salmon and Galena to ensure early interception over the Bering Straits. *See also* SOVIET UNION.

TUPOLOV TU-22. Designated as Blinder by North Atlantic Treaty Organization, the Tu-22 was a twin-engined supersonic jet flown by the Aviatsiya Voenno Morskova Flota (AVMF) and equipped with six cameras in the bomb bay and deployed mainly against Swedish targets in the Baltic. *See also* SOVIET UNION.

TUPOLOV TU-95. Designated as Bear by the North Atlantic Treaty Organization, the Tu-95 came into service in 1956 as a strategic bomber but was identified in a reconnaissance role for the Soviet Naval Air Service (AVMF) in September 1964 during an exercise codenamed TEAMWORK. With a speed of 500 miles per hour and a ceiling of 41,000 feet, the Tu-95 had a range of 7,700 miles with a payload of 11 tons, but could fly twice that distance without weapons and also boasted an in-flight refueling capability. In 1970, Bear-D and Bear-F aircraft began regular patrols between Murmansk and José Martin airfield in **Cuba**. In August 1976, a Bear-D crashed into the Atlantic, 230 miles off St. John, Newfoundland, with the loss of the entire crew of 10. A salvage operation in September enabled the Red Fleet to recover much of the airframe and the equipment from the ocean floor.

The Tu-94 was later replaced by a variant, the Tu-142, and from 1987 by the **Blackjack**. *See also* SOVIET UNION.

TUPOLOV-126. The Tu-126, designated as Moss by the North Atlantic Treaty Organization, was a military reconnaissance variant of the Tu-114 airliner, equipped with a large radome on the top of the fuselage and operational mainly in the Baltic. In 1985, it was replaced by the Mainstay, a modified Il-76 transport aircraft. *See also* SOVIET UNION.

TUSHINO. Observations made by the U.S. air attaché at Tushino during the annual Soviet Aviation Day celebrations in 1947 led to a miscalculation of the number of **Tupolov Tu-4** bombers in the Red Air Force. The four prop aircraft, designated as Bull by the North Atlantic Treaty Organization, was based on the B-29 and was the first Soviet long-range bomber capable of reaching the United States. *See also* SOVIET UNION.

TWA 800. On 17 July 1996, Trans World Airlines flight 800, a Boeing 747 with 230 crew and passengers aboard, blew up near the east coast of Long Island, having taken off minutes earlier from John F. Kennedy International Airport. A lengthy investigation conducted by the U.S. National Transportation Safety Board and the Federal Bureau of Investigation (FBI) concluded that the loss had been an accident caused by an electrical short-circuit in the center fuel tank, which had been filled with hot, volatile vapor. James Kalltrom, who led the FBI's team, ruled out all other theories, including a terrorist attack and a missile fired in the vicinity during a naval exercise.

TYURATAM. The site of a prewar quarry, the **inter-continental ballistic missile** (ICBM) test site at Tyuratam in the Kazakhstan desert was discovered in August 1957 during a **U-2** overflight codenamed **SOFT TOUCH** that mapped the Moscow to Tashkent railway southeast from Aralsk, along the bank of the Syr Darya river. Located at the end of a spur 15 miles into the desert and codenamed TASHKENT-50 by the Soviets, who had commenced its construction in May 1954, it was marked on a **Mil-Geo** map of 1939. Initially, the only launch pad, designated as Launch Complex A, handled all the *Sputnik*, Luna, and ICBM tests, but in 1959, **TOUCHDOWN** found a second site, Launch Complex B, which had been constructed 10 miles to the east, serviced by a new rail link, for the SS-6 Sapwood, known to the Soviets as the Semyorka R-7, which proved to be the model for all future Soviet ICBM launch pads. The SQUARE DEAL overflights in 1960 revealed a third launch pad, Launch Complex C, used to test the SS-7 Saddler. In any public statements, the Soviets often referred to the site as Cosmodrome Baikonur without identifying its location, which is actually 188 miles southeast of the city. Telemetry from the site was monitored by National Security Agency intercept stations at Meshed, Kabkan, and Behshahr in Iran. *See also* SOVIET UNION.

– U –

U-2. Designed in 1954 by Lockheed's **Clarence Johnson** to cruise at an altitude of 70,000 feet at 540 miles per hour (or Mach 0.8), with a range of 3,000 miles, the Utility-2 aircraft, codenamed Project AQUATONE, consisted of a fragile aluminum airframe powered by a single Pratt & Whitney J57 turbojet engine. The first test flight took place on the Watertown Strip (later redesignated as **Area 51**) in July 1955 and the first U-2 of an initial order of 55 entered service later the same year. It was intended to operate as Detachment A from **Royal Air Force** Lakenheath, Suffolk, under cover of the Weather Squadron (Provisional) 1, but after a report of the mysterious aircraft had been published in the 1 June 1956 edition of *Flight* magazine, Detachment A was hastily moved to Wiesbaden. The first overflight of the Soviet Union, in a series codenamed HOMERUN, was completed successfully on 4 July 1956 and the 24th and last was the **SOFT TOUCH** mission flown by **F. Gary Powers** on 1 May 1960. Two of the flights from Incirlik, in December 1959 and February 1960, were flown by RAF pilots, Squadron-Leaders Robert Robinson and John MacArthur.

The U-2, with an early stealth treatment codenamed RAINBOW, was intended to escape detection by Soviet **radar** but each of the first eight overflights was spotted, and President Dwight D. Eisenhower banned further missions for 15 months. A further prohibition followed when the president authorized a single overflight, which was also detected and was the subject of a protest from the Kremlin. After July 1959, five further missions were flown until SOFT TOUCH.

Between July 1956 and May 1960, a total of 24 overflights were made of the Soviet Union by the U-2, creating 1,285,000 feet of film covering 1.3 million square miles of the country, being about 16 percent of the Soviet landmass, and including all 24 **inter-continental ballistic missile** (ICBM) sites.

Exactly how the Soviets learned of the U-2 operating altitudes remains a mystery, although the GRU mole Piotr Popov reported to his **Central Intelligence Agency** (CIA) handler George Kisevalter in April 1958 that the KGB had acquired full details of the aircraft. This may either have been a deliberate leak of a bogus flight manual, allegedly fabricated by Lockheed at the CIA's request or, as some believe, was the result of espionage at the Atsugi airbase where Lee Harvey Oswald was posted in September 1957. In May 1960, when Powers was shot down, Oswald was living in Minsk, whence he had moved in January, since his arrival in Moscow the previous October. He would remain in the Soviet Union for 20 months, until June 1962, when he returned to New York on an ocean liner.

After SOFT TOUCH, all further U-2 incursions were banned, and only one took place, accidentally, on 30 August 1962 on a mission from Japan that drifted over Sakhalin Island on the return leg from the Kuriles. No missiles were fired, probably because of the proximity of interceptors, and when the Soviets protested a formal apology was issued by the U.S. State Department, acknowledging that a weather flight had encountered unexpectedly strong currents at high altitude.

The aircraft was equipped with the HR-73B camera with a 36-inch focal-length lens that caught astonishing detail on the ground from an altitude of 14 miles. The camera was fed by two 6,500 foot rolls of nine and a half inch film that could produce 4,000 frames that would be processed at a special facility at Suitland, Maryland, before being studied by the photo interpreters at the **National Photographic Intelligence Center** in Washington, D.C.

Stereo imagery produced by the U-2 dramatically altered American assessments of Soviet power because the huge liquid-fueled SS-6 Sapwood missiles, 34 feet in diameter, were transported from the factory to the test facility and launch site by railway. The U-2 therefore mapped every railway in the Soviet Union, identified Semipalatinsk, Tyuratam, Kapustin Yar, and the warhead factory at Alma Ata as critical sites, and was able to demonstrate an almost complete absence of

SS-6 rockets. CIA analysts interpreted this as evidence that the Soviet ICBM program had run into difficulties that had delayed production, whereas the Air Force claimed the absence was proof that the Soviets had concluded their tests and had moved straight into production. This disparity became known as the **missile gap**.

The total number of U-2s built is unknown but is around 100, of which a proportion was shot down. Major **Rudolf Anderson**'s plane was shot down over Banes, **Cuba**, in October 1962 by a Soviet-launched SA-2 missile, and at least nine were destroyed by the Chinese. U-2 flights over **China**, which began in 1960 and concluded in 1974, were flown by Chinese Nationalist personnel.

In 1962, two U-2As were launched from the carrier USS *Kitty Hawk*, and in 1964, two U-2Gs took off from the USS *Ranger*. In November 1969, a U-2 landed on the USS *America*.

In 1967 a new version was built, designated as the TR-1, and 12 were delivered in 1968. By 1978, 35 had been built, and some included direct downlinks to earth stations, which were developed in 1971 to relay signals intelligence intercepted over Vietnam to Thailand. These aircraft were deployed to Cyprus in 1974 and to Korea in 1976, and during the 1980s flew drug interdiction missions over the Caribbean. The most modern versions are equipped with satellite uplinks, enabling the aircraft to operate out of line-of-sight from ground stations, and continue to be flown although exact production figures are unavailable.

U-BOAT WAR. Air intelligence played a crucial role in the Allied efforts to defeat the U-boat. Aerial reconnaissance of the shipyards on the Baltic provided vital information about U-boat production and their deployment to the operational pens in Nazi-occupied France and Norway. When combined with signals intelligence derived from decrypted Kriegsmarine Enigma traffic, intelligence analysts were able to provide astonishingly accurate figures for the U-boat fleet. For example, the estimated monthly production of U-boats during 1943 was put at "not more than 25 a month," whereas the correct figure was actually 24. *See also* WORLD WAR II.

UNITED NATIONS (UN). Although the UN does not maintain its own independent intelligence agency, it established an information unit in March 1999 to support the work of the recently created Special Commission (UNSCOM) and the Monitoring, Verification and Inspection Commission (UNMOVIC). To undertake its mission in Iraq, UNSCOM was dependent on air intelligence supplied by commercial satellite imagery, American **U-2** flights from Saudi Arabia, and by French Mirage aircraft, together with information from Germany. An offer from Moscow of the use of a Russian AN-30 could not be taken up because there was to be a charge.

UNSCOM was responsible for supervising the destruction of an unknown number of Al-Fatah missiles and 72 Al-Samoud-2 missiles, out of an estimated Iraqi arsenal of 100, when it was discovered that the weapon's range could be extended beyond the 150 kilometers allowed under the UN cease-fire agreement by the addition of a second rocket engine, an expedient pioneered in India.

UNITED STATES. Since **World War I**, the United States has consistently made the greatest investment in air intelligence technology, ranging from the Bolling Commission of 1917, sent to Great Britain to study modern military aircraft design, to the development of **satellites** and the deployment of **unmanned aerial vehicles** in Afghanistan.

Successive American administrations, following the uncoordinated muddle of 1941 exposed by the failure to anticipate the Japanese attack on **Pearl Harbor**, have acknowledged the importance of air intelligence as a source of reliable information by allocating resources to reconnaissance aircraft, building the **U-2** and **SR-71**, and creating a vast industry devoted to increasing the capability of **satellites**. First, **World War II** provided the environment required to stimulate air intelligence, and then the **Cold War** made the discipline a potential key to survival in the 40-year period of East-West confrontation.

In the post–Cold War era, air intelligence has played an essential role in the American interventions in Panama and in two Gulf Wars, although campaigns conducted in Grenada in October 1983 and Somalia 20 years later demonstrated that sophisticated technology cannot guarantee military success in low-intensity counterinsurgency operations.

UNITED STATES INTELLIGENCE BOARD (USIB). Created in 1957 to advise the director of central intelligence, Allen Dulles, on intelligence priorities, the USIB set targets for satellite reconnaissance programs. Its name was changed by President John F. Kennedy to the President's Foreign Intelligence Advisory Board (PFIAB), but was abolished in 1977 by President Jimmy Carter. The PFIAB was restored in October 1981 by President Ronald Reagan, who appointed 14 nominees to monitor and improve the quality of intelligence collection.

UNMANNED AERIAL VEHICLE (UAV). Widely operated by U.S. forces in **Vietnam**, remotely piloted aircraft, then known as **drones**, were developed by the Israeli Defence Force, which deployed the innovative Mastiff in **Lebanon** during 1982. Being unmanned, the UAV eliminates the risk of a pilot being captured or killed and, being smaller in size than conventional reconnaissance platforms, can linger over a target area relatively quietly without attracting hostile attention from the ground.

The first American UAV was the distinctive, twin-tailed **Pioneer**, powered with a reciprocating engine and a pusher propeller, which saw service during **DESERT STORM** in 1991. It was followed by the miniaturized Dragon Eye, used by U.S. Marines. More recent systems have included the **Predator**, **Darkstar**, and the **Global Hawk**. In March 2003, a flight made by an Iraqi UAV was cited as an example of a breach of UN sanctions, and Saddam Hussein's regime belatedly acknowledged having developed a primitive reconnaissance aircraft powered by a two-stroke motorcycle engine, with a range of 55 kilometers, a payload of 30 kilos of video equipment, and a claimed flight duration of just 30 minutes.

The latest generation of UAVs deployed in Iraq and Afghanistan include the ScanEagle, operated by the U.S. Marines, which provides a gimballed platform for a color video camera; the Skylark, with a seven foot wingspan and used for short-duration reconnaissance missions; and the Silver Fox, a low-cost UAV designed to carry sensors and controlled by a ground station that can handle up to 10 Silver Foxes simultaneously. The highly sophisticated X-45C, a Joint Unmanned Combat Air Systems project, is likely to be the next innovation in remotely controlled pilotless aircraft. *See also* PIONEER; RYAN; SHADOW; WATCHKEEPER.

UNMANNED COMBAT ARMED ROTORCRAFT (UCAR). Developed by the Defense Advanced Research Projects Agency, the UCAR is planned to enhance the ability of U.S. forces to penetrate hostile airspace and conduct offensive operations, including reconnaissance and the suppression of defenses, without endangering a pilot.

URGENT FURY. The U.S. codename for the invasion of the Caribbean island of Grenada in October 1983, following the assassination of prime minister Maurice Bishop and his replacement by the pro-Soviet Bernard Coard. A U.S. Navy battle group led by the carrier USS *Independence* was diverted from its mission to the Middle East to participate in the assault, but a lack of intelligence left the Rangers, Delta, and other Special Forces unaware of the numbers of Cuban troops on the island, so a **Central Intelligence Agency** officer was dispatched to make observations and, in particular, to test the depth of the runway tarmac at Point Salines Airport to establish whether it could sustain landings by troop transports. Her report suggested it was safe for the planes to land. The operation proved to be an expensive debacle, with 18 American troops killed, some by "friendly fire" and 116 wounded. An estimated 29 Cubans were killed and 59 wounded. It remained a hard lesson for the Pentagon on the necessity of acquiring reliable air intelligence before mounting any operation involving an airborne assault.

U.S. *See* UNITED STATES OF AMERICA.

– V –

VANSITTANT, ROBERT. Formerly the permanent undersecretary at the Foreign Office, Lord Vansittant was appointed the British government's chief diplomatic adviser in 1938. He developed his own private intelligence network. He was heavily reliant on Group Captain **Malcolm Christie** for information about Nazi air rearmament, and his reports that circulated in Whitehall were contradicted by the official Air Staff assessments. Although his opinions were considered controversial by the government, led by Neville Chamberlain, his information was accurate and his pessimistic interpretation was supported by Winston Churchill's intelligence adviser, Major Desmond Morton. Vansittant's unique role, intended to isolate him from exercising his determined anti-German influence, actually enabled him to conduct an unofficial campaign against Chamberlain's policies, which he assessed as appeasing the Nazis.

V-BOMBERS. The **Royal Air Force**'s strategic bomber force consisted of Valiant, Victor, and Vulcan aircraft, which remained the principal British nuclear deterrent until the introduction of the submarine-launched Polaris missile in 1968. As the sole means of delivering nuclear free-fall weapons deep into the Soviet Union, the RAF was reliant on air intelligence, both as a means of reaching targets by avoiding ground defenses, and for the accurate identification of military and industrial installations suitable for inclusion on the bomb list. Thus, air intelligence played a vital role in maintaining the effectiveness of a credible deterrent and placed a heavy burden on the war planners to provide up-to-date details of suitable routes, avoiding hostile radar, SAM sites, and fighter airfields, and to undertake ground-mapping of potential targets. These requirements were eliminated when the British government opted for the largely American-supplied naval alternative.

VELA. The Spanish word for "watchman," VELA was the codename for a secret **U.S.** Air Force surveillance **satellite** project that commenced in October 1963 to monitor Soviet and Chinese nuclear detonations and continued until the launch of VELA 12 in April 1970. An improved VELA satellite was credited in September 1979 in detecting a possible nuclear explosion in the South Atlantic, between South Africa and Antarctica, later presumed to be an Israeli atmospheric test conducted with a missile fired from international waters by a South African warship. In 2006, a former **Central Intelligence Agency** station chief in Pretoria, Tyler Drumheller, disclosed in his autobiography, *On the Brink*, that he had confirmed the test had taken place following his arrival in South Africa in 1983.

VIETNAM WAR. Air intelligence played a crucial role in the Vietnam War when American forces became increasingly dependent on information about the size and location of their largely hidden adversary. Both **U-2** and **SR-71** strategic reconnaissance aircraft were deployed over the combat area, and at lower altitudes Lockheed EC-121M Super Constellations collected signals intelligence while Huey UH-1H helicopters attempted to gather the enemy's tactical radio chatter. In addition, the U.S. Army Security Agency flew single-engined de Haviland RU-A Beavers and twin-engined RU-8D Seminoles on similar missions.

To reduce air losses, especially on raids over North Vietnam, the **U.S.** Air Force received intelligence about ground defenses and the deployment of MiG interceptors from the National Security Agency intercept site at Nakhon Phanom in northern Thailand, which monitored enemy voice channels, **radar** emissions, and other communications.

Despite a huge technological advantage over the Vietcong and North Vietnamese regular forces ranged against them, U.S. ground forces were disadvantaged because successive American administrations were unwilling to escalate the conflict by taking the decisive action required to deny foreign air and sea supplies to Hanoi, enforce the demilitarized zone, and eliminate the safe-haven assembly areas in neutral Laos. Thus, while the United States developed increasingly ingenious countermeasures to detect movement along the Ho Chi Minh trail, the principal resupply route from north to south, the traffic was never interrupted for more than short periods, thereby allowing the enemy to build up significant concentrations of troops and matèriel in and around Saigon, the city that eventually fell in April 1975. Whether the ultimate outcome was inevitable, or whether the South Vietnamese could ever have prevailed, given the willingness of Hanoi to sustain appalling losses, remains a matter of debate.

VINCENNES, USS. On 3 July 1988, an Iran Air A-300 Airbus was shot down over the Persian Gulf by a missile fired by the USS *Vincennes* when it was mistakenly identified as a hostile F-41 fighter. The accident, resulting in 290 deaths, was a consequence of failures aboard the cruiser and served to exacerbate already strained relations between Iran and the **United States**, even though liability was admitted and compensation paid. Flight 655 had taken off from Bandar Abbas and was climbing toward the warship at 12,000 feet when the Aegis **radar** system identified it as a target. The *Vincennes* was on patrol, confronting Iranian gunboats harassing oil tankers in the Gulf, when Captain Will C. Rogers III gave the order to fire two missiles.

VOISKA PROTIVOVOZDUSHNOI OBORONY (VPVO). The Soviet air defense force was a separate armed service responsible for the protection of the motherland from attack. The VPVO was an integrated organization with an air wing of interceptor fighters, ground radar, and an early-warning chain of target acquisition stations sited along the country's periphery linked to surface-to-air missile (SAM) sites and flak batteries. The VPVO was itself a priority target for Western air intelligence and the introduction of each new aircraft or SAM required a review of existing operating procedures. The MiG-15 posed no threat to high-altitude intruders, but in 1953, the MiG-17 Fresco entered service, which posed a serious risk to the RB-47, as did the Fresco-B variant with interceptor radar and the Fresco-C fitted with an afterburner. *See also* SOVIET UNION.

VORTEX. Codename for a **U.S.** signals intelligence **satellite**, one of which was deployed over Kiev following the destruction of reactor 4 at the Chernobyl nuclear power plant in April 1986. *See also* BYE-MAN.

V-WEAPONS. In 1943, the Nazis developed two weapons, the **Fi-103** Doodlebug flying-bomb and the **A-4** ballistic missile, which were known as *vergeltungswaffen* ("vengeance weapon"). The first, which was launched operationally against London from sites in northern France in June 1944, flew conventionally, powered by a ramjet, and descended onto its target after its supply of paraffin fuel had been cut. The V-2 was a less accurate missile that carried a warhead containing a ton of high explosives. Allied countermeasures were coordinated by the **CROSSBOW** Committee in London that evaluated the first reports of a German secret weapon, and then collated the intelligence relating to the launch sites. The V-1 was vulnerable to attack at its assembly plants in Germany, and the distinctive "ski-jump" launchers proved easy to identify from the air because they were aligned with

London. In contrast, the V-2 did not require a permanent launch site and was only visible for a few hours as it was prepared for launch from a mobile transporter.

Although the V-weapons had no long-term strategic impact on the prosecution of the war, this was in large measure a result of coordinated air intelligence that filtered reports of the projects from the earliest news contained in the **Oslo Report**, and then monitored the development at **Peenemünde**, made an accurate assessment of the threat, and recommended the appropriate countermeasures. *See also* WORLD WAR II.

– W –

WADDINGTON. A **Royal Air Force** base established before **World War II** as a center of aerial reconnaissance operations, Waddington in Lincolnshire has been the home of 54(R) Squadron for 89 years. In May 2007, having been disbanded in April 2005, the squadron was reformed to cope with the demands of commitments in Afghanistan and Iraq, and to train crews for the AWACS E-3D Sentry, Nimrod R1, and five Sentinel aircraft, delivered as part of the Astor Project to train 170 aircrew a year in two courses a year.

WAR OF ATTRITION. Between June 1967 and August 1970, Egypt conducted a war of attrition, mainly across the Suez Canal, to inflict unsustainable casualties on the Israeli Defence Force. When a ceasefire agreement was made in July 1970, the Egyptians possessed 16 SAM sites, with only one within 19 miles of the canal, but immediately afterward, more SAM batteries were moved into the Suez zone, in breach of the agreement. The Israeli Air Force flew reconnaissance missions in August and October 1970 that established 50 SAM sites, 42 of which were judged to be operational. Four of them were located within 13 miles of the canal, bringing them within the 12.5-mile range of the missiles, and 16 were manned by an estimated 3,000 Soviet personnel. This analysis was subsequently confirmed by a **U-2** mission completed on 29 August 1970. Despite protests, the Egyptians retained the SAM sites, which gave them a significant advantage in subsequent peace negotiations. *See also* GUIDELINE.

WATCHKEEPER. Codename for an advanced British **unmanned aerial vehicle** under development for deployment in Iraq and Afghanistan.

WATTON. The **Royal Air Force** (RAF) base in Leicestershire that during **World War II** had been the home of 192 Squadron, later disbanded to become the Central Signals Establishment. In September 1948, a Lancaster and Lincoln B-2 converted for signals interception duties were added and deployed to Habbaniya in Iraq for flights along the Soviet border.

192 Squadron was reformed in July 1951 with Avro Lincolns and four Washingtons (the RAF version of the B-29), and in March 1953, a Lincoln was shot down in East Germany just outside the Hamburg air corridor, with the loss of six of the seven aircrew. On the same day, MiGs attacked another Lincoln near Kassel.

In February 1953, Wyton was equipped with **Canberras** carrying a third, extra member of the crew, a Russian-speaking intercept operator. ELINT collection missions were flown on behalf of GCHQ to and from Bodo in Norway and Akrotiri in Cyprus. The squadron participated in MUSKETEER, the invasion of the Suez Canal zone in October 1956, learning that Egyptian **radar** operators routinely switched off their equipment soon after midday, and in 1955 was credited with the discovery that MiG fighters had been equipped with airborne radar. The Squadron had a forward operating base in Germany at Wunsdorf and later at Wildenrath, and in August 1958 it was redesignated as No. 51 Squadron. In April 1957, the Washingtons were replaced by the first of three Mark 2 Comets with a range of 3,060 miles, a cruising altitude of 40,000 feet, and provision for 10 intercept operators and 12 other passengers.

WHIFF. The North Atlantic Treaty Organization designation of the SON-4 E-band fire control radar, the first Soviet-built system, which was introduced into service in 1947, having been copied from the American SCR-584.

WIGGLESWORTH, H. E. P. The prewar deputy director of Air Intelligence at the British Air Ministry, Wing Commander Wigglesworth undertook an inspection of intelligence facilities in the Far East and

in March 1938 submitted a damning report recommending the introduction of a **Far East Combined Bureau** to eliminate interservice ri-
valry and improve liaison.

WILHELMSHAVEN. Within an hour of war being declared in September 1939, a Blenheim from **Royal Air Force Wyton** flew a photographic reconnaissance flight over Wilhelmshaven in anticipation
of the first air raid on the German fleet. *See also* WORLD WAR II.

WILLOW SAND. Codename for a classified **U.S.** procurement program initiated after the collapse of the Soviet Bloc to acquire
Scud-B missiles for test purposes. The weapons were fired from Aur
Atoll in the Pacific during the development of the Patriot ballistic
missile defense system. After their launch, Patriot batteries on Kwajalein Atoll were deployed to destroy the Scuds in flight. The original Scud missile was a Soviet-built IRBM with a range of 185 miles,
accurate to within about half a mile, carrying a half-ton warhead. The
next generation, the Scud-B, designated as the R-17E by the Soviets,
was 37 feet long and three feet in diameter, and it was exported
widely. In Iraq, the Scud-B was modified to become the Al-Hussein,
armed with a smaller, 1,000-pound warhead but longer, at 41 feet,
with a range of 472 miles. Another version, built from cannibalized
Scuds, was the Al-Habbas (later renamed the Al-Hijarah) with an
even longer range of 465 miles, but with a reduced warhead of 650
pounds and rather less accuracy.

WILTON PARK. The **World War II** interrogation center at Latimer in
Buckinghamshire where captured **Luftwaffe** personnel underwent
questioning by skilled Combined Services Detailed Interrogation
Centre interrogators. Enemy aircrew taken prisoner were processed
initially at Trent Park, Cockfosters, before being selected for further
attention. Wilton Park later became the British government's principal language school following the closure of **Royal Air Force** (RAF)
Bodmin in Cornwall and RAF **Crail** in Scotland. *See also* PRISON-
ERS OF WAR.

WINDOW. British codename for metal foil strips, 30 cm long and 1.5
cm wide, which emulated the **radar** echo of an aircraft and were de-

veloped in 1942. Some 2,000 strips, deposited into the slipstream, produced the return of a heavy bomber and the countermeasure was used to overwhelm and mislead German radar by producing clouds of blips on their screens to make ghost fleets of planes. WINDOW was tested at Tantallon Castle, on the Firth of Forth, where captured German FREYA, WURZBURG, and SEETAKT radar equipment was studied by air intelligence experts.

WINDOW was known to the U.S. Army Air Force as CHAFF and to the Germans as DÜPPEL. *See also* WORLD WAR II.

WINTERBOTHAM, FREDERICK. Appointed the head of the Secret Intelligence Service's (SIS) Air Section in January 1930, Wing-Commander Fred Winterbotham was a pioneer of aerial reconnaissance and with his fellow pilots Sidney Cotton and Cyril Mills undertook numerous clandestine overflights of Nazi airfields prior to **World War II**. Operating from Heston and flying a twin-engined Lockheed 12A equipped with concealed Leica cameras, the pair established a commercial cover in Paris, the Aeronautical Research and Sales Corporation, and successfully completed missions along the length of the Maginot Line.

SIS's air unit, designated as Section IV, was founded in 1930 by Winterbotham, who would be succeeded in 1943 by Squadron-Leader John Perkins. In SIS's postwar reorganization, the air section was renamed R2, with Perkins moving to R8, the Coordination Section, responsible for assessing requirements with agent production capabilities. Thereafter, R2 would be staffed by a single officer, Squadron-Leader Sofiano, seconded from the Air Ministry, until 1964 and the establishment of the Defence Intelligence Staff at the Ministry of Defence.

Winterbotham left SIS in 1945 to join British Overseas Airways Corporation, and after his retirement in 1948, returned to pig farming in Devon. Winterbotham wrote three books, including an autobiography, *Secret and Personal*, and a controversial exposé of the wartime Anglo-American cryptographic cooperation, *The Ultra Secret.*

WOODBRIDGE. Early on the morning of 13 July 1944, a Junkers 88 nightfighter landed at **Royal Air Force** Woodbridge in Suffolk, when an inexperienced pilot suffered a compass failure. As his aircraft approached the airfield, it had been mistaken for a returning Mosquito and given a green signal, and the crew would not realize their error until a bus driven by an equally surprised airman arrived to collect them from the apron. The plane was found to be equipped with the new German SN-2 **radar** and the FRENSBURG homing device, and tests conducted at Farnborough proved that the nightfighter could detect the MONICA tail-warning device fitter to all Bomber Command aircraft at a range of 130 miles. As a result, MONICA was withdrawn within a few days. *See also* WORLD WAR II.

WORLD WAR I. The first military aircraft to be flown over the front lines during World War I were unarmed scouts on reconnaissance missions, and the planes only acquired armaments in an effort to shoot their enemies down and deny them this source of valuable intelligence. Artillery spotting and trench-mapping eventually gave way to aerial photography, replacing the more vulnerable tethered balloons. Zeppelins also made a contribution to the collection of air intelligence, as did flying-boats on operations against submarines.

In the **United States**, before President Woodrow Wilson's declaration of war, Captain Billy Mitchell, the War Department's head of the European intelligence section since 1912, advocated the use of aircraft for intelligence collection. In 1916, reconnaissance missions were flown by Jenny biplanes during General John Pershing's campaign in northern Mexico against Pancho Villa. In June 1917, the head of the U.S. Army Signal Corps Aviation Section, General George Squier, sent Colonel Raynal C. Bolling to Great Britain on what became the Bolling Commission to gather technical information about Allied aircraft, including the de Haviland 4. From these initial, tentative steps into the field of air intelligence, the disciplines of air reconnaissance and technical intelligence would develop, assisted by experiments with cameras conducted by No. 3 Squadron of the Royal Flying Corps, which resulted in films being developed in the air, before landing, to save time. During the Allied offensive in the Meuse-Argonne, in September 1918, some 56,000 prints were distributed to American artillery batteries and infantry commanders; some of the images were delivered within 20 minutes of the pictures being taken.

The German Military Aviation Service also built a large aerial reconnaissance capability, amounting to 505 of the 2,047 aircraft deployed along the western front, and by the end of 1917 up to 4,000 images a day were being delivered to the Kaiser's staff.

WORLD WAR II. With only limited knowledge of Luftwaffe strengths and production statistics, the Air Ministry's **Air Intelligence Branch** entered World War II at a significant disadvantage, and with a minimal understanding of the enemy's order-of-battle that anyway would change dramatically with the occupation of France, Belgium, and the Netherlands. Conversely, the Luftwaffe's grasp of the **Royal Air Force** (RAF) was considerable, partly because of the very public debate in Great Britain on the subject of relative fighter and bomber squadrons, but also because of the espionage of Dr. **Herman Goertz** in 1938, who had visited and sketched numerous RAF airfields in southern and eastern England. Nevertheless, the German Air Ministry never fully appreciated the scale of RAF losses in France in 1940, amounting to 944 aircraft, including 450 fighters, leaving Fighter Command with only 502 planes with which to defend the country from the long-dreaded assault on London from the air, an offensive that had been anticipated since the aerial bombardment of Madrid, Guernica, and Barcelona.

The shortcomings of British details of the Luftwaffe would be rectified during 1940 by aircrew interrogations and, latterly, signals sources including Enigma intercepts and radio direction-finding. Thereafter, technical intelligence became predominant, with German and British scientists making research breakthroughs at an astonishing pace in an effort to gain an edge over the enemy. Both sides pursued proximity fuses, atomic weapons, jet engines, guided bombs, pilotless aircraft, rockets, **radar**, and electronic countermeasures, and some of the German projects were to be disclosed to the Secret Intelligence Service in the **Oslo Report**.

In strategic terms, the confrontation between the Luftwaffe and the RAF during the summer of 1940, which came to be known as the Battle of Britain, proved crucial, as Adolf Hitler's plan for an invasion depended on establishing air superiority. However, handicapped by obsolescent Heinkel 111 bombers and the poorly performing but more modern Junkers 88, the Luftwaffe's tactic of concentrating on the destruction of the RAF on the ground and in the air was canceled at the end of August, just when it was achieving its objective. Hitler's intervention, and his insistence on transferring the attacks to London, enabled the RAF to regroup just as it was on the point of collapse. Poor Luftwaffe intelligence resulted in the High Command's failure to grasp how successful the Messerschmitt-109s had been. On 13 August, the German offensive began in earnest with 702 single-engined fighters, 227 twin-engined Me-110s, 875 serviceable bombers, and 316 dive bombers, ranged against 749 Hurricanes and Spitfires, a strength improved by the introduction of 490 aircraft built during July. The Luftwaffe lost 45 planes, compared to 13 RAF fighters, and six of the RAF pilots survived to fly again. On the next day, the Luftwaffe had 19 aircraft shot down to the RAF's eight. On 15 August, the Luftwaffe lost 75 planes to the RAF's 34, and on 16 August the results were much the same, with 45 German aircraft destroyed for only 21 RAF fighters. On 18 August, 71 intruders were shot down for 27 defenders, but the Luftwaffe aircrews had greatly exaggerated their claimed successes so German air intelligence estimated the RAF was down to its last hundred planes, whereas on 23 August, having been replenished, it actually had 700 serviceable fighters. During August, the RAF had lost 359 aircraft for 653 enemy planes, and the shortage was not in fighters, but qualified pilots, whose numbers were running dangerously low. However, the real turning point was an accidental German attack on London on 25 August for which a reprisal air raid on Berlin was launched. Infuriated, Hitler ordered London to be flattened, and on 7 September a force of 300 bombers, with 600 escorts headed toward the Thames and were met by 23 RAF squadrons. Forty German planes were shot down, compared to 28 RAF fighters. These statistics mystified the Luftwaffe analysts, who on 8 September had calculated the RAF's fighter strength at 465, of which only 345 were likely to be serviceable, but since then German pilots had claimed 288 kills, thereby theoretically leaving the RAF with only 177 planes.

On Sunday, 15 September, 300 RAF fighters flew against the largest raid ever and shot down 60 intruders for the loss of 26 defenders (even though the BBC claimed 185 raiders were shot down); this final conflict persuaded Hitler that the air supremacy required for a successful cross-Channel invasion had not been accomplished, so he ordered an indefinite postponement of Operation **SEELÖWE**. Early in October, with the weather deteriorating, the Luftwaffe abandoned all further daylight missions over England, and the attempt to eliminate RAF Fighter Command was over. From 10 July until the end of October, the Luftwaffe lost 1,773 aircraft, compared to the RAF's 915, and there was not a single week during that period that the raiders inflicted greater losses on the RAF.

While, for the **United States**, **World War I** had been essentially a land conflict, World War II started and finished with an air raid. The surprise Japanese attack on Pearl Harbor in December 1941 had been intended to eliminate the U.S. Navy's Pacific Fleet, and the bombing of Hiroshima and Nagasaki brought hostilities to an abrupt conclusion. In between, air superiority had been the key to successful land and sea operations.

WRINGER. Codename for a program conducted during the 1950s in which returning German prisoners of war who had worked at the Soviet rocket development laboratories at Khimka were interviewed after their release to the West. *See also* SOVIET UNION.

WURZBURG. The German codename for a fire-control **radar** system manufactured by Telefunken and introduced into service in 1940. British air intelligence received photographs of the antenna, placed on the top of flak towers near Berlin Zoo, from the American embassy in 1941, but an example of the apparatus was not recovered until Operation **BITING** in February 1942. The British countermeasure for the radar was **WINDOW**. *See also* WORLD WAR II.

WYTON. In 1950, the **Royal Air Force** concentrated its photographic interpretation facilities at RAF Wyton, in Cambridgeshire, which became the operational base for air reconnaissance flights throughout the **Cold War**. Canberra PR-3s of No. 540 Squadron were established in March 1953, and were followed by Nos. 58 and 82 Squadrons. In May 1954, No. 542 Squadron was reformed with Canberra PR-7s, and they would be joined in November 1955 by Vickers Valiants of 543 (Strategic Reconnaissance) Squadron. The 51 Squadron was equipped with the Canberra B-6 ELINT variant, which was deployed regularly to Laarbrüch, Wildenrath, and Akrotiri. Later, seven de Havilland Comet R2 aircraft of 51 Squadron were posted to Wyton, and in 1974 the Comets were replaced by the **Nimrod** R-1.

– X –

X. Codename for a source in prewar Nazi Germany who supplied Group Captain **Malcolm Christie** with accurate information about the strength of the **Luftwaffe**. X's true identity is unknown, but he is believed to have been a colonel in the German air ministry. *See also* WORLD WAR II.

X-16. The official **U.S.** Air Force designation of the Bell model 67 experimental high-altitude reconnaissance aircraft that flew in the spring of 1956 with a ceiling of 59,500 feet.

X FLIGHT. A **Royal Air Force** Special Duties flight based at Gambut, Egypt, X Flight was equipped with four Liberator bombers to fly clandestine missions from north Africa until March 1943, when it was reformed as 148 Squadron and provided with Halifaxes that flew into the Balkans. After the invasion of Italy, it was relocated to Brindisi, with a Lysander flight, and undertook long-range operations to Poland until late 1944, when it also covered northern Italy, Austria, and southern Germany. In June 1945, the unit was transferred to Foggia for transport duties, and it was disbanded in Egypt in January 1946.

X-GERÄT. German codename (literally "X-device") for a **World War II** navigation beam developed by Lorenz to assist **Luftwaffe** precision bombing during air raids over England.

– Y –

YAK-28. On 6 April 1966, a Yak-28P interceptor, designated as Firebar by the North Atlantic Treaty Organization, crashed into the Havelsee in Berlin's British sector, killing the pilot and navigator. British army personnel salvaged the airframe and intelligence analysts studied the advanced SKIPSPIN **radar**, but the recovery operation was delayed by the need for divers to disarm the ejector-seat charges. Eventually the aircraft was lifted onto a barge and returned to the Soviets. *See also* SOVIET UNION.

YAKOVLEV-25. The principal Soviet reconnaissance aircraft, designated as Mandrake by the North Atlantic Treaty Organization, the Yak-25RV entered service in 1960 and was estimated to have a ceiling of 65,000 feet, a range of 1,180 miles, and a cruising speed of 400 miles per hour. Originally designed as a fighter, the reconnaissance variant of the Yak-25 was operational over Greece, Turkey, **China**, Pakistan, and India until 1972. *See also* COLD WAR; SOVIET UNION.

YAMAMOTO, ISOROKU. A former **Japanese** naval attaché in Washington, D.C., and Harvard University language student, Admiral Isoroku Yamamoto was commander-in-chief of the Japanese Imperial Navy during **World War II**, but in April 1943, the aircraft carrying him on an inspection tour of airfields in the Solomon Islands was intercepted en route from Rabaul to Buin and shot down over Bougainville by 18 **U.S.** Army Air Force P-38 Lightnings of the 70th Fighter Squadron operating from Guadalcanal. The fighters had been vectored to their target for the purpose of assassinating Yamamoto, following the successful decryption in Pearl Harbor of an enemy wireless message that compromised his route and schedule. In Operation VENGEANCE, authorized personally by President Franklin D. Roosevelt, two Japanese Mitsubishi Betty twin-engined bombers, escorted by six Zeroes of the 309th Fighter Squadron, were shot down, with the loss of a single American plane, and only three fighters survived to land at Kahili. The bodies of Admiral Yamamoto and the three staff officers accompanying him, the fleet medical officer Rear Admiral Takata, Commanders Ishizaki and Toibana, together with the two pilots, were recovered from the wreckage of their aircraft, which had crashed in thick jungle, not far from Kahili. To conceal the cryptographic source of the information concerning Yamamoto's movements, the American aircrews were told that the tip had come from Australian coast watchers.

Y-GERÄT. German name (literally, "Y-device") for a night navigation system introduced in 1940 based on pulses transmitted as a single beam from sites in France at Poix and Cassel, which enabled **Luftwaffe** bombers to reach their targets in England. Known to the British as BENITO, the countermeasure was codenamed **DOMINO** and jammers were built at Highgate and Alexandra Palace. *See also* WORLD WAR II.

YOUNIS, FAWAZ. In September 1987, a joint operation conducted by the **Central Intelligence Agency** (CIA) and the Federal Bureau of Investigation (FBI) lured Fawaz Younis to a yacht moored off Cyprus. Younis had been the hijacker of a Royal Jordanian Airlines jet in Beirut on which three Americans had been murdered. Believing he was about to clinch a major drug deal, Younis had joined the yacht, encouraged by two bikini-clad FBI special agents. Once aboard, he was taken to international waters, formally arrested, and then transferred to a U.S. Navy warship for trial in Manhattan. He was sentenced to 30 years' imprisonment at a federal penitentiary in Kansas.

YURI ISLAND. On 7 October 1952, a **U.S.** Air Force **RB-29** of the 91st Strategic Reconnaissance Squadron was shot down by a Soviet fighter over Yuri Island, the disputed Soviet territory closest to Hokkaido, Japan. None of the eight crew survived.

– Z –

ZACHARSKY, MARIAN. A senior Polish intelligence officer, operating in California under commercial cover, Marian Zacharsky was convicted in December 1981 of having paid William H. Bell, a project manager at the **Radar** Systems Group of Hughes Aircraft in El Segundo, California, $150,000 for details of stealth technology. Hughes gave evidence against Zacharsky, who remained silent under interrogation and during his trial, and was sentenced to life imprisonment. He was released in a spy-swap in June 1985, and Bell received a sentence of 10 years.

ZAPATA. The **Central Intelligence Agency** (CIA) codename for the invasion of **Cuba** in April 1961. The precursor to the operation was to be the fake "defection" of one of Fidel Castro's pilots, who would fly his B-26 bomber to Miami, claim political asylum, and announce that the Cuban Air Force had rebelled. This was to be the cover story for the subsequent air raids on Cuban airfields intended to eliminate the air force, conducted by Cuban aircraft displaying Cuban Air Force livery. Actually the pilot, Mario Zuniga, was part of Brigade 2506 and had flown not from Cuba but from the CIA base at Puerto Cabezas, and his tale was disbelieved when it was pointed out that his aircraft did not have the Plexiglas nose characteristic of the Cuban Air Force's B-26s.

ZENITS. Daily early morning Luftwaffe meteorological missions from Norway, France, and Italy during **World War II** provided important cryptographic data for Allied code breakers. The flights were known as Zenits and were left deliberately undisturbed by Allied fighters because their wireless signals, encrypted in the *Aufklaungs unKampfflieger Signalstafel Land und See* (AuKa-Tafel) code and transmitted every 15 minutes, was relatively easy to solve and included helpful position reports that referred to a grid system. The messages were invariably reenciphered at their base on an Enigma circuit, thereby providing significant assistance to the cryptographers.

ZHIRYAKOV, BORIS A. The Soviet pilot of an LA-11 fighter, Boris Zhiryakov intercepted and destroyed a **U.S.** RB-29 over Yuri Island on 7 October 1952. *See also* COLD WAR; SOVIET UNION.

ZIRCON. British codename for a signals intelligence satellite planned in 1979 for introduction by the Government Communications Headquarters (GCHQ) in 1988 over the Eastern Bloc and the Middle East. The project, costing £500 million and described officially as a military communications system in the SKYNET series, was abandoned because of the financial burden and because of premature disclosure in the *New Statesman*, a radical journal published in London in January 1987. As a result of the publication, police raids were mounted against journalists and BBC offices to recover classified documents, but the investigation showed that the information had been pieced together from open sources by assiduous researchers and a film documentary was broadcast in September 1988. When ZIRCON was abandoned, GCHQ was instead offered the opportunity to contribute to the funding of the **MAGNUM** system that was launched in 1994.

ZOMBIES. During the **Cold War**, civil aircraft from Eastern Bloc countries straying out of recognized flight paths were identified as Zombies by the North Atlantic Treaty Organization air traffic controllers. Among the offenders were LOT Polish airlines, East Germany's Interflug, Hungary's Malev, Czechoslovakia's CSA, Romania's Tarom, and Balkan Bulgarian Airlines. Also categorized as Zombies were aircraft from Albania, Libya, and the People's Republic of China.

Appendix

U-2 HOMERUN OVERFLIGHTS OF THE SOVIET BLOC

Date	Mission No.	Pilot	Base	Target
June 1956	2003	Carl Overstreet	Wiesbaden	Prague, Warsaw
July 1956	2013	Hervey Stockman	Wiesbaden	Leningrad
4 July 1956	2014	Carmine Vito	Wiesbaden	Moscow
9 July 1956	2020		Wiesbaden	Lithuania
9 July 1956	2021		Wiesbaden	Kiev, Minsk
10 July 1956	2023		Wiesbaden	Crimea
20 Nov 1956	4016	F. Gary Powers	Incirlik	Armenia
10 Dec 1956	4018		Incirlik	Bulgaria
10 Dec 1956	2029	Carmine Vito	Giebelstadt	Yugoslavia
18 Mar 1957	4020*			
25 Apr 1957				Albania
7 June 1957	6002		Eielson	Kamchatka**
19 Jun 1957	6005		Eielson	Kamchatka
5 Aug 1957	4035	Eugene Edens	Pakistan	Aralsk
11 Aug 1957				Camera failure
20 Aug 1957	4045	Sammy Snyder		Tomsk
20 Aug 1957				
21 Aug 1957	4050	James Cherbonneaux	Pakistan	Sary Shagan
21 Aug 1957				
21 Aug 1957				China, Tibet
28 Aug 1957	4058			Tyuratam
10 Sept 1957			Incirlik	Kapustin Yar
15 Sept 1957	6008			Klyuchi
13 Oct 1957	2040	Hervey Stockman	Giebelstadt	Severomorsk
28 Jan 1958				Albania
1 Mar 1958	6011	Tom Crull	Atsugi	Sovetskaya Gavan

Date	Mission No.	Pilot	Base	Target
9 Jul 1959	4125	Marty Knutson		Sverdlovsk
6 Dec 1959	8005	Robert Robinson	Incirlik	Saratov Engels
10 Feb 1960	8009	John MacArthur	Incirlik	Kazan
9 Apr 1960	4155	Bob Ericson	Peshawar	Sary Shagan
1 May 1960	4154	F. Gary Powers	Peshawar	Sverdlovsk

* accidental incursion
** mission aborted

Bibliography

CONTENTS

INTRODUCTION

Air intelligence has always been especially sensitive because of the discipline's dependency on technology and the ease with which it can be compromised. Accordingly, those governments with access to high-resolution imagery have been reluctant to demonstrate the accuracy of their product because, by doing so, its limitations would be revealed, thereby offering opportunities to defeat it. Almost as soon as aerial reconnaissance developed as a means of observing a potential adversary, there were countermeasures that could be taken to foil the cameras. Camouflage is but one of the most obvious ways of misleading the inquisitive, but during World War II, with the widespread adoption of bombardment from the air, local efforts to disguise armor, troop concentrations, and the location of airfields and industrial targets evolved into strategic deception. The skill of studying imagery was the role of the photo interpreter, first described by Constance Babington-Smith in 1957. She had been credited with having spotted the first evidence of Hitler's V-1 secret weapon, on imagery taken in June 1943 by a Spitfire over Peenemünde.

As camouflage became increasingly important, we now know from declassified documents of the extraordinary attempts made, for example, to conceal the Suez Canal, move Tobruk harbor a few miles to the west, and create an entirely bogus assembly of infantry, artillery, tanks, and landing craft in southeast England in anticipation of a cross-Channel amphibious assault on the Pas-de-Calais in 1944. Details of Operation FORTITUDE, arguably the most successful deception of all time, would become known through the publication of Roger Hesketh's account of the campaign in 1999.

Because of the relevance of the methods introduced during World War II to any future conflict, the entire subject of air intelligence remained somewhat taboo, although the loss of a U-2 aircraft over Sverdlovsk in May 1960 revealed to the Soviets the tremendous advances that had been achieved in the manufacture of high-resolution cameras and of film sensitivity. The incident also provoked considerable unwelcome interest in the plane, and several books of varying accuracy were published, including *Operation Overflight* by the pilot, but the most comprehensive account would have to wait until 2001, when Norman Polmar released his magisterial *Spyplane: The U-2 History Declassified*.

The loss of the U-2 over the Soviet Union served to compromise the aircraft's capabilities so external commentators found it easier to document its vital contribution during the Cuban missile crisis, as detailed in James Blight's *On the Brink*. The confrontation was quickly resolved, but in its aftermath two lessons emerged. First, the Soviets appeared to have made no effort to disguise the deployment of their strategic rocketry, and second, the Americans remained reluctant to show publicly the tremendous detail caught on the U-2 film, until Dino Brugioni's *Eyeball to Eyeball* in 1991.

The satellite era heralded another period of top security. It is not surprising that the open literature is necessarily limited, but in 1986, William Burrows revealed in *Deep Black* more about America's covert satellite program than in all the previously published literature. He was followed by Jeffrey Richelson's *Secret Sentinels* in 1990.

At the conclusion of the Cold War and the change in the balance of global politics away from superpower confrontation and into a new era of small wars, terrorist atrocities, and insurgency movements, the security context has changed, almost out of all recognition. High-resolution satellite imagery is available instantly on the Internet, the entire CORONA program has been declassified, made available commercially, and described by Curtis Peebles in 1997, and even the most unsophisticated terrorist knows his cell phone can betray conversations and movements. While there remain understandable restrictions on the circulation of some imagery, readers can now benefit from what hitherto has been confined to classified archives.

For the newcomer seeking a broad perspective of the topic, Dick van der Aart's *Aerial Espionage* remains the most accurate and detailed survey of the entire topic, even if it was first published in 1985.

GENERAL AND REFERENCE WORKS

Department of the Air Force. *Photographic Interpretation Handbook*. Washington, DC, 1954.

Gunston, Bill. *Spy Planes and Electronic Warfare Aircraft*. New York: Arco, 1983.

Kahana, Ephraim. *Historical Dictionary of Israeli Intelligence*. Lanham, MD: Scarecrow Press, 2006.

Pringle, Rovert. *Historical Dictionary of Russian and Soviet Intelligence*. Lanham, MD: Scarecrow Press, 2006.

Turner, Michael. *Historical Dictionary of United States Intelligence*. Lanham, MD: Scarecrow Press, 2005.

West, Nigel. *Historical Dictionary of British Intelligence*. Lanham, MD: Scarecrow Press, 2005.

———. *Historical Dictionary of International Intelligence*. Lanham, MD: Scarecrow Press, 2006.

———. *Historical Dictionary of Cold War Counterintelligence*. Lanham, MD: Scarecrow Press, 2007.

———. *Historical Dictionary of World War II Intelligence*. Lanham, MD: Scarecrow Press, 2007.

WORLD WAR I

Gray, Peter, and Owen Thetford. *German Aircraft of the First World War*. London: Putnam, 1962.

James, Sir William. *The Eyes of the Navy*. London: Metheun, 1955.

Raleigh, Walter. *War in the Air*. London: Oxford University Press, 1922.

WORLD WAR II

Babington-Smith, Constance. *Evidence in Camera*. London: Chatto & Windus, 1957.

Bleakey, Jack. *The Eavesdroppers*. Melbourne: Brown, Prior Anderson, 1992.

Clory, David A. *Rocket Man*. New York: Hyperion, 2003.

Craven, Wesley, and James Case. *The Army Air Force in World War II*. Washington, DC: Office of Air Force History, 1983.

Cumming, Michael. *Beam Bombers*. Stroud, Gloucestershire: Sutton Publishing, 1998.

David, Burke. *Get Yamamoto*. New York: Random House, 1969.

Hamilton, Alexander. *Wings of Night*. London: William Kimber, 1977.

Hesketh, Roger. *FORTITUDE: The D-Day Deception Campaign*. London: St. Ermin's Press, 1999.

Infield, Glenn B. *Unarmed and Unafraid*. London: Macmillan, 1970.

———. *The Poltava Affair*. London: Robert Hale, 1973.

Jackson, Robert. *The Secret Squadrons*. London: Robson Books, 1983.

Jones, R. V. *Most Secret War*. London: Hamish Hamilton, 1978.

———. *Reflections on Intelligence*. London: Heineman, 1998.

Kramish, Arnold. *The Griffin*. Boston: Houghton Mifflin, 1980.

Leaf, Edward. *Above All Unseen*. Yeovil, Somerset: Patrick Stephens, 1997.

McCall, Gibb. *Flight Most Secret*. London: William Kimber, 1981.

Merrick, K. A. *Flights of the Forgotten*. London: Arms & Armour Press, 1989.

Nesbit, Roy Conyers. *Eyes of the Royal Air Force*. Stroud, Gloucestershire: Sutton Publishing, 1996.

Oliver, David. *Airborne Espionage*. Stroud, Gloucestershire: Sutton Publishing, 2005.

Pleskett, S. John. *Strange Intelligence*. London: Robert Hale, 1981.

Price, Alfred. *Instruments of Darkness*. London: William Kimber, 1967.

COLD WAR

Arnold, David Christopher. *Spying from Space*. College Station, TX: Texas A & M University Press, 2005.

Ball, Desmond. *Soviet Ears in the Ether*. Canberra: Australian National University, 1984.

Bottome, Edgar. *The Missile Gap*. Rutherford, NJ: Fairleigh Dickinson University Press, 1971.

Burrows, William E. *Deep Black*. New York: Random House, 1996.

Clark, Phillip. *Aspects of the Soviet Photoreconnaissance Satellite Programme*. Journal of the British Interplanetary Society, April 1983.

Day, Dwayne, John Logsdon, and Brian Latell, eds. *Eye in the Sky*. Washington, DC: Smithsonian Institution Press, 1998.

Heaps, Leo. *Operation Morning Light*. London: The Paddington Press, 1978.

Hochman, Sandra, with Sybil Wong. *Satellite Spies*. New York: Bobbs-Merrill Company, 1976.

Hough, Harold. *Satellite Surveillance*. Port Townsend, WA: Loompanics Unlimited, 1991.

Killian, James. *Sputnik, Scientists and Eisenhower*. Cambridge, MA: MIT Press, 1982.

Klass, Philip. *Secret Sentries in Space*. New York: Random House, 1971.

Lashmar, Paul. *Spy Flights of the Cold War*. Stroud, Gloucestershire: Sutton Publishing, 1996.

Lindgren, David. *Trust but Verify: Imagery Analysis in the Cold War*. Annapolis, MD: Naval Institute Press, 2000.

McMullen, David. *Chinook! The Special Forces Flight in War and Peace*. London: Simon & Schuster, 1998.

Miller, Jay. *Lockheed SR-71*. Arlington, TX: Aerojax, 1985.

Peebles, Curtis. *Guardians*. Novato, CA: Presidio Press, 1987.

———. *The Corona Project*. Annapolis, MD: Naval Institute Press, 1997.

Penkovsky, Oleg. *The Penkovsky Papers*. Garden City, NJ: Doubleday, 1965.

Richelson, Jeffrey T. *America's Space Sentinels*. Lawrence, KS: University of Kansas Press, 1999.

Taubman, Philip. *Secret Empire*. New York: Simon & Schuster, 2003.

Taylor, John W. R., and David Monday. *Spies in the Sky*. New York: Charles Scribner, 1972.

KOREAN WAR

Hyuan Hee, Kim. *The Tears of My Soul*. New York: William Morrow, 1993.

VIETNAM WAR

Castle, Timothy N. *One Day Too Long*. New York: Columbia University Press, 1999.

Robbins, Christopher. *Air America*. London: Macmillan, 1979.

———. *The Ravens*. New York: Crown Books, 1987.

BAY OF PIGS

Aguilar, Luis. *Operation ZAPATA*. Frederick, MD: University Publications of America, 1981.

Ferrer, Edward B. *Operation PUMA*. Miami, FL: International Aviation Consultants, 1982.

Immerman, Richard. *The CIA in Guatemala*. Austin: University of Texas Press, 1982.

Johnson, Haynes. *The Bay of Pigs*. New York: Norton & Co, 1964.

Wyden, Peter. *Bay of Pigs*. New York: Simon & Schuster, 1979.

CLANDESTINE FLIGHTS

Bechloss, Michael. *Mayday: Eisenhower, Khrushchev and the U-2 Affair*. London: Faber & Faber, 1986.

Blight, James, and David Welch. *On the Brink*. New York: Pantheon, 1993.

Brookes, Andrew. *Photo Reconnaissance*. London: Ian Allen, 1975.

Brugioni, Dino. *Eyeball to Eyeball*. New York: Random House, 1991.

Burrows, William. *By Any Means Necessary*. London: Hutchinson, 2002.

Leary, William M. *Perilous Missions*. Tuscaloosa, GA: University of Alabama Press, 1984.

Marchetti, Victor, and John D. Marks. *The CIA and the Cult of Intelligence*. New York: Alfred A. Knopf, 1974.

Powers, Francis G. *Operation Overflight*. New York: Holt, Rinehart, 1970.

White, William. *The Little Toy Dog*. New York: Durron, 1962.

Wise, David. *The U-2 Affair*. New York: Random House, 1962.

STRATEGIC INTELLIGENCE

Aart, Dick van der. *Aerial Espionage*. Shrewsbury, Wiltshire: Airlife Publishing, 1985.

Ball, Desmond. *Pine Gap*. Sydney: Allen & Unwin, 1988.

Bamford, James. *The Puzzle Palace*. Boston: Houghton Mifflin, 1982.

Blix, Hans. *Disarming Iraq*. New York: Pantheon Books, 2004.

Crickmore, Paul. *Lockheed SR-71 Blackbird*. London: Osprey, 1986.

Drumheller, Tyler. *On the Brink*. New York: Carrol & Grag, 2006.

Gann, Ernest. *The Black Watch*. New York: Random House, 1989.

Gavin, James. *War and Peace in the Space Age*. London: Hutchinson, 1959.

Goddard, George. *Overview: A Lifelong Adventure in Aerial Photography.* New York: Doubleday, 1969.

Hersh, Seymour. *The Target Is Destroyed.* New York: Random House, 1986.

Mann, Wilfred. *Was There a Fifth Man?* Oxford: Pergamon Press, 1982.

Osborn, Shane. *Born to Fly.* New York: Random House, 2001.

Pocock, Chris. *Dragon Lady: The History of the U-2 Spyplane.* Shresbury: Airlife, 1989.

Polmar, Norman. *Spyplane: The U-2 History Declassified.* Osceoloa, WI: MBI Publishing, 2001.

Rich, Ben, and Leo Janoe. *Skunk Works.* London: Little, Brown, 1994.

Richelson, Jeffrey. *America's Secret Eye in Space.* New York: Harper & Row, 1990.

Stockwell, Richard. *Soviet Air Power.* New York: Pageant, 1956.

Taylor, John, and David Mondey. *Spies in the Sky.* London: Ian Allen, 1972.

Yonay, Ehud. *No Margin for Error.* New York: Pantheon Books, 1993.

Ziegler, Charles, and David Jacobson. *Spying Without Spies.* Westport, CT: Praeger, 1995.

TERRORISM

Gertz, Bill. *Breakdown.* Washington, DC: Regnery, 2002.

Grey, Stephen. *Ghost Plane.* London: Hurst & Co, 2006.

Leppard, David. *On the Trail of Terror.* London: Jonathan Cape, 1991.

St. John, Peter. *Air Piracy, Airport Security and International Terrorism.* New York: Quorum Books, 1991.

Wilkinson, Paul. *Aviation Terrorism and Security.* London: Frank Cass, 1999.

WEBSITES

France

French Armee de l'air: www.defense.gouv.fr/air/index.html

Great Britain

British Army Intelligence Corps: www.armyintelligence.mod.uk

British Defence Intelligence Staff: www.mod.uk/DefenceInternet/About Defence/WhatWeDo/SecurityandIntelligence/DIS/ICG/IntelligenceCollection Group.htm

Eye Spy: www.eyespymag.com
Global Security: www.globalsecurity.org/
Government Communications Headquarters (GCHQ): www.gchq.gov.uk
Secret Intelligence Service (MI6): www.mi6.gov.uk/

Russia

Agentura (Russian secret services): www.agentura.ru/english/
Russian Foreign Intelligence Service (SVR): www.pravitelstvo.gov.ru

United States

Air Force: www.af.mil/
Air Force Intelligence, Surveillance and Reconnaissance Agency: www.aia
    .af.mil/
Army: www.army.mil/
Center for Naval Intelligence (CNI): www.npdc.navy.mil/cennavintel/index
Central Intelligence Agency (CIA): www.cia.gov/
Coast Guard: www.uscg.mil/default.asp
Department of Defense (DoD): www.defenselink.mil/
Department of Energy: www.energy.gov/
Defense Intelligence Agency (DIA): www.dia.mil/
Defense Joint Intelligence Operations Center (DJIOC): www.defenselink.mil/
    news/NewsArticle.aspx?ID=1089
Department of Homeland Security (DHS): www.dhs.gov/index.shtm
Federation of American Scientists: www.fas.org
Joint Intelligence Operations Centers (JIOC): www.defenselink.mil/news/
    newsarticle.aspx?id=15475
Marines: http://hqinet001.hqmc.usmc.mil/DirInt/default.html
National Geospatial-Intelligence Agency (NGA): www.nga.mil/portal/site/
    nga01/
National Reconnaissance Office (NRO): www.nro.gov/
National Security Agency (NSA): www.nsa.gov/
Navy: www.navy.mil/
State Department's Bureau of Intelligence and Research (INR): www.state.gov/
    s/inr/

About the Author

Glenmore Trenear-Harvey served in the Royal Air Force as a jet fighter pilot, station intelligence officer, and at Signals Command Headquarters, Medmenham, in the Air Ministry Book Production and Distribution Centre, supervising the handling of confidential ciphers. Between 1969 and 1997, he worked in the Far East and Africa for the British intelligence community. He is an acknowledged air intelligence expert, lectures at the British Defence Intelligence and Security Centre, Chicksands, and is a member of the Royal United Services Institute for Defence Studies and the Security and Intelligence Study Group. He is also an associate editor of *Eye Spy* magazine, editor of the London-based *IntelDigest*, and heads a consultancy, IntelResearch.